Praise for *Sav*

"*Saving Our Own Lives*
perience in and comm...
practice. This is a book grounded in deep love for those who are most marginalized in our society, and it respectfully documents their stories and emancipatory analyses. This open-hearted book is illuminating, informative, and inspiring. It will have a forever place on my bookshelf." —**Mariame Kaba**, author of *We Do This 'Til We Free Us*

"This vital book is a spark, a balm, an agitation, a blessing, a celebration. Through narrative and research and conversation and reflection, *Saving Our Own Lives* tears down the myths perpetuated by the medical-industrial complex and prison-industrial complex and shows us how communities have been building ways to survive and heal in spite of—and against—these systems. Shira Hassan's book is at once expansive and personal, far-reaching and like coming home. I'm going to return to it again and again, and you will too." —**Maya Schenwar**, coauthor of *Prison by Any Other Name* and editor-in-chief of *Truthout*

"Grounded, brilliant, and generous, *Saving Our Own Lives* offers key tools, histories, testimony, and analysis to deepen our everyday work to support ourselves and our beloved communities. As always, deep gratitude to the visionary Shira Hassan for this luminescent collection, resplendent with the power to shift hearts and minds. A must-read for organizers, educators, and all of us working to do more than struggle and survive. —**Erica R. Meiners**, coauthor of *Abolition. Feminism. Now.*

"This brilliantly moving book—at once a generous love letter to our freedom movements and an urgent demand for radical, transformative work—will inspire readers not only to think about harm reduction differently but to actually live in ways that reflect a commitment to its liberatory potential. Shira Hassan has brought together an amazing chorus of voices that includes freedom fighters, political educators, cultural workers, BIPOC leaders, and Disability Justice activists, whose analyses and reflections offer exactly the kind of collective wisdom and encouragement that we need right now. Indeed, the possibility of a radical, queer, abolitionist future is closer because Shira Hassan has so beautifully helped us understand the potential for freedom when we engage in a process of saving our own lives." —**Beth E. Richie**, coauthor of *Abolition. Feminism. Now.*

"*Saving Our Own Lives* is one of the most important books that I have read in a long time. Shira Hassan defines and emphasizes the necessary intersections of multiple growing movements for Reproductive Justice, Transformative Justice, Disability Justice, anti-criminalization of sex work, Healing Justice, and abolition. This is the first book that has explicitly brought our movements together to highlight the importance of our shared analyses and commitments. *Saving Our Own Lives* is also a tribute to leaders, organizers, care workers, and icons who have long been at the forefront of liberatory struggles but have been historically neglected or deemed disposable by mainstream and leftist movements. This book weaves together painful stories, astute political insights, research, theory, and lived experiences to remind readers of the importance of community and our commitments to one another. For those of us who have been at the outskirts of multiple spaces and places, this is a guide, an affirmation book, a welcome mirror, an entire embrace. This book reminds us that the power has always been with us, and it welcomes everyone else to learn from and to join us." —**Connie Wun**, cofounder of AAPI Women Lead

"With *Saving Our Own Lives*, Shira Hassan has yet again provided an immensely practical, grounded, inspiring, indispensable tool for our struggles. This book will introduce a whole new generation of organizers who got involved in anti-police mobilizing

and COVID mutual aid projects to the history, principles, and practices of Liberatory Harm Reduction, which are essential for ensuring this work resists paternalistic charity dynamics, brings everyone along, and actually builds the new world we need rather than just tinkering with the broken institutions that currently dominate us. *Saving Our Own Lives* is packed with compelling stories that show what Liberatory Harm Reduction is and what it can do, and what tensions surround its practice that need to be attended to with care by its practitioners. Shira shares her particular wisdom, gleaned from years of practice in communities most harmed by policing and coercive social services and healthcare models, showing paths forward that generate community-based solutions that we can all start working on right now. This book is easy to read and ready to inspire us all as we take the difficult and urgent next steps confronting the unfolding crises of our times."
—**Dean Spade**, author of *Mutual Aid*

"*Saving Our Own Lives* is a courageous, insightful, and vulnerable offering from Shira Hassan, pulled from three decades of her life and movement history. Part narrative of how she saved her own life along with those of many others, part handbook on how practicing harm reduction creates liberatory and resilient movements, and part history lesson illustrating the role of harm reduction for decades past and decades to come, this book is an essential read, as oppressed communities are co-figuring how to survive these times together." —**Ejeris Dixon**, executive director of Vision Change Win

"As someone who has had the privilege of learning from Shira Hassan and her community of Liberatory Harm Reductionists, I know what an incredible gift it is that now the rest of the world can too. *Saving Our Own Lives* fiercely reclaims the roots of harm reduction in disabled, Indigenous, Black, queer, trans, sex working, drug using, and migrant communities, and challenges conventional wisdoms around treatment, service provision, violence, trauma, survival, resilience, empowerment, and change in ways that are absolutely essential, in the current moment and to build the futures we want. Whether we are looking for lessons on how to tackle the opioid crisis, interrupt and heal from violence, or ensure Reproductive Justice for all, the chorus of voices gathered in this volume offers incisive, insightful, and practical real talk from the front lines. Simultaneously irreverent and serious as a heart attack, *Saving Our Own Lives* tells it like it is and as it needs to be if we are all going to survive what is unfolding now and what is to come." —**Andrea J. Ritchie**, cofounder of Interrupting Criminalization and coauthor of *No More Police*

"*Saving Our Own Lives* is truly a priceless gift to the world. Each chapter or revolutionary love note recounts the beautiful, brilliant, and, at times, painful histories of the family of Black, Indigenous, and People of Color organizers, people in the sex trade, sex workers, young people, queer people, trans people, and those whose street-based strategies for survival and love created what we now know as 'harm reduction.' There are so many lessons on each and every page, all exquisitely written to document stories that we should already know and principles of liberation that we should be practicing every day. This book should be read page by page by everyone and held close at hand for constant reminders of those to whom we owe so much. Shira Hassan, in collaboration with her revolutionary harm reduction family, has created an incredible book that has such relevance to our continued co-creation of a liberatory abolitionist future." —**Mimi Kim**, founder of Creative Interventions

Saving Our Own Lives

A Liberatory Practice of Harm Reduction

Shira Hassan
Edited by Deana G. Lewis
Foreword by adrienne maree brown
Introduction by Tourmaline
Afterword by Rosario Dawson

Haymarket Books
Chicago, IL

Published in 2022 by
Haymarket Books
P.O. Box 180165
Chicago, IL 60618
773-583-7884
www.haymarketbooks.org
info@haymarketbooks.org

ISBN: 978-1-64259-841-4

Distributed to the trade in the US through Consortium Book Sales and Distribution (www.cbsd.com) and internationally through Ingram Publisher Services International (www.ingramcontent.com).

This book was published with the generous support of Lannan Foundation and Wallace Action Fund.

Special discounts are available for bulk purchases by organizations and institutions. Please email info@haymarketbooks.org for more information.

Cover artwork by Marcus Rogers. Cover and text design by Rachel Cohen. Interior illustrations by Lizartistry. "Revolutionary Love Notes" illustration by Marcus Rogers.

Printed in Canada by union labor.

Library of Congress Cataloging-in-Publication data is available.

10 9 8 7 6 5 4 3 2 1

For Miss Major. For Chloe. For Kelly. For Jada Safari. For all of Young Women's Empowerment Project past, present, and future.

I am here because the part of me that wanted to survive joined forces with other people who wanted us to survive—my guides were the aunties and uncles of street youth, who were street youth themselves, who believed that building us up—building our individual and collective power—is a resilience practice and is the key to our cultural, political and individual survival. The gift of being able and of wanting to write this book came directly through the investments my community made in me when I was a young person. And this book, in turn, is my gift back to the community that created Liberatory Harm Reduction, who saved me, who taught us how to save our own lives. And you.

Contents

Foreword

adrienne maree brown
author of Emergent Strategy, Pleasure Activism, We Will Not Cancel Us, *and* Holding Change

I walk around with the principles of harm reduction remixing in my mind, in my heart:

Accept what is: drugs exist and people use them, societal structures impact use, and the result can be pleasure, relief, ease, comfort, addiction, and tragedy.

Embrace the complexity of drug use, including the spectrum of using and not using, and acknowledge that there are safer ways to use any substance.

Acknowledge that we live inside intersecting systems of egregious harm.

Remember, relearn, that no one is disposable.

Honor the sovereignty of each person over their own paths and choices, and let users hear each other and shape the support they receive.

Set down whatever judgment or coercion arises and focus on the quality of life and connection.

See each person's humanity.

Harm reduction was a revelation for me as a twenty-one-year-old who'd just flunked out of college (I failed my French oral exam, but not for lack of trying), and then been fired from my first job recruiting people to that college, because, well, they couldn't have a recruiter who had failed at college.

It was NYC at the turn of the century, and I wanted to taste everything. When I learned through an online job search that the National Harm Reduction Coalition (NHRC) existed, I was thrilled. When I went in to interview, I saw the most beautiful badass group of humans I'd ever witnessed in one place, from all backgrounds, with tattoos, shaved heads or wild manes, style, and, most of all, an honest way of being with what they needed and what they did. I spent two years doing the administrative work to support the training program, and along the way I learned about syringe exchanges, safe injection sites, what it looks like when someone is on heroin, how to test ecstasy pills, the framework of "drug, set, and setting," the power of sex worker survival strategies, that gender and sexuality were constructs and spectrums, that people with HIV/AIDS were learning to thrive, and that I wasn't alone in my crazy, my depression, my coping, my trauma, or my needs. I also learned that harm reduction was a movement and societal reframe bigger than any single institution or conference could hold.

I remember people who are now ancestors, teaching me to be freer and more exacting about collective freedom. I remember in particular the late Keith Cylar, long and dynamic, dancing and still, teaching me that pleasure was a worthwhile, important pursuit. I remember the late Don McVinney, my first supervisor at NHRC, explaining who the trainers of the program were—survivors, innovators, fighters, people who had learned what they were offering from lived experience.

I remember Shira Hassan walking into that space, gorgeous, glamorous, fat, and disabled, with her head held high. She was there to run a training, but I instantly realized that Shira is someone who teaches both in the formal settings of a classroom and in the informal setting of a conversation, in the way she holds the space and relationships around her. She walks with her history intact, both fluid and precise, meaning she might forget the exact timing of when a conversation happened, but she will remember the exact rhythm of it, and what we were wearing, and what we believed, and both how and why those beliefs changed. Shira is not easily impressed and will not pretend untrue things are true for the sake of polite company. This means she is trustworthy in a long-term fight because her visionary nature guides her to speak what is true in the present moment, clarifying which fight we are actually in.

Years later I would write books in which I referenced concepts and teachers I gathered from my time in harm reduction work. In each book, I had to be a writer who knew Shira was going to read my work, so I had to know what I knew and not pretend to know more. When I reached an edge of my own knowing around Transformative Justice, I ceded the pages to Shira's experience. It is rare that I publish anything major without checking in with Shira. I have also called on her to help me and others through the murky territory of learning to be an accountable human being—accountable to the truth of my own body and needs, accountable to the movements we serve, accountable to our overlapping purpose of liberation.

When she first told me that she was writing this book to tell the story of harm reduction as Transformative Justice, as Disability Justice, as Healing Justice, as an act of reclamation of the Black and Brown root systems of this brilliant framework, I literally clapped my hands in celebration. Because I know that Shira Hassan will tell us the truth, will help us see ourselves through a liberatory lens, and will help us understand how we practice harm reduction together by reminding us that it is how we have been surviving; it is our intuitive lineage of offering radical care and generating belonging in the face of oppression.

The structure of this book is very much like holding Shira's hand while moving through a gathering of harm reductionists not bound by space or time. There's theory, practice, humor, correction, political education, and so much deep and brave experimentation.

This book is such an important piece of history, told to set the stage for changing the paradigm of how we understand drugs and justice. It is a weaving together of storytelling, conversation, analysis, and practical tools. It is a kaleidoscope of identities that have shared needs and healing journeys. It is a gift, and I am so grateful it is in your hands.

Introduction

TOURMALINE

We have always been saving our own lives. When the state deems certain people disposable, we don't disappear. We turn to one another, prop each other up, and provide the care and solutions that no governing body ever could or would. In *The Faggots and Their Friends Between Revolutions*, Larry Mitchell writes, "We gotta keep each other alive any way we can 'cause nobody else is goin' do it." And we continue to.

Harm reduction isn't a single organization, or even one set of stable beliefs. But you know it when you see it: taking PreP before an all-nighter with a client. Telling your friend suffering intimate partner violence that they can call you anytime they need anything—you'll keep your phone on—and you won't question why they can't *just leave.* Doing drugs around people you love, rather than using alone. Going with a friend to a doctor to advocate for fair treatment on their behalf.

Before the nonprofit-industrial complex ever uttered the words "harm reduction," trans women of color were developing its best practices. Sex work and our efforts to keep one another safe are inextricably linked; the street-based hustling Marsha P. Johnson and Sylvia Rivera participated in fueled their own need for innovative harm reduction practices—as they were exposed to constant risk and violence—*and* funded the work they did to keep even more vulnerable and younger girls safe.

Marsha was fiercely protective of everyone she loved; they called her Saint Marsha. But just because she was a saint didn't mean she wouldn't fight back if she needed to, didn't mean she wasn't prepared to protect herself. She would say, "I carry my wonder drug everywhere I go—a can of Mace. If they attack me, I'm going to attack them, with my bomb." Her bomb! That's harm reduction: acknowledging the risks we take to stay alive and doing our best to value and protect our lives within that framework of risk. It wouldn't make sense to tell Marsha, *Oh, just get a different job.* A different job wasn't available, and a different job wouldn't pay the rent on STAR house. But it did (and still does) make sense to make sure that all the sex workers you knew had pepper spray on them, and knew how to use those bombs with precise accuracy if push came to shove.

Harm reduction happens in the pockets of exquisite care we show our loved ones, without questioning or judging their life choices, or imagining that we know better than they do. It's extending a belief system of true autonomy and self-determination: *I trust you, I'm not afraid of you, here are tools that might be useful to you, do with them what you will.* It's not about abstinence or punishment.

Since Marsha, Sylvia, and Miss Major Griffin-Gracy, countless harm reductionists have taken on the mantle of keeping their friends and communities alive, fed, housed, safe(r). As HIV spread through prisons in the 1980s and '90s, sick people who were locked up were left for dead; we can't forget that it was other incarcerated folks who learned and practiced ways to treat HIV-positive friends safely and effectively, and how to offer end-of-life palliative care. It's always been us—queer and trans sex workers, friends, organizers, healers, drug users, those of us who are disabled, without health insurance, reliant on systems that extract value from us without offering anything in return—who figure out what needs to be done to make one another's lives more livable, and who proceed to *do it*. Who believe that we all deserve lives of joy, comfort, abundance, and care, and commit big and small acts every day to turn those deserving dreams closer to a beautiful reality. We have been thinking through risk forever: how to face gendered violence, structural racism, contagion, the violence of poverty, the ravages of the dominant culture that tries time and again to disappear us. We have laid the groundwork, dug the foundation. And we do not have to do it alone: we save each other's lives, back and forth, always.

Welcome

I am not a trained writer by most definitions. Other than my own zines, I have only written with my sisters and comrades using circles, butcher paper, and hours of sharing. I am also not a trained historian, but I have been gathering the stories of my community, the people I love, for nearly three decades. This book was pulled from those of us who are street healers and radical activists after what has felt like a decades-long divination. My collaborators, many of whom I have lived and worked with toward our collective liberation for more than twenty-five years, held me in this writing process through online coworking dates, virtual hand-holding, edits, rewrites, and endless conversations about my own truth and the beauty of our intersecting realities that this book is reclaiming and renaming Liberatory Harm Reduction.

In many ways, the writing of this book is an example of Liberatory Harm Reduction in action. Loved ones surrounded me and moved with me at the pace of fear while I panicked every time I sat down to try to honor to this precious information painstakingly assembled through more than sixty interviews with queer, trans, Black, Brown, Indigenous, and People of Color who have breathed life into the daily practice of saving our lives.

Every interview I did contained a prayer for our people, a crafted wish that our discussions would lead us to a formula that could make clear the interweaving radical actualizations of care and fight.

The purpose of this project is to reclaim the history and creation of harm reduction as a liberatory strategy that was developed by Black, Indigenous, and People of Color (BIPOC) who were sex workers, queer, transgender, using drugs, young people, people with disabilities and chronic illness, street-based, and sometimes houseless. This project seeks to make a clear distinction between our practices of harm reduction and the ways that public health and social work[*] have co-opted their messages and meaning. We need to reclaim harm reduction and our voices, history, and legacy within it. We need to document our values that are the basis for this care work.

This book is titled *Saving Our Own Lives* because that's what we did—and do—every day. And those of us who do not survive whisper the secrets of how to be safer to the next generation through cherished platforms like handwritten instructional zines and song, protest chants, and the stories our communities share through our vast oral histories.

This book is about what happens when those of us who are targeted by the intersections of structural violence—by forces such as institutional racism, settler colonialism, ableism, capitalism, misogyny, Islamophobia, homophobia, fatphobia, and transphobia—survive, thrive, and build power together.[†]

This book is an invitation.

It is an invitation to BIPOC communities; to yransgender and queer communities, to sex-working and drug-using communities, to disabled and chronically ill communities, to young people, to

---

* When I say *social work* in this book, I am referring to the field as a whole. However, it is important to note there is a huge difference between *carceral social work*, which intentionally aligns itself with the police and supports increased criminalization, and *abolitionist social work*, which intentionally works to undermine state violence and end prisons and policing. Abolitionist social work seeks to disrupt the idea of social workers as arms of the state including the medical-industrial complex (MIC), children's services, and other systems of institutional violence.

† In this book, I use the term *structural violence* to describe the many ways forces of oppression impact our lives. This list is incomplete.

all of us who are survivors of violence—including those of us who have not survived—to recenter our history and see our cultures as the creators of this hard-working magic that has been gifted to us through memories and generational resilience.

This book is an invitation to public health departments and social workers to get clear about the meaning, history, and praxis of Liberatory Harm Reduction so that those institutions can begin to honestly acknowledge their theft of a people's generations-long practice. The inclusion of harm reduction inside public health and social work is a necessary, critical strategy to reduce the combined impact of the deadly medical-industrial complex (MIC), the prison-industrial complex (PIC), and the treatment industry on the lives of the people it claims to serve with dignity and respect. But public health must own that it cannot practice a Liberatory Harm Reduction inside those dehumanizing, ableist, and death-making systems, and it must admit that it did not create, grow, or honor the roots of this praxis.*

How to Read This Book

I asked loved ones, comrades, and thought partners to review the drafts of this book, and so many people gave me feedback that what is contained in these pages builds the heart and takes time to absorb. In order to write this, I accessed some of my deepest vulnerability and did my best to navigate the line between sharing enough to make the book feel alive and connected to our communities and yours, and maintaining a political, grounded meta-analysis. And I am only half joking when I say that during

* I am using the word *ableism* to refer to able-bodied and able-minded supremacy. Defined by Sins Invalid in their *Skin, Tooth, and Bone* primer (2020), *able-bodied* is a system that reinforces the superiority of nondisabled people. *Able-minded* is similar to *able-bodied* and refers to people who don't have mental health disabilities, psychiatric impairments, developmental disabilities, learning disabilities, and so on.

this two-year writing process, which felt like an excavation, I exhausted my highly competent and talented therapist, and my service dog needed to re-up his training.

I have often thought about Aurora Levins Morales's note in her book *Medicine Stories*: "Repetition is a method, a rhythm of meaning that must be maintained, a beat to my message." As themes repeat, it isn't a mistake, she says. This holds true in this book as it has my whole life as a student of my community, a student of my trauma memory that keeps me forgetting and remembering. The invitation in the repetition is maceration—to hold and release, to speed up and slow down.

One of the scariest parts of this project was deciding which of my own stories could serve this book, without sharing too much with you or challenging my deeply private nature. I hold close the value I learned from Young Women's Empowerment Project that one person's story should not be elevated above that of the collective or it risks simplifying us—making all our stories the same and making us targets—in the eyes of the world. I repeat Poly Styrene's lyrics *I am a cliché*, to remind me that nothing that I have experienced is terribly unique, freeing me from the shame of being alone with my trauma and opening me up to a whole community of people. I am afraid to share my stories because my memories are skewed by pain and yet remain my truth. I am afraid to tell my stories because I have made so many mistakes, caused others grief, suffering. I am afraid to share my stories because of what you will or won't think, say, believe about me and others like me. I offer these intimacies with understanding that each one—in the words of my palm reader Amelia—are both significantly powerful and powerfully insignificant in our practice to reclaim our resilience strategies.

I am choosing to be brave by sharing these stories because as Chicago Liberatory Harm Reduction practitioner, Mayadet Patitucci Cruz, said to me, "Liberatory Harm Reduction is different because it asks us to self-reflect, holds space for us to grow, let go of shame, to change or not change, to make mistakes and keep showing up anyway." I hope that this book offers a space for us to dislodge our shame and live into the beauty of our mess. Because doing that can be heavy work, I invite you to be cozy with it, to read this with friends, comrades, chosen family, and loved ones; skip around chapters and interviews; get lost in the beautiful images by Lizartistry; and put the book down when you need to.

I am sharing the guidelines we use in our Just Practice Collaborative (JPC)* workshops because I want this book to be a space where you can go full mer-person—dive deep and come up for air. The space of this book holds you—all of you—and invites care for you on your own terms and at your own pace.

> This book space is generous and generative.
>
> This book space honors mistakes. There is no perfection here.
>
> This book gives us space to transform shame.
>
> This book space knows that curiosity and judgment cannot coexist. We know and believe that multiple truths can co-exist. We answer judgment with curiosity, with a question.
>
> This book space holds our pace, our questions, our grief, our joy, and our self-care and our collective care.

---

* Cofounded by Mariame Kaba, Deana Lewis, Rachel Caïdor, Ana Mercado, Keisa Reynolds, and me in 2014, Just Practice Collaborative's mission is "to build our communities' capacity to effectively and empathically respond to intimate partner violence and sexual assault without relying on police or other state-based systems. Our work seeks to create a world where survivors and their communities can feel believed, feel held, like healing is possible, and where prisons and police no longer exist."

Saving Our Own Lives

Saving Our Own Lives is not a book about addiction,* the War on Drugs, or the history of syringe exchanges; it is not the story of building AIDS Inc or of how ACT UP created access to HIV medications domestically and internationally.

There are so many heroes this book could be about, including Edith Springer—considered the godmother of US harm reduction by many—for her thousands of trainings and clinical support to multiple organizations. It could be about radical women of color and queer People of Color like Keith Cylar, Bali White, Jon Paul Hammond, Paula Santiago, Imani Woods, Rhoda Creamer, Mona Bennett. It could also be about Alan Clear, Donald Grove, and Don McVinney, or it could be about those radical thinkers who formed the first National Harm Reduction Coalition: a combination of Black, Latinx, queer, and antiracist white organizers that created a national body for grassroots education and policy work—still the only one in the country. So many people—too many—have gone unacknowledged.

This book is not even the partial story of the incredible activists who were arrested multiple times for giving clean needles and supplies to drug users to stop the spread of HIV and hepatitis C,† beginning in 1982 with Jon Stuen-Parker in New Haven, CT, and continuing with Diana McCage in New Brunswick, NJ, in the 1990s.

---

* I am choosing to use the word *addiction* over the current term *substance use disorder* because I am not just writing about substances or use disorders in this book. I am reclaiming the word *addiction*, releasing the shame and owning it as a part of me. I am practicing honoring *all* of my coping strategies, even the stigmatized.

† Jon Stuen-Parker was arrested numerous times in many places but primarily lived and worked in New Haven, CT. See PBS, "Needle Exchange: A Primer," May 30, 2006, https://www.pbs.org/wgbh/pages/frontline/aids/past/needle.html, as well as the documentary *Chasing Heroin*, Maria Galva, writer/director (Frontline Films, 2016), https://www.pbs.org/wgbh/frontline/film/chasing-heroin/transcript.

This book is not the story of Dan Bigg, who, along with Sarz Maxwell and Karen Stanczykiewicz at the Chicago Recovery Alliance, turned the tables on the opioid epidemic in Chicago by putting naloxone, a drug that reverses opioid overdoses, directly into the hands of drug users.

It is not the tale of the philosophy of Housing First, a model that radically states that housing is a human right, and *all* people should be given homes, not just sober people.

This is not a book about Dave Purchase, who founded the Tacoma-based syringe exchange, Point Defiance AIDS Projects, in 1988, and then went on to start the North American Syringe Exchange Network: the first network of syringe exchanges that at the time was mostly made up of underground and illegal exchanges. Nor is it about Mary Howe, who became an icon in peer-led work with young people who inject drugs, through the founding of Homeless Youth Alliance in San Francisco in 2006.*

Even though I am indebted to each of these incredible, hard-working activist visionaries whose work informed this book and harm reduction in social services and public health settings, this book is not about them.

This book is about Liberatory Harm Reduction as a political philosophy, lifesaving strategy, and set of concrete tools. These tools seed liberation movements through maintaining compassionate and complex relationships, the belief that none of us are disposable, and, most important, through the daily practice of love, the making of chosen family, and the whispers of our ancestors who taught us how to keep going in a country that would rather see us

* For the incredible history of the evolution of harm reduction syringe exchange, drug policy, and activism in the US, please read Maia Szalavitz's *Undoing Drugs: The Untold Story of Harm Reduction*.

become ghosts than leaders. This book exists as the demonstration of love in practice in BIPOC communities.

While some of us know that street-based people, queer and trans people, young people, drug users, and all those whose survival is criminalized have been critical leaders in mass movements for change, many do not know that people in the sex trade and sex workers—especially BIPOC—have conjured the majority of our models of collective safety, including harm reduction: the glitter lighting our paths.

Saving Our Own Lives challenges the widespread and mistaken beliefs that harm reduction is only a public health model or only a behavior change model. I want to show you that while harm reduction is most often thought of as a set of practical strategies used to address injection drug use, it is actually a liberatory approach to community preservation and a value-based creation that can be used to address everything from violence to eating disorders to policing.

As a coherent philosophy and set of pragmatic practices, harm reduction emerged from a careful, alchemical balance of death and durability, love and boundaries, creativity and loss, and survivorship and empowerment. It is essential for our collective survival to recognize that harm reduction, which achieved widespread recognition in the 1980s through the critical strategy of syringe exchange, evolved through decades and decades of liberatory awareness and organizing.

Harm reduction teaches us how to practice the politic *no one is disposable* demanded by Transformative Justice, another strategy developed by BIPOC searching for solutions to end violence without using state systems. Liberatory Harm Reduction gives us the concrete tools to make sure that our marches, protests, rallies, campaigns are truly led by those of us who are experiencing the most harm from the systems we are living under. Harm reduction knows that *we are not the problem—we are the solution.** When

* This is quote from the Young Women's Empowerment Project (YWEP), a

we understand and believe that harm reduction is the street-based revolutionary's gift back to our larger community, then we can begin to ensure that we are *all* engaged in work that advances freedom and liberation.

Saving Our Own Lives: A Liberatory Practice of Harm Reduction was written because I owe my life to my community's practice: a practice that holds trauma, resistance, resilience, joy, creativity, passion, anger, and heart. This book is about *my* community's practice and an homage to as many elders and ancestors that I could get into these pages. It is my humble and incomplete offering back to the hours of investment that so many mentors, community members, and chosen family made in my work and survival. When I feel small in the face of this project and inadequate next to the legendary activists who gave life to the rituals of love that is Liberatory Harm Reduction, I remember that my ultimate hope is that is that this book will help create an avalanche of books about you and how your community's liberatory practice of Liberatory Harm Reduction operates in your town, city, or rural life, so that none of us can be erased from our own work.

Maybe you are or were using drugs, trading sex for money, disabled or chronically ill, practicing self-injury, fighting for a world without prison, policing, violence and harm, fighting for your children and family, both given and chosen, so that you can understand your lineage, where you come from, and the fact that we are here because our warriors whispered messages like "Fuck safe and shoot clean," and showed us how to cook enough food from one can for the whole block—without electricity.

This book is a gift to you—you beautiful, complicated, powerful, messy, and precious survivor.

---

project that was led by and for young People of Color in the sex trade and street economy in Chicago, IL, from 2002 to 2014.

Liberatory Harm Reduction Saved My Life

Southwest Asian North African (SWANA) people know my background as soon as I say my name and it makes my mixed ethnic origin transparent.* What may be less apparent is that I am an anti-Zionist queer femme who grew up in a mixed-class household filled with drug use, drug sales, and a lineage of physical, sexual, and emotional abuse. I somehow survived addiction, a life in the sex trade,† sex work, the street economy, multiple physical and learning disabilities, and sleeping rough more nights than I can remember. I got through college and social work school with the help of case workers, tutors, and learning disability specialists.

It's odd for someone like me—who has mostly been known as a hooker who gives good workshop, who gets young people out of the trunks of pimps' cars, who busts people out of psych wards,

* I am of a blended SWANA ancestry, with my people coming from Dagestan, a small country on the Caspian Sea. I am of Ashkenazi, Moroccan, and Turkish descent, and I've been a vocal anti-Zionist since my teens.

† Like many young people, I didn't understand that the activities I was participating in were considered part of the sex trade until I met Claudine O'Leary in 2000.

who can find safe housing across the country for those who don't have identification, and who works to solve problems without cops or the state—to be asked what I think and believe about the world.

What I know is this: in the simplest and most complicated of ways, harm reduction saved my life.

I ran to New York City from the suburbs of Philadelphia because I was desperate to do something—anything—that would get me out: out of danger, out of erasure, out of fear. For about three years, I lied to everyone in my life and went back and forth from outside of Philly to Tompkins Square Park on the Lower East Side of New York City. I went home with different men many nights, stayed out all night in clubs,* slept under the shrubs in the park, and, on lucky nights, some angel from the squats on 7th Street would invite all the girls in the park to sleep inside. I got the best sleep at a Ball† or in a club. The music, the drugs, the fashion, and the darkness were so comforting that even now, as a mostly sober person, I have to fall asleep listening to the radio, music, or television to calm my brain.

I became a client at Streetwork Project in NYC as a young person because a punk-looking, Brown queer person handed me a pile of clean syringes and told me where I could take a shower.‡ That interaction changed my life. It was the first time in a long

---

* Shout out to the angels who ran the club Shelter in NYC for feeding us breakfast before closing down at the end of the night. This is a precious example of one of my favorite harm reduction interventions in queer public spaces.

† Balls and the House community are a critical part of BIPOC queer and trans culture. Beginning in the nineteenth century in Harlem, they thrived in NYC in the 1980s and 1990s and are still evolving and alive in many places today. Their impact on the development of harm reduction practices and implementation of everything from testing and hormone safety to condom distribution at Balls is well known. For more information, please read Marlon M. Brandon's *Butch Queen Up in Pumps* and watch Luna Luis Ortiz's *The Luna Show* on YouTube.

‡ Streetwork Project began in 1984 as a grassroots harm reduction project in the Times Square neighborhood of NYC working with street based and houseless youth. It has expanded to work with young people all over the city.

time that I had thought about taking care of myself beyond just surviving. I kept in touch with that outreach worker for more than two decades. The care I received did more than prevent me from getting HIV: it introduced me to an invisible web of support, transmitted through messages like "Make sure your socks stay dry," and "Cotton underwear will help your coochie heal after sex."

I know that I wouldn't have graduated high school if the same Streetwork outreach worker hadn't come around the Lower East Side looking for me a few times per month. She asked me real questions, like, "Do you want to graduate high school?" and listened. She told me I had options because I hadn't been kicked out of school yet and that she would help me figure out the best way to live with whatever choices I made. Those conversations kept me going back and forth to high school and helped me remain connected enough to my mom's suburban house to graduate. When I finally finished with a D-minus average, I registered for a summer program for young people who had "fallen on hard times," which, at its conclusion, enrolled our desperate asses in college.

I worked my way through college on a rape crisis line and in a women's prison in Pittsburgh, PA. I became a peer educator at a syringe exchange and started going back to Twelve-Step meetings (I went to Alateen when I was thirteen). After leaving a cult due to the rampant sexual violence by leaders, at twenty-one I eventually made my way back to New York. I got a job working with boys, aged sixteen to eighteen, who were incarcerated at Rikers Island because they were being charged as adults for crimes of sexual violence. We talked about how to stay alive, gang rules, consent, feminism, and queerness. Working in prisons made me believe in the concepts underlying prison abolition and Transformative Justice before we started using these terms.

I owe my life to sex workers, to drug users, and to people called "mad" and "criminal" by much of the world. I owe my life to Black and Brown trans women, who worked daily to survive sometimes bone-deep violence. Through their commitment to themselves and to community building, they led and mentored us and all of the crooked and wounded and glorious children who were dancing and clawing our way to safety through fashion and family. I owe my life to the House community, whose Balls and club scenes were places where I felt my body was safe, where I was relaxed and simultaneously visible and invisible. I owe my life to queers, to queens, to dykes, to butches and studs, to weirdos, to the community who knit family and meaning into the sacred mundane like meals and bathing.

On Sex Work, the Sex Trade, and Street Economy

I am making a conscious choice not to isolate the sex trade and sex work from the rest of the book in a special chapter, because to do so would be to separate our contributions into a single, easily digestible, easily dismissable section. Much of the mainstream harm reduction movement that operates alongside public health has historically treated people in the sex trade as an afterthought. It's as though the most important intervention ever contributed to the field of harm reduction is syringe exchange and that sex workers, even those of us, like me, who also shot up drugs, are not a central part of the creation of this life-affirming philosophy. The few books that are written about harm reduction barely touch on sex work and focus entirely on drug use. *Saving Our Own Lives* centers the roles and lives of people in the sex trade, sex work, and survivors of all kinds as the breath work of Liberatory Harm Reduction because, although this may sound uncomfortable to many, we place the importance of relationships and care work at the core of everything that we do.

My own lineage can be traced back to friends and chosen family who are made up of the same young people I met in the

1990s—Black, Brown, queer, and trans survivors. We laced together into a family. As someone who started trading sex for money, housing, and drugs at an age earlier than this book documents, I have woven sex work and sex workers seamlessly throughout these pages. The fight for freedom from violence for people who trade sex or sexuality for money, drugs, or other survival need—for instance, documentation, immigration paperwork, diapers, or in exchange for not being arrested or detained—is not only integral to the story of Liberatory Harm Reduction but also integral to my own survival story and politicization.

My experience in the sex trade, sex work, and street economy needs no explanation or disclosure.* I will not be regaling you with the wonders and horrors of what it is/was like to be involved in sex work as a teen and adult. Nobody with life experience trading sex for money—whether due to force, for pleasure, or for economics—should have to recount their experiences in order that others recognize the basic principles of body autonomy and Reproductive Justice.

However, to understand some information in this book, it is necessary to clarify some basics. First, let me offer some language. *The sex trade* is an umbrella term that can include many different ways of being sexual in exchange for many different kinds of resources. Some people in the sex trade may identify their activity as a job while others, especially young people, may not think of their activities explicitly as work and may just say, "I do some things for money." As defined by Young Women's Empowerment Project (YWEP):

---

* At YWEP, we had a strong value of not publicly telling our stories about the sex trade, for so many reasons. The most important reason is because we became targets of violence. One person's story can easily become the dominant version in someone's mind. We also did this because our stories are so often co-opted by mainstream news media and told the same way over and over again. Our stories are ours—no one else's—and they must be earned.

> The sex trade is any form of being sexual (or the idea of being sexual) in exchange for money, gifts, safety, drugs, hormones, or survival needs like housing, food, clothes, or immigration [paperwork] and documentation. Our definition of the sex trade also includes girls who are trafficked, sold for sex through family and pimps, or are ritual abuse survivors. People from all backgrounds can be involved in the sex trade.

I love this definition because it includes the critical component of bartering sex and sexuality, honors that not all experiences in the sex trade are consensual, and does not require people to name their involvement as an identity. This brings me to the terms *sex work* and *sex worker.* Coined by Carol Queen in the 1970s, the term *sex work* has been critical to labor rights and organizing to decriminalize consensual sex work for people considered adults. Generally, the term *sex work* is used by adults (but not always), and, generally, it is a term used by people who identify their activities as a job (but not always). The sex workers' rights movement has played an essential role in the establishment of harm reduction. I will be using both the terms *sex work* and *the sex trade* throughout this book, because it is important to recognize that people relate to their experiences, and name them, differently.

It is also important to recognize that people can have experiences that are good, bad, and/or neutral, and they do not cancel each other out. I have experienced force, fraud, and coercion—*and* freedom, independence, and self- determination. If you believe that people in the sex trade and sex workers can only be either victims or empowered, then you are missing the reality of the lived experiences of those of us who have complex histories. Which is to say, you're missing the whole thing. Sex work and the sex trade are complicated and cannot be neatly summed up for public consumption and legibility.

The term *street economy* is often used to describe any activity that happens in exchange for cash that is not taxed. The most common examples are drug sales and some parts of the sex trade. There is an enormous overlap between the sex trade, sex work, and the street economy. However, it is important to note that there are many ways to be in the sex trade that are legal and taxed sex work. For example, phone sex and strip clubs are not necessarily a part of the street economy because they have business licensing and are taxed establishments with employees. That said, many clubs operate a legal, tax-compliant, public-facing front while also operating a shadow business hidden from most of the public and the IRS.

Revolutionaries and the Gift of Liberatory Harm Reduction

The story of the evolution of harm reduction predates the AIDS crisis. As Tourmaline writes in her introduction, Liberatory Harm Reduction came to us through leaders like Marsha P. Johnson, Sylvia Rivera, and Miss Major Griffin-Gracy and their comrades, trans women of color who were sex workers and street based, who, together, created shared housing to ensure that young people had safer places to sleep. Liberatory Harm Reduction came through the Black Panthers' creation of free breakfast programs to feed and nourish a revolution, and through the Young Lords' occupation of Lincoln Hospital in the Bronx to demand—and ultimately operate—community-run, accessible drug treatment programs.*

People in helping professions either don't know or actively ignore these founding facts. Literature about harm reduction makes it sound as though it either sprang fully formed from the veins

* I will use the terms *treatment programs* or *treatment industry* to refer to the business side of addiction. Treatment programs have a poor success rate, documented in too many studies to list. The treatment industry keeps treatment programs propped up and relies on criminalization and stigmatization of drug users to do so.

of white needle users or was created by departments of health or white savior do-gooders. In that story, harm reduction is best known for its game-changing impact of stemming the tide of the HIV/AIDS epidemic through practical and evidence-based interventions, such as providing immediate and easy access to condoms in prisons and syringe exchange, that are championed by public health departments and social workers as critical strategies that significantly reduce the person-to-person transmission of HIV and hepatitis. Yet even those who know that harm reduction did not start in departments of public health largely credit white male needle users with the invention of these principles.

Liberatory Harm Reduction came into being because people in the sex trade, People of Color, queer people, and transgender, gender-nonconforming, and two spirit people saved our own lives. This is a collective story of Bad Date sheets passed between sex workers in Portland; it is the story of clean syringes "liberated" from empathetic doctors' offices to be passed between punks in the East Village squats by leaders like Isabel Dawson, an early AIDS activist, who made sure that everyone had syringes and knew how to use them. Her daughter, Rosario, writes more about Isabel's work in the afterword.

The Gift of Liberatory Harm Reduction

The values and methods of Liberatory Harm Reduction were passed on to me by BIPOC, and antiracist white activists. After an experience of pro-police racism in the mid-2000s at one of the largest syringe-exchange conferences, I became obsessed with understanding and then widely sharing the true roots of Liberatory Harm Reduction.

I trace my own Liberatory Harm Reduction history back to 1997, a year before I fell in love with and started dating Chloe Dzubilo. Chloe was a downtown art goddess, the white front woman for a punk band called Transisters, coconspirator of Transexual Menace,* and she became the primary staff person for the first-ever syringe-exchange program in the United States run by and for transgender people in New York City. This syringe exchange, called the Transgender Initiative, was started by Bali White, spoken about later in this book by Kiara St. James. Bali collaborated with Imani Henry, Kelly McGowan, and Arlene Hoffman at Positive Health Project in Midtown to create the first federally funded syringe exchange† run by and for trans people in the country. When I quit the job that had me working at Rikers Island, Chloe sent me toward Edith Springer's project called New York Peer AIDS Education Coalition (NYPAEC).

I was finally home. At NYPAEC I met Kelly McGowan, a white, antiracist, queer, cis woman who had also run away and lived in the squats on the Lower East Side. Kelly and Chloe were the first antiracist white people I met. Together they had cofounded syringe exchanges and projects for trans people and people in the sex trade. Kelly conducted the United States' first HIV Needs Assessment for Transgender Adults, completed in December 1999. The findings are still relevant today, and the study remains one of New York City Department of Health's most requested documents.

Edith Springer, in collaboration with Kelly and a host of others, created NYPAEC as a harm reduction peer education network for young people ages twelve to twenty-four who were street based, involved in the sex trade, shooting up, transgender, queer,

---

* Transexual Menace was one of the first direct action groups formed in the early 1990s to challenge the exclusion of trans people from LGB Pride marches, centers, and the Gay Games.

† It is important to note that federal funds have never (and still cannot) be used to support syringe distribution, according to the CDC. The Transgender Initiative got HIV prevention dollars to support sex workers via peer education and made sure to distribute syringes and carefully track and document the cash flow to both honor their grant agreements and push back on the state.

Black, and/or Brown. I was twenty-two when, in 1997, I became the peer program director of NYPAEC. Three nights a week, we ate warm food together, studied harm reduction, and mass distributed condoms and life-saving information to other young people living on the piers of New York City's West Side, to the strolls in the meatpacking district, and spots like the Port Authority building in Midtown, where so many young people in the sex trade and street economy were working. We were sick, disabled, and mad—half of us vogued our way through every conversation while the other half cried, slept, or sang off-key. We were community. We helped each other, healed each other, and figured out how to hold each other accountable when things "went missing" or partners were "stolen."

Kelly became my weekly support person, offering me structured intentional leadership development and mentoring. These exchanges provided a template for how to offer thoughtful, whole-person accompaniment to young people with complex histories of trauma, drug use, and the sex trade. Through this relationship, I learned how to make queer family, as Kelly reparented me with careful teachings on how to stay steady in long-term crisis, and how to invest in the people you love and who love you for all of your flaws and fuckups.

I moved from New York to Chicago in 2002, after a year of anti-Arab death threats following 9/11. I was lucky to move there and enter into a collective of women, trans people, and girls with current or former experience in the sex trade and street economy who were in the process of founding a social justice organizing group called Young Women's Empowerment Project (YWEP). Claudine O'Leary, a white, lesbian-identified person with life experience in the sex trade and street economy was working to establish a social justice project where young people could organize, protest, talk to each other, and work with our community from a place of lived authenticity. Claudine became the first director, and she invited me to help develop YWEP's peer-to-peer outreach project in 2002, using the model Kelly had cocreated with Edith Springer at NYPAEC more than ten years earlier.

I was in love with YWEP and the young people working there. Like NYPAEC, YWEP was not a social service provider but instead was staffed and run by young People of Color from age twelve to twenty-four who worked as outreach workers, member leaders, directors, and coordinators. In 2011, YWEP hired Dominique McKinney—a member of YWEP since the age of fifteen—to be the executive director. This meant that our project had achieved its goal of becoming the only organization in the country run by and for young BIPOC with current or former experience in the sex trade and street economy. Dominique became one of the youngest Black executive directors of a nonprofit organization in the country and ran the project brilliantly until YWEP closed in 2014 as a result of anti-trafficking legislation that criminalized certain harm reduction practices. In 2014, Dominique and several YWEP leaders spun off another justice-based organizing project called Street Youth Rise UP! (SYRU).

Throughout this book, I use examples of my learning with YWEP. I am referring to the years I was most heavily involved, 2004–2011, so that the cofounders who began working together in 2001 can, at some point, tell us how this sacred project evolved, should they choose to. Dominique McKinney, Daphnie Williams, and C. Angel Torres—who continued to lead the project into the creation of Street Youth Rise UP!—Dr. Laura Janine Mintz, Stacy Erenberg, Alissa Hull, and Tanuja Jagernauth have been consulted about the stories contained within these pages, and I hope that this book gives them the recognition they deserve for their powerful leadership that changed the conversation about young people in the sex trade in the United States.

From roughly 2006 to 2013, YWEP led the only syringe exchange in the country that was operated by and for young BI-

POC who were involved in the sex trade and street economy. We reached five hundred young people a year though our peer-to-peer outreach and an additional two hundred young people through our syringe exchange.

Our syringe exchange was dubbed SEXXY (Syringe Exchange Expansion for Youth). It was a body-loving project that distributed safer injection information and equipment for young people injecting hormones and/or shooting drugs. Many of our participants were under the age of eighteen, which placed the operations of our exchange outside Illinois law, as it was legal to distribute clean needles only to people eighteen and over.

In the mid-2000s, we learned about a giant conference for people operating syringe exchanges, and we were so excited! We pooled our resources, got some travel assistance to attend, and about eight of us boarded a plane in Chicago to head to the West Coast. The idea of meeting other BIPOC, queer, and trans young people slinging syringes and talking about the sex trade was a dream for us.

The morning of the first conference event we woke up and got fabulous. With clothes strewn all over the hotel floor, it took us hours to untangle everything and dress each other, get our makeup flawless, and straighten our neckties so our queerness would be visible from outer space. We floated into the huge hotel ballroom set with banquet tables covered with long, super-white tablecloths, passing signs like "Someone I Love Is a Drug User" and people in T-shirts that read, "Be Nice to Sex Workers." We were in heaven and had never been in a public place that felt so drug-positive and sex worker–led. But as we continued to walk deeper into the conference space, we quickly realized we were the youngest, brownest, and queerest people in the room. We suddenly felt smaller, more protective, aware that our lives in the street economy were glaring.

At some point during the main plenary, a white police officer, who had been invited by the organizers, was introduced as the next speaker. The white man who introduced him was a well-known harm reductionist working in a majority Black and Brown city on the East Coast. The harm reductionist stated that the biggest challenge facing syringe exchanges was the lack of relationships with police and argued that syringe-exchange programs that prioritized building connections with police officers would see a decrease in arrests of their participants. He was proud of his relationship with this white police officer—his friend—and he wanted us to listen to the officer and consider building relationships with the police as a form of harm reduction.

Our table was stunned. We looked at each other, first in confusion and then in anger, as his words sank in. We realized immediately that we needed to act. One YWEP leader stood up with their fist in the air and shouted, "No Justice! No Peace!" The rest of us followed quickly. We stood up, chanting together and interrupting the cop's speech, and walked out loudly with our heads held high and fists raised. We gathered outside of the hotel to rage at what we had just experienced. It was a shock to us; we had no idea there were people who believed in harm reduction who also believed that policing was just.

For the rest of the conference, the only people who spoke to us were the very few other sex workers present. Not one conference organizer checked in on us, even though most of them had known me for ten years by that point. They were completely uninterested in honoring the roots of what I now think of as Liberatory Harm Reduction. In fact, no bridges were built between YWEP and the mainstream harm reduction community locally or nationally during our entire lifespan as a project. We left that conference early and never went back to another until Monique Tula, a Black activist with a long history of organizing, became the executive director of the National Harm Reduction Coalition and reached out to us to rebuild our relationship.

The experience of being in such a large conference space with hundreds of white people who were excited about the police revealed the stark contrast between our worlds. I had been brought up by activists with an overarching politics about the dehumanizing role of state violence in our lives. Harm reduction, at YWEP, at NYPAEC, and in countless examples demonstrated to me during the entire previous decade, was not only about navigating individual experiences of drug use and safer sex but also about the daily impact of the racist War on Drugs and of colonialist cisheteropatriarchy in BIPOC communities.

The disillusioning and infuriating experience at that conference marked the beginning of YWEP's choice to understand our lineage as activists and caregivers who believed in harm reduction as a liberatory philosophy and strategy, and as people who were working toward a revolution for Black, Indigenous, immigrant peoples, and People of Color. The event made clear to us that we needed to better understand the connections that harm reduction identified between the sex trade and Islamophobia, between harm reduction and colonization, among trans liberation, squatters' rights, the MIC, Disability Justice, and capitalism. We wanted to connect the dots for ourselves, make our inheritance clear to our communities, and link these beliefs with the possibility of living freely, without the fear of violence, police, or prisons.

By 2007, YWEP was the first organization openly led by young People of Color in the sex trade and street economy to make these links publicly, using data that we collected independently.* We were vocal and explicit about our life experience in the sex trade and the first to develop campaigns, to conduct ongoing research on institutional violence, and, importantly, to say clearly, "We are prison abolitionists." YWEP's analysis was

* Shout out to Different Avenues' *Move Along: Policing Sex Work in Washington, D.C.*, published in 2008. This participatory action research project led by and for adult sex workers was groundbreaking, inspiring, and still highly relevant today.

always grounded in the root causes of violence in our lives, including capitalism, cisheteropatriarchy, racism, and other systemic oppression, as well as the agents of these oppressions: cops. Cops are known to be violent individuals who would often use the threat of arrest to coerce sex workers. For example, many of the young people who formed YWEP had experience with cops who would say, "Sleep with me or I will arrest you," but then, after the act, they were arrested anyway.

Along with our individual experiences, leaders like Sylivia Rivera and Marsha P. Johnson, through their anti-police analysis at STAR, informed our political analysis as we realized the widespread impacts of police, policing, and prisons as forms of violence. To this day, I often hear this analysis credited to adult-run, mostly white-led, sex workers' rights groups or to Instagram accounts run by adult sex workers. Let me be absolutely clear: they got it from YWEP, from young People of Color, and from STAR. YWEP trained the larger sex workers' rights organizations and activists in our analysis—and they argued with us, insisting that advocating for "sex workers' rights" was the answer to the legal risks that people face in the sex trade. The slogan of the sex worker movement has been "Only rights can stop the wrongs." At YWEP, we knew the root cause of violence against people in the sex trade cannot be fixed with a "rights" framework, because to do so overfocuses on the law and fundamentally excludes people under eighteen, who are not recognized by most laws proposed by adults. Additionally, the law does not have much to do with how people are targeted by police; that targeting is rooted in racism, colonialism, and cisheteropatriarchy.

The reality is that while laws against the sex trade need to be removed and sex work *must* be decriminalized, the acts of violence against us will not be stopped unless we organize from an anti-criminalization framework. Anti-criminalization includes ending prisons and racist policing—this work is connected to prison abolition and has been happening for generations. Decriminalization of the sex trade and sex work is, in a sense, a policy-based harm reduction strategy. The idea is that removing the laws that target us is a small but essential step in reducing violence. "Decrim," as it is often abbreviated, is a reform that all of us, from Women with a Vision in New Orleans to nationally known activists like Monica Jones, have been working toward. We know that decriminalization of the sex trade and sex work is part of our long-term goal of ending criminalization and, ultimately, of prison abolition. YWEP made it clear in our politics, workshops, trainings, and writing, that decrim is not the ultimate goal—we were fighting for an end to profiling, police violence, rape, and prisons.

The revelation at the syringe-exchange conference brings me to one of the critical messages of this book: harm reduction must be viewed in the larger context of the revolutionary organizing that laid the kindling for harm reduction to catch fire. Those sparks were lit by the Young Lords and Black Panther Party during the 1969 Lincoln Hospital takeover in the Bronx; continued to burn brightly with Silvia Rivera and Marsha P. Johnson when they founded Street Transvestite Action Revolutionaries (STAR), a housing/mutual aid project started in the early '80s; and grew into a bonfire with thousands of illegal syringe-distribution projects, drug user unions, and sex worker organizing projects.

THE *Activist History* OF LIBERATORY HARM REDUCTION

Critical Lineage

- MS. MAJOR GRIFFIN-GRACY

- INDIGENOUS RESISTANCE PRACTICES
- SEX WORKERS
- DRUG USERS & AIDS ACTIVISTS
- PEOPLE'S PROGRAMS

THE BLACK PANTHER PARTY FOR SELF-DEFENSE 1972 TEN-POINT PROGRAM

THE YOUNG LORDS & THE B.P.P. & THE PEOPLE'S DRUG PROGRAM AT LINCOLN HOSPITAL

- UNDERGROUND ABORTION PROVIDERS
- S.T.A.R.-STREET TRANSGENDER ACTION REVOLUTIONARIES

MARSHA P. JOHNSON & SYLVIA RIVERA

What Is Liberatory Harm Reduction?

Liberatory Harm Reduction is not new; it was born from decades of revolutionary practice. This section was written in reflection with queer and trans activists and practitioners, almost all of them BIPOC, some of whom I have been lucky enough to be in practice with for nearly thirty years. I spoke to them as I was trying to sift and sort through the distinctions in the work both inside and outside of institutions and social services. Everyone here has either been a young person in harm reduction or has worked with young people as an organizer. We have also all been working to end violence—without the state and social services—using harm reduction strategies. The definitions and concepts in this section were discussed, refined, and reviewed by Erica Woodland, Priya Rai, adrienne maree brown, Monique Tula, Kelli Dorsey, Emi Koyama, Micah Hobbes Frazier, Benji Hart, La Tony Alvarado-Rivera, Bonsai Bermúdez, Mayadet Patitucci Cruz, Sarah Daoud, Xavier MaatRa, Dominique Morgan, Monica Jones, Andrea J. Ritchie, Mariame Kaba, Deana Lewis, Rachel Caïdor, Dominique McKinney, Kelly McGowan, and Dr. Laura Janine Mintz.

In a conversation with Micah Hobbes Frazier, a comrade I met through harm reduction work in my twenties, Micah reflected:

> In Liberatory Harm Reduction work we say let's get underneath and get to the root cause of things because if we don't get to the root of things, then we're going to constantly be responding to instead of creating new ways of being in new conditions, really setting ways for people to be their best selves, be safe, be well. Instead of continuing to respond to crisis, to trauma, to violence, to harm, Liberatory Harm Reduction can pull out those roots and then plant something different.
>
> Is it white supremacy? Is it patriarchy? Is it someone's trauma? Like what allowed and supported this risk to happen in

> the first place? That's our work. Condoms, yes, of course—but challenging police violence is how we really reduce risk.

At the end of the day, public health, social work, and medicine are not concerned with putting themselves out of business, and they are not concerned with building our collective power.* Keeping the lights on and thousands of people employed, keeping the institutions lawsuit free and the system intact, is the primary purpose of hospital administrators and most corporate nonprofits. And while I do, in fact, want both systems of healthcare and social services to center harm reduction, we need to acknowledge that liability laws make the application of Liberatory Harm Reduction almost impossible. In the words of Sarah Daoud, an anticarceral queer and trans Arab social worker who works with LGBT houseless young people in Chicago:

> So often, we can't use Liberatory Harm Reduction. Liability laws and other bureaucracy make the practice of honoring what people want to do with their bodies nearly impossible. We'd get fired, licenses revoked, maybe even arrested. So, we're given public health harm reduction, and told that it's the same thing. That it's good enough. It's like what they say in cooking shows—if you can't make your own, store bought is fine. But most of the time, state-sanctioned harm reduction isn't fine. It's the site of harm.

I offer the following definition of Liberatory Harm Reduction with humility and with the full hope and expectation that it will change over time as it is honed by activists and practitioners seeking to name the intangible. As Dominique Morgan, the executive director of the Okra Project, said, "Shira—Liberatory Harm Reduction is grace in practice."

---

* Please read *The Revolution Will Not Be Funded* by Incite! Women, Gender Non-Conforming, and Trans People of Color Against Violence for more history about the term *nonprofit-industrial complex* and how nonprofits were created and used to subvert the people's power and revolution.

Liberatory Harm Reduction *is a philosophy and set of empowerment-based practices that teach us how to accompany each other as we transform the root causes of harm in our lives.*

We put our values into action using real-life strategies to reduce the negative health, legal, and social consequences that result from criminalized and stigmatized life experiences such as drug use, sex, the sex trade, sex work, surviving intimate partner violence, self-injury, eating disorders, and any other survival strategies deemed morally or socially unacceptable.

Liberatory Harm Reductionists support each other and our communities ***without judgment, stigma, or coercion,*** *and we do not* ***force*** *others to change. We envision a world without racism, capitalism, patriarchy, misogyny, ableism, transphobia, policing, surveillance, and other systems of violence.* ***Liberatory Harm Reduction is true self-determination and total body autonomy.***

LIBERATORY HARM REDUCTION

A PHILOSOPHY & SET OF EMPOWERMENT-BASED PRACTICES THAT TEACH US HOW TO ACCOMPANY EACH OTHER AS WE TRANSFORM THE ROOT CAUSES OF HARM IN OUR LIVES.

WE PUT OUR VALUES INTO ACTION USING REAL-LIFE STRATEGIES TO REDUCE THE NEGATIVE HEALTH, LEGAL, AND SOCIAL CONSEQUENCES THAT RESULT FROM **CRIMINALIZED AND STIGMATIZED LIFE EXPERIENCES SUCH AS DRUG USE, SEX, THE SEX TRADE/SEX WORK, SURVIVING INTIMATE PARTNER VIOLENCE, SELF-INJURY, EATING DISORDERS,** AND ANY OTHER SURVIVAL STRATEGIES DEEMED MORALLY OR SOCIALLY UNACCEPTABLE.

LIBERATORY HARM REDUCTIONISTS SUPPORT EACH OTHER AND OUR COMMUNITIES WITHOUT JUDGMENT, STIGMA, OR COERCION, AND WE DO NOT FORCE OTHERS TO CHANGE. **WE ENVISION A WORLD WITHOUT RACISM, CAPITALISM, PATRIARCHY ABLEISM, TRANSPHOBIA, POLICING, SURVEILLANCE, AND OTHER SYSTEMS OF VIOLENCE.**

LIBERATORY HARM REDUCTION IS

True Self-Determination & Total Body Autonomy

The idea of keeping our community safe from harm through the practices of abundance, love, and welcoming each other as whole people is deeply rooted in the cultural practices of many Black, Indigenous, Latinx, and other People of Color who find ways to survive in the United States. The risks of harm we are reducing derive from the long-term impacts of structural violence on our bodies, families, and communities. I believe that one of the key differences between public health harm reduction and Liberatory Harm Reduction is that the latter builds collective power through the unabashed and unconditional support of self-determination and body autonomy. This practice reflects that support for our individual control over our choices builds our resilience and is the basis for empowerment that goes beyond the individual to encompass all of us surviving and becoming a groundswell—together.

I had a conversation with Kelli Dorsey, a Black sex worker from the US South who has been doing sex worker organizing for more than twenty years. She said:

> What most people in public health don't understand is that harm reduction practices are the way Black people make home. We feed people, we figure out how to be different, love different, and fight while sharing a table, a living room, and making a life that is better for all of us together.

Through relationship and community building, Liberatory Harm Reduction focuses on transforming the root causes of the oppression that increases the risks of illness, death, and incarceration in our communities. In countless workshops and trainings with social workers and health department staff, this is the part that leaves them baffled: Liberatory Harm Reduction hinges on the relationships we have with each other, not the rules of a program or the liability concerns of an agency. Safety is created through the investment we make in each other and the acceptance and holding we offer in a world that wants to see us dead or locked up. We are invested in each other's lives and in our abilities to make choices for ourselves.

Daoud's point, that honoring people's self-determination is not the point of public health, is well proven. The idea that people can choose to stop taking psychoactive medication, for example, is not tolerated within systems set up to manage problems rather than solve them. Xavier MaatRa, a youth worker in Chicago who has been a community organizer for nearly two decades, told me this story about how harm reduction is the throughline from his family to political organizing to his work with street-based young people:

> The idea that people can be changed and redeemed, and you meet people where they're at, and that you don't throw people away because they have habits or because they've been through things or they have mental health things, that's just always been something that's been a part of how I grew up with my family's legacy.
>
> For me, Harm Reduction aligns with being a community organizer because it's how I do grassroots organizing. You meet the people where they're at. You support the people to make the choices that they need, to decide how they want to address their issues. And to me, that translates to Harm Reduction.
>
> You ask questions—motivational interviewing: "Where are you at? What's going on? What's the next step? What makes sense? How can we pull off a little piece, to start here and there?" Western public health doesn't care anything about social-political context, or history, or all those pieces. But I think, for those of us who come from the communities that we're working with, harm reduction has to connect to liberation because oppression is at the root of all the things we are experiencing.
>
> Public health says, "Rather than solve the fact that there are this many houseless people, or this many people struggling with addiction, instead, let's just try to make sure that it doesn't go completely out of control." Versus what a liberatory organizer who practices harm reduction says: "Let's give our people what they need so that they can be free and so that they can

decide for themselves what freedom and liberation mean for them, right? And how to reduce the harm in their lives so that they can reach their goals." Harm reduction is a framework for supporting people's self-determination and supporting people's ideas around what freedom means to them and how they relate to their body and the people around them.

If you go to any city in this country, you're going to find, probably, often, some Black woman roaming the streets trying to give people everything that they need whether it's condoms, or food, or a talking-to, or to know where the needle exchange is. It's just because she out there trying to love her people and trying to take care of her community.

Additional Liberatory Definitions of Harm Reduction

The definition of Liberatory Harm Reduction isn't static or finite. It's ever changing and organic. We can look to organizations like YWEP to understand how deep Liberatory Harm Reduction was in their practice. As a peer-run, grassroots organizing project, YWEP changed Chicago and, arguably, the world.

From YWEP's mission statement:

> YWEP Harm Reduction means that we give practical options, no judgments, and we respect the choices that young people make. We will work with anyone to find resources that they think will be helpful. We believe that **We Do What We Have to Do to Survive,** and we don't question why someone is involved in the sex trade or street economy, instead we ask them what they think they need to stay safe, feel supported, and take care of themselves.
>
> Harm reduction means finding safer ways to practice a risky behavior. We define risk as anything that might put someone in harm's way. HIV, violence, STDs, theft, or depression are all examples of harmful things we can survive with information and support.

We help young people take responsibility for their actions and their choices by having honest conversations about real risks and real ways of avoiding risk.

We also believe that harm reduction is a philosophy that can work for any circumstance, not just for high-risk situations. For example, wearing a seatbelt in a car is harm reduction. Or taking a day off work to sleep and relax when you are really stressed out is harm reduction too. Here are some ways we practice Harm Reduction at YWEP:

- We offer realistic information and education about DRUGS and the SEX TRADE to anyone who needs it.
- We offer syringe exchange to anyone who wants it. We have needles for hormones and can teach safer injection to anyone using needles for any reason.
- We give out condoms, lube, safer piercing kits, insertive condoms and more to anyone who wants it.
- We offer birth control information and abortion support.
- We will help find whatever information or resources needed-like a testing kit for ecstasy or naloxone to reverse an opioid overdose.
- We give legal information about people's rights and risks.
- We stress self-care and empowerment and incorporate these values into our program.

At YWEP, we would practice Liberatory Harm Reduction by giving young people the space to say what they need and then honoring their requests. Sounds simple. But how often are young people in the street economy treated as experts in their own lives? The reality is that young people, particularly young femmes and trans People of Color in the sex trade, are told how to live their lives, all day and every day, by someone that they don't know. They are told, "This is the right way" for them. A doctor knows what is right for their bodies; a social worker knows where they should live. But at YWEP we would say clearly, "You are the boss of you. What do you think should happen next for you?" And then we would piece together their visions for their futures.

Liberatory Harm Reduction values self-determination, a relationship to the self and to community, including those engaged in what is considered "high-risk" behavior. Moreover, Liberatory Harm Reduction is a belief that laws, capitalism, and carceral systems (including—gasp—social work and medical settings) are harmful, and must be transformed or eliminated altogether so that we can access the kinds of help and healing that work for our bodies and communities.

Liberatory Harm Reduction offers us rare opportunities to reclaim our imaginations from the mainstream clinical and abstinence-only approaches that have become dogma regarding addictions, self-injury, the sex trade, and street economy. It also offers us the even rarer chance to restore radical trust in our intuition. Rather than taking the view that we are broken, Liberatory Harm Reduction asks us, "What do I need? What does my community need?" Rather than asking us, "Are you clean and sober?" Liberatory Harm Reduction asks us what we want to survive. These questions about our basic well-being remind us that our intuition works for us, not against us. This restoration is a slow process because we are consistently force-fed the idea that we are worthless because we use drugs, self-injure, participate in the sex trade, are fat, and/or have disabilities. Liberatory Harm Reduction gives us the chance to take baby steps, honoring each one. And when we can't hear our own voices, we can meet with someone at a needle exchange or other peer-run program that can reflect back our possibilities.

This book helps us think through these questions: What does Liberatory Harm Reduction look like in action? How do we establish relationships that are complex enough to challenge and hold people through long and complex changes, such as interrupting cycles of violence? What does Harm Reduction look like in action when someone is houseless, sixteen years old, and trading sex for money? These are just some of the questions I have struggled with as I moved back and forth between my own drug use, life in the sex trade, and personal struggles to heal from violence; as I worked with my peers and, later in my life, with people much younger, who were living through sometimes very similar and at other times very different life experiences.

I remember calling Kelly McGowan in a panicked search for support because a young person in the sex trade I had known for years showed up to one of my peer education jobs with a life-threatening, violently inflicted wound. The young person absolutely insisted that we not call 911, and that they did not want to go to a hospital or other social service agency for assistance. In that moment, harm reduction was the realest it could ever be because the basic values of respecting body autonomy, self-determination, and empowerment clashed with my overwhelming urge to "rescue" and presume I knew what was best.

Should I use motivational interviewing, a communication tool used by longtime harm reduction practitioners, to resolve the young person's reluctance to seek professional medical help? In other words, do I convince her to go to the emergency room? Or should I treat this injury myself and fall back on my odd collection of makeshift medical knowledge picked up over years of doing emergency wound care when friends, chosen family, participants in syringe exchanges, and even neighbors showed up with abscesses caused from injection drug use? Should I try to do what this young person was asking me to do: treat her wound?

As I paced around the room and screamed at my mentor into my tiny flip phone, the young person sat there, being tended by other youth leaders in the space. They were given herbal tea, an ice pack, herbs for anxiety; to me, they were shockingly relaxed despite this serious wound on their body. Even though they were totally terrified of going anywhere else for help, they knew they were in a safe place in our harm reduction project, that they would be heard and listened to, and that together we would figure out a plan, which we did. And it was okay.

Introducing the Revolutionary Love Notes

I knew from the moment I set out to write things down that I wanted to speak to the erasure of BIPOC, sex workers, and young people from the mainstream dialogue on harm reduction. Liberatory Harm Reduction was and is a BIPOC philosophy and set of practices and so many of the first syringe exchanges were started by Black queer and Black trans people.

In books and at conferences, white people discuss BIPOC communities as having been reluctant to embrace harm reduction or as having rejected harm reduction concepts until the HIV epidemic took hold. The narrative repeated by journalists and public health experts alike is that the impact of the crack epidemic and veterans returning from Vietnam with opioid dependence made BIPOC communities supportive of the War on Drugs and abstinence-only approaches. Time and again, I have heard white experts say, "People of Color believe that harm reduction is only for white people" and that harm reduction could not apply in a given situation because being a Person of Color who is an active drug user means increased risk of incarceration, home loss, violence, and a disproportionate impact of drug stigma. This argument is used to explain why there aren't more People of Color attending harm reduction conferences, publishing articles, or directing nonprofits.

My goal is for this book to push back against this white-centric argument to show that not only are BIPOC communities essential to the emergence of harm reduction principles, values, and practices, but also that these ideas actually originated inside BIPOC, queer, and feminist-led resistance movements. The work of the

Black Panthers, the Young Lords, The Janes, multiple Indigenous rights and land sovereignty groups, and Sylvia Rivera and Marsha P. Johnson gave political framing and precedence to the subsequent wave of AIDS activists who sparked illegal syringe exchanges all over the country in the late 1980s.*

I suggest that it isn't the values and politics of harm reduction that BIPOC communities have resisted, as those values and politics were already alive within them. Instead, it is the co-optation of harm reduction by public health and social services that watered down its meaning and turned something that was originally intimate, interpersonal, loving, and liberation based into something that became steeped in the language and tools of the medical-industrial complex (MIC).

As with all things in this book, this theory is supported by evidence from the complex communities of care I have been a part of since the early 1990s. I made it to adulthood through the collective models of care that so many took the time to teach me. The people who taught me were some of the first activists to create the world of Liberatory Harm Reduction work. I was surrounded by some of the most powerful and prolific organizers in the United States, but they were largely unknown. It has been shocking, yet somehow unsurprising, to witness in real time how, for example, the work of YWEP has been virtually unacknowledged both within mainstream harm reduction and the sex workers' rights movements. In some ways, though, this erasure of BIPOC-operated syringe exchanges has become part of the larger story of harm reduction.

Tracing back through my own lineage of harm reduction through interviews with elders, peers, and comrades, I realized that I was taught by people who created some of the first syringe

* Shout out to Allen Kwabena Frimpong, my decades-long thought partner, for making visible the work of his mentor, Black Panther Party member Dhoruba al-Mujahid bin Wahad, who played a pivotal role in exposing the racism fueling the War on Drugs.

exchanges in the country. It is very difficult to document with absolute certainty who created the first syringe exchanges, or where, because they were illegal and therefore underground and clandestine.* Catlin Fullwood, one of my precious mentors in this work—a Black, queer antiviolence and HIV activist who taught and guided YWEP in participatory action research—started what I think are the first two Black, queer, and transgender syringe exchanges in the United States. Similarly, when my longtime comrade and friend Deon Haywood sat down to talk about Women with a Vision (WWAV), a harm reduction project that has always been run by Black lesbians in New Orleans, it became clear that WWAV was also one of the first syringe distribution projects in the country and was specifically started to serve sex workers. Bali White, as mentioned earlier, started the first syringe exchange program to receive federal funding in the US run by and for trans people.

In the pages that follow, Kiara St. James, founder and director of New York Transgender Advocacy Group (NYTAG), lifts up Arlene Hoffman and Bali White: two Black, trans social workers who, along with Chloe Dzubilo, Imani Henry, and Kelly McGowan, codeveloped the first syringe exchange in the country run by and for transgender people. The Native Youth Sexual Health Network (NYSHN) helps us see how Indigenous values, beliefs, and practices infused Liberatory Harm Reduction. Monique Tula speaks to the Black Panthers as the original harm reductionists, and an interview with Vicente "Panama" Alba from the Young Lords helps us understand how Healing Justice and Liberatory Harm Reduction have always been intertwined. Kelly McGowan and Isabel Dawson, two housing rights activists living in the 7th Street squat on New York City's Lower East Side, were among

* We do know that Jon Stuen-Parker is the first individual to be public about, and arrested for, his syringe-exchange work, around 1982. However, he did not form the organization AIDS Brigade until 1986. By this time there were at least four other projects led by queer and trans BIPOC groups that had building power in their communities for several years.

the firs to destribute syringes in New York City in 1986. Kelly, who is still a tireless AIDS activist, went on to help establish at least three of the first syringe exchanges and was a critical part of the squatters' rights movement in New York City.

Kelli Dorsey is a Black queer sex workers' rights organizer and the former executive director of Different Avenues, one of a handful of sex workers' organizations that worked with both youth and adults and was run by Black queer people in Washington, DC.

Leah Lakshmi Piepzna-Samarasinha writes about how the disabled community has always used harm reduction strategies to keep each other alive. You will read revolutionary love from Dominique Morgan and others who have built and continue the radical legacy of Liberatory Harm Reduction in BIPOC and sex workers' communities.

The words of Lilla Watson, a Murri artist and activist living and working in Australia, were hand painted on a banner that stretched across an entire wall at YWEP. For me, this quote perfectly explains the basis of Liberatory Harm Reduction:

> *If you have come here to help me you are wasting your time, but if you have come because your liberation is bound up with mine, then let us work together.*

revolutionary love notes

People Power and the Original Harm Reductionists: *The History of a Movement*

MONIQUE TULA

Monique Tula is the former executive director of the National Harm Reduction Coalition.

I was maybe six or seven years old the first time I saw Angela Davis.

She imprinted herself upon me like a mother duck as she walked across the courtroom with her fist in the air. I fell in love with her bouncy afro and broad, gap-toothed smile. She radiated strength, power, and resistance. And if for a second you doubted her Blackness because of her light skin, the moment you looked into her eyes she dared you to think she was anything other than the fiercest of African queens.

Looking back, I realized that Angela—by virtue of her broadcasted image on a screen—introduced me to a new archetype that day, one who made light-skinned mixed girls like me feel seen and less ashamed of our complex lineage. And I saw in her something I wanted: her terrible beauty and her battle scars. The power held in her fist. Although Angela wasn't officially a Panther, she—alongside Elaine Brown, Assata Shakur, Kathleen Cleaver, and all the lesser known but equally powerful Panther sisters—stood in the face of the patriarchy as unapologetic Black women, committed to the total elimination of social and economic disparities and institutional violence perpetrated by a white, capitalist government.

Besides my own biological and chosen family, the most influential Black people in my life are still the Black Panthers. Both courageous and fallible, the Panthers sought to transform the system of racial oppression by staring the opposition in the face and showing that the exercise of power would not go uncontested—not unlike the tribe of harm reduction warriors I found two decades after meeting Angela.

The Original Harm Reductionists

When I stumbled into harm reduction in the mid-nineties, there were no textbooks or classes that could be taken at a school of social work, even at a super-liberal university.

Earning a "degree" in harm reduction consisted of attending the early harm reduction and needle exchange conferences; reading *Harm Reduction Communication*, a zine-like newsletter produced by the National Harm Reduction Coalition; reading *Pedagogy of the Oppressed*, written in 1968 by popular-education pioneer Paulo Freire; learning Black feminist theory, such as the Combahee River Collective Statement from 1977; learning about the fierce public health activism of the Young Lords, who launched the People's Program, a volunteer-run methadone detox program at Lincoln Hospital in the Bronx in 1970; or reading anything you could get your hands on about the Black Panthers' social programs.

The unifying theme of all this work was the bold commitment to name and dismantle oppression, be it racial, gender, sexual orientation, or socioeconomic status. Harm reduction gave me a political home, tools, a new lexicon, and a community of self-taught radical activists who were learning how to save ourselves from state-sanctioned violence. We were following in the footsteps of the people who laid the foundation of harm reduction, long before it had a name.

The Panthers and the Lords brought a new message of self-determination to the post–civil rights environment. The Black Panther Party manifesto (usually referred to as the Ten-Point Program), updated in 1972 by Elaine Brown, included an explicit demand for free healthcare for all Black and oppressed people. The Young Lords' seven demands for Lincoln Hospital included nutrition, treatment for drug addiction, and preventive care programs for children and the elderly. The Panthers' and Lords' bold visions and long-term strategies sought to destroy a five-hundred-year hegemonic legacy of white patriarchy. They knew the likelihood of their success and persisted because inaction led to death.

By the end of the 1960s, the FBI considered "extremist" political groups like the Black Panther Party and the Young Lords to be the greatest threat to national security. With the full force of the federal government against them, they eventually fell: COINTELPRO and, later, the drug war on Black and Brown communities made sure of it. By 1989, even Huey P. Newton, embattled cofounder of the Black Panther Party, was assassinated by a member of the rival Black Guerilla Family, allegedly for extorting BGF drug dealers.

As abruptly as their story seems to end, the legacy and power of the Panthers and the Lords—along with the Combahee River Collective and popular education pioneers—shaped the future of social and public health activism, including harm reduction.

The Drug War

The War on Drugs is just one example of the legacy of social control tactics used by the patriarchy to uphold white supremacy.

While it was sold to the American public as a means to end drug addiction, crime, and violence, all it's done is widen the poverty gap and destroy families.

Like me, many of you reading this come from Black and Brown communities that were ground zero of the US drug war, where open-air drug markets became battlefields in the '80s and '90s, like the one in West Oakland where Huey Newton died. As the CIA flooded our streets with crack, our families were systematically torn apart as our mothers, fathers, sons, and daughters were sentenced for "drug crimes" or "sex crimes." At the time, Los Angeles was named the crack capital of the world, and its growing Skid Row became home to many, including my father.

In that cauldron of death and despair, many of my father's friends contracted viruses like HIV and hep C that lurked in the barrels of shared needles and crack pipes. Many succumbed to unmitigated trauma and mental illness, compounded by the daily physical and emotional violence experienced living on the street. Many were stepped over, were ignored, and died on those streets before the words *harm* and *reduction* were ever put together and uttered in the same sentence.

Harm Reduction: A Cultural Shift

Tired of waiting to be saved by the government, a small group of visionary activists took it upon themselves to care for drug users dying from AIDS. Along with other HIV activists, harm reduction advocates in the '80s forced the American government to confront its shameful abdication of leadership over the AIDS epidemic. As a result, we witnessed the birth of the harm reduction movement, composed of grassroots activists, public health and drug treatment advocates, people who use drugs, and sex workers.

Drawing on the wisdom of the ancestors, the foundational Principles of US Harm Reduction, written by the National

Harm Reduction Coalition in the late '90s, specifically state, "The realities of poverty, class, racism, social isolation, past trauma, sex-based discrimination, and other social inequities affect people's vulnerability to and capacity for effectively dealing with drug related harm." Harm reduction is a natural outgrowth of our ancestors' legacies.

One of the earliest and most powerful voices to emerge from the harm reduction community is Imani Woods. A Black woman trained as a social worker and substance use counselor, Imani wasn't always a believer in harm reduction. Her essay in the Spring 1997 issue of *Harm Reduction Communication* poignantly captures her journey to harm reduction. "I'm here to represent all of us who believe in abstinence," she defiantly states, and then continues:

> I was from the Clarence Thomas school of substance abuse counseling. But the arrival of HIV disease turned me around . . . [to] ask, "What is more important? That people stay alive or that people not use drugs?" As a person who has followed the teachings of Malcolm X, one of the things I've learned is that it's okay to be wrong. . . . What I had to do was really start looking at me and start examining how I was thinking about stuff. I came to understand as time went on that my job was really about healing and not curing, not about changing, and not about determining what other people's paths should be.

Like Imani, many people in Black and Brown communities unsurprisingly struggled to embrace harm reduction. Many of the nationally known harm reduction leaders were white and primarily cis men, some of whom were exceptionally polarizing in the way they preached (and practiced) harm reduction. Imani was one of the few Black women who took an early stance on harm reduction and spoke on it in a way that resonated with those of us who experienced the violence of the drug war very differently than white folks. She unapologetically pointed out these distinctions: "Now for you white people, I must tell you: y'all use most of the drugs.

Y'all just don't go to jail. Y'all live in nice neighborhoods, you have social acceptability and employment, and financial status—and some of us Black [and Brown] folks be livin' there too. But y'all come from that naturally, and we come from this."

Reckoning

What was set in motion half a century ago will continue to define us for decades to come. The civil rights movement begat a lineage of social justice movements that dared to imagine a just society: from the Panthers and Lords to Black feminism; from women's and reproductive rights to the HIV/AIDS, harm reduction, sex worker, and trans/GNC rights movements. Working more or less in tandem, each movement led us to the current paradigm shift: one that is bringing out both the best and the worst in humanity.

The movement toward personal transformation, self-awareness, alternative healing, and spiritual awakening is accompanied by (if not driven by) major increases in depression, suicide, anxiety, stress, and drug use, both pharmaceutical and recreational. At the societal level, we're witnessing the rise of fundamentalism, polarization, racism, xenophobia: all deeply harmful forms of "othering" and fear mongering.

Transformation is never a painless process. Along with growth and expansion comes inevitable pain and suffering. But society must break down in order for something new to emerge. Some people are preparing for this shift by reimagining a world that shifts power and resources to people most harmed by structural violence. To achieve this ideal in the midst of such social and political upheaval, we need unified strategies that are undergirded by radical love and Transformative Justice, both of which are at the core of harm reduction.

Like the Panthers and the Lords, harm reductionists believe that everyone has the right to health, well-being, and participation in public policy dialogue. True harm reduction demands that no one is left behind, regardless of their behavior, beliefs, or mistakes. Yet, for all of our claims of unity, inclusion, and acceptance, harm reductionists are some of the most judgmental folks I know. Constantly fighting for people pushed to society's bulging margins for centuries, we're exhausted, and sometimes we take it out on each other.

We fear co-optation, and for good reason. The broader acceptance of our philosophy outside of traditional harm reduction environments has the potential of decentering people who use drugs, who should be driving every step of this movement. As a microcosm of the macro, the harm reduction community is in a state of transition—and it's a painful place to be. For a movement that espouses nonjudgment, we're not above being judgmental. Imani said it back in the day, and it still rings true:

> I think through the work of the National Harm Reduction Coalition and people like you, and those of us who get mad at each other and cuss each other out and all that kind of stuff, we're gonna have all that in harm reduction. Everybody thinks that they're in charge. Everybody thinks they're right, including me! With all that, you know it's gonna be a mess. But if we don't do it, nobody's gonna do it. Somebody's got to make the change.

Some of us have lost faith in the movement. Some of us do not see ourselves reflected in the community—sex workers and Black and Brown people have been telling us this for years. We're suffering from collective trauma—the overdose epidemic isn't just at our doorstep, it's in our house. We're losing our elders, struggling to manage our grief and survivor guilt, and sometimes that results in lashing out at each other.

Longstanding, unaddressed divisions between different factions of this movement have the potential to weaken our collective impact. bell hooks once said that forgiveness and compassion are always linked: “How do we hold people accountable for wrongdoing and simultaneously remain in touch with their humanity enough to believe in their capacity to be transformed?” This is the core of Transformative Justice and harm reduction. Forgiveness, compassion, and second chances.

Today’s harm reduction movement is larger and more diverse than ever. But we are indelibly inked by the blood of our ancestors. Indeed, our community is a microcosmic reflection of the new world being born, and I’m hopeful that we’ll find ways to manage our collective trauma by embodying the principles and values of harm reduction. I ain’t sayin’ we gotta take other people’s shit. But we do need to remember we’re on the same side, because ain’t nobody else coming to save us.

Power to the people.

A Conversation with P. Catlin Fullwood

P. Catlin Fullwood is a Black queer activist and visionary and cofounder of the People of Color Against AIDS Network—the first queer, Black, and People of Color–led harm reduction organization in the United States.

Harm reduction is notoriously difficult to evaluate, because change comes from inside long-term relationships and cannot be tracked through easy-to-capture indicators like stopping drug use, ending self-injury, leaving the sex trade, and so on. These are not our goals. We can't count how many people quit something during a twenty-eight-day program the way most treatment agencies can claim the number of people who "graduated." Participatory Evaluation Research (PER) allows the people most impacted to learn evaluation skills, to become researchers.

I met Catlin when YWEP applied for a grant to learn PER because we were having trouble measuring the impact of our work on our community. We were awarded a grant by a foundation, but we were also required to work with Catlin Fullwood. I don't think any of us knew at the time how much fate was involved in those decisions. Although we didn't have any idea who she was, other than a very strict and rigorous teacher, we grew to love Catlin because she spent so much time breaking down complex ideas, reminding us that we already had all the information we needed to change the world and showing us how to do it. I think Catlin taught us as much about ourselves, and what we were capable of, as she did about research. She taught us how to write our truth to power and how to show the receipts with care and pride.

When we invited Catlin to our office—something that required prior approval from YWEP's youth membership because we never allowed outside adults to come into our office—we were sure that she had never been in an office like ours before. We were wrong, so wrong, and that day we learned about one of the first syringe exchanges started by queer Black People of Color in Seattle, Washington, and run by people like us.

Shira: I think that one of the reasons I think of you when I think about harm reduction is because of People of Color Against AIDS Network (POCAAN) in Seattle, WA. I'd love to hear that story.

Catlin: Yeah. At that point, I was working for American Friends Service Committee (AFSC). And I was doing this project that was . . . I was a generalist. They're big on generalists. And my areas were immigration, homophobia in the clerical communities and the various religious communities, and how racism and homophobia intersected. I was new to Seattle. My wife at the time and I were sort of feeling our way along the margins of the gay community. Because it was all gay. We didn't have so much lesbian. We didn't have all the initials at that point; you just said the gay community. That was it. So, feeling our way along the margins of that. And at the same time when I was working at AFSC, there was a woman who was the office manager who was as nerdy as I was. And when they came out . . . I think it was *TIME* magazine came out with one of the first in-depth articles about AIDS.

What year was this?

This was 1986, I would say. Yeah. So, she and I decided that we wanted to delve further into AIDS. And at the same time, there was a big report that came out talking about the disproportionate impact of the epidemic on Blacks and Hispanics. It was a real deal. The report didn't say this, but our political analysis was that the cofactors for AIDS weren't necessarily medical cofactors. They were the cofactors of our lives, which were poverty, limited access, racism, homophobia. All the things that kept people from being able to be safe.

This is at the very beginning. It was still very much a white gay men's disease, particularly in the Pacific Northwest. But a group of People of Color came together, and we decided that we needed to have a different conversation. We needed to have a different conversation about the disease, beyond the epidemiological discussion. We needed to have a conversation beyond "to quarantine or not to quarantine." And we needed to have conversations about how that epidemic was going to affect communities of color; once again, the white man gets a cold, and People of Color get pneumonia. We knew that it was going to have tremendous economic impact, and gendered impact. It was going to be huge.

We had an opportunity to actually do prevention. And we all knew that effective prevention is based in a lack of being judgmental. Let me just say it like that. You can't do prevention and blame, or chastise, or sort of judge the people that you're working with. Because people will smell that a mile away, and people will shut down. So, when we put together our staff, we did it with an intentionality—we had people working with us who had been in this life for a very long time. And people who were young community organizers. And people who were very political and very radical Black and Puerto Ricans. It was the first group of its kind, I think—especially in the Pacific Northwest.

The chair of the board was Kazas Jones, who was just this beautiful, powerful Black queen who had been kicked out of the military. He was a captain or something and had been kicked out of the military for being gay and HIV-positive. When he came with me to start POCAAN, he said, "I just want you to know. I don't have AIDS. I'm HIV-positive." And I said, "Okay. Yeah. I understand." Because we were making a movement. We were understanding more deeply what this meant, and what it meant to have a virus, as opposed to having a disease syndrome—which carries so much more judgment. To say that I have a disease or a virus, as we well know now, people are either—I don't know, either going to go one way or the other.

We did this whole project, I'm sure I told you about it before, funded by the CDC, that Sheila Robinson ran. Sheila was a woman who had been in the life, in the sex trade that is, for most of her life, and was this incredible educator. Sheila would go out and say, "I'm going to go save some lives today." And everybody loved her, everybody believed her—she would save lives every day. She'd have her condoms, she'd have her bleach bottles, which was what we had at the time—we didn't have needle exchange at that point. But these were her tools.

Mostly what she had was her belief in other people. Her belief that people could change. Her belief in herself that she could change. She relapsed once while she was working for me, and the staff were trying to cover it up because they were afraid I was going to fire her. I'm like, "What the fuck? You crazy? She's my best outreach worker. I'm certainly not going to fire her. We're going to get her into treatment if that's what she wants, or we will do whatever she wants us to do to support her."

And that's what we did. That's what we did with all the people who worked with us. We were the only organization that hired people who were active drug users. We hired people who were actively involved in the street economy, whether it was in terms of sex for drugs, or sex for money, whatever, sex for survival. Saving our communities required us to understand and to develop a new narrative and a new discourse about how you actually address something that is so vast and so complicated in the ways it affects people's lives, and the ways it affects communities. We knew we had to do it through the eyes—and with the understanding of the people—who were most deeply affected. That was our way. You can't do prevention in a crack house if you're not in a crack house to get some crack. This was our belief.

Our work involved many, many ways of engaging with people that we hoped had integrity. We understood the value that they brought to us, in terms of being willing to do this kind of work among their peers. Because, often times, that led to ostracism. People who did harm reduction and people who were identified as peers lost their status and credibility within their own peer community, because it meant that you were changing your life for a job, and doing needle exchange was not really accepted. So, when people became peer educators about drugs or the sex trade, in some ways they lost their peers—they were people who were engaged in the life but had managed to get into the work of harm reduction.

We had to deal with this whole understanding of what it means to be a peer, and what it means to be engaging with people from a position with a changed power dynamic. How to work with people you care about without being judgmental, because even though we believed in change we also weren't "selling or pushing" change . . .

Our peer educators were just like, "Here's what you can do to stay safer, and if you don't want to do that, here's something else you can do. But if you don't want to do that either, then you can do whatever you want to do. You can just keep on doing what you want to do. And if you want to come down here, and if you want to hang out, and if you want to talk, and if you want to do this, you want to do that, that's cool, too."

Then we started to use harm reduction to address violence against women and people of all genders in intimate violence relationships. And infant mortality. Because the infant mortality rate in Black and Brown communities was over the top, and it's the same cofactors at play: poverty and lack of access. Harm reduction is essential to thinking about so many things that threaten us.

But back then, the needle exchange discussion had just been started. And within our organization and certainly within our communities of color, that was a big deal. People didn't like it—no communities liked it—but our communities really didn't like it. It really fostered drug use, from their perspective. We had to lean into that belief system and try to understand it to offer options for people to make decisions about what they were going to do, and how they were going to keep themselves safe.

I think our approach to preventing an epidemic was very much based in cultural connections with the people we were working with, and who worked for us. People used to say that if you've been kicked out of your house for being queer, if you have a record, if you're a felon, I know a place you can go and get a job—POCAAN. And that's who we were. We were all about understanding the importance of a lived experience. And a certain kind of ability to see the world, and to see their peers in ways that were not judgmental and not holier-than-thou, and not chastising, and . . . It wasn't AA, in other words. Everybody who worked on our staff went to AA. But I think it was more of a pickup joint, actually.

I have to say I came up that way, too. Where harm reduction programs were filled with people in Twelve-Steps, and vice versa.

Harm reduction has been positioned as the opposite of Twelve-Steps, but in my experience it's a pretty open continuum.

Right. I think that's absolutely true. And I think that's one of the reasons for the folks who were a part of POCAAN, whether they were peer educators, or outreach workers, or whatever their role there was. . . . What they needed was connection and community. It was all about the social networking. That's what I mean when I talk about POCAAN as a dating service, because everybody there had dated each other at some point or another. But it was really just about knowing that you were with someone who understands where you're at, and where you're coming from. And those relationships were what kept people going and kept people feeling connected and safe. We know about domestic violence, as well as about drug use, it's about isolation often. Or you get isolated by the behavior itself. Because people judge you. Your family kicks you out. There are all these ways that . . . external exclusion happens.

And then there's the internal exclusion that happens. For us, within our organization, the peer model and the harm reduction approach and ideology really was the only way that people could stay afloat. It's one thing to say, "I'm not going to do it today." But when you say, "I'm not going to do it ever." And people say, "You're shitting me. That's not true. You know it's not true, I know it's not true. But you're okay anyway. You're okay with me, anyway."

Who were the founders or cofounders of POCAAN? And what year was it?

It was me. I was a primary initiator, Tenny Tafaya, Jeff Sakuma, Kara Hartfield, George Freeman, Don Matt, and Kazas Jones—Kazas was my first board president. And it was in 1987.

Wow.

Is that right? It was 1986 that we got our first $20,000. And we got it because we were really the only game in town. We were multiracial. We were multi-sexed. It's like we ran the gambit of every kind of fluidity that one could possibly think of. And we had structure. And we sort of understood . . . I understood, and most of our people understood, organization development. The board, they worked for Group Health. They worked for the health department. They worked for institutional places, universities, that sort of thing. But they were an interesting bunch of people. And I don't know why they always put up with us, but they did. They were willing to take risks for our communities.

POCAAN started in '87 with you and Kazas. So, two questions. One is, what was the conversation around being explicitly BIPOC-led? Then two, what was the conversation like when you started syringe exchange, and around when did you do that?

Syringe exchange started through an outreach program that was, actually, funded by Group Health. It came through the National Institute on Drug Abuse (NIDA), before the Substance Abuse and Mental Health Services Administration (SAMHSA). They did this huge, huge, huge, huge, huge, interview-based study of IV drug users. It was a research project. So, it went through the Washington Health Department. And then Group Health found Imani Woods. Group Health hired Imani Woods to set up the initial needle exchange downtown, and they called it Street Outreach Services (SOS). But see, the Health Department was sort of pitting POCAAN against SOS. Interestingly enough, as a public health harm reduction tool, what SOS did was critical. But their ideology and their philosophical stance was very much opposed to the engagement of active users—you had to be in recovery. You had to want to go into recovery to get syringes. We were at odds with that. We didn't feel that people had to go into recovery. We felt that people could determine their own lives. And just stay safe.

Then does that make you the first syringe exchange in Seattle?

No. SOS was the first syringe exchange in Seattle, but they were *not* a harm reduction project and they were *not* led by BIPOC, drug users, or people in the sex trade. We were the first BIPOC–run organization that did a combination of outreach, peer engagement, and also harm reduction in the country. We were one of the first. And we were queer.

It was pretty amazing. And it wasn't like, oh well, we're leading something. We were just figuring it out as we went along. When the clinical trials started, we had clinical trials for AZT and the first combination cocktail. We knew that we were going to have an uphill battle getting women and getting BIPOC into the clinical trials, both from them and from the Health Department. There was talk about, well, should we take that over? We'll do that in-house, and then people won't have to go to the Health Department. And I said, "Well, that's not how things should work." They get the money to offer these services. And they should be available to every person who needs them.

So, we created this position called a community-based services liaison, Victor Rivera, and he ensured that if you wanted to get into a clinical trial, you would. If you wanted to know about how to get any of the treatments that were available at that time, which was primarily AZT, you could. And for women, there were a couple of research studies that were looking at women and infant mortality. If you wanted to get additional services as a woman, we would also arrange for that to happen.

This young guy, Victor Rivera—he was so young and so beautiful. He came from New York. He was part of the Vega Clan.

The Vega Clan—actually, several of the family members worked in POCAAN. Judith was the first one. . . . She was one of the first ones I started the organization with. Then we hired her mother, who was also a community-based services liaison, to make sure that women were getting the services they needed around child-care and their own care. Then we hired her dad, who was an active drug user, to be a peer education and outreach worker. And then we hired Victor to be the community-based services liaison to ensure that people got into the services they needed. The thing about Victor was that he was gorgeous. Two, he was young. Three, he had AIDS. And people wanted to be with him. People wanted to talk to him. People trusted him on both sides, the health department side as well as the community side.

It was just another way of thinking about how to make health services available without saying, "Okay, we'll take your leftover 25 cents and provide services to all these people that you won't." Or to say, "Fuck that. You get five hundred dollars for this and you'll use all of it to provide services for these people." It was like a different way for the Health Department to think about how they approached service provision overall.

You have always been one of my biggest heroes. And this conversation is so personally meaningful. I felt myself starting to cry at five different points. I'm just so grateful for all the work that you've done in this movement and for all the work you did that I don't even know about that saved us all.

Imani Woods, Fred Johnson, and Liberatory Harm Reduction

KELLI DORSEY

Kelli Dorsey is a part of my queer BIPOC sex worker family. We met back in 2005, when she was directing one of the few Black- or BIPOC-led harm reduction organizations led by sex workers in the United States, and we talked for about six hours the first day we met. Kelli is a radical Black, queer sex worker who has organized in harm reduction, Reproductive Justice, and Transformative Justice for nearly three decades. She engages in various underground economies and is one of the few people who publicly challenges the mainstream harm reduction community to better understand the fluidity of the street economy and to include the fight for drug dealers in how they address decriminalization and dismantling the War on Drugs. Kelli's national legislative organizing work to decriminalize the sex trade, sex work, and street economy is some of the most comprehensive, radical, and long-term work in that area that I know.

Harm reduction in radical communities of color is my movement home. Fred Johnson, my mentor who taught me the deepest compassion for those of us whom society deems unworthy, introduced me to harm reduction in the late 1990s. As an empath, harm reduction became the first place that alleviated my deep grief for the suffering of my people.

To write this piece, I interviewed Fred Johnson, who thought it was important to name the Black folks across the country in primarily Black cities who supported him and taught him how to show people how to use drugs safely. Fred Johnson, Imani Woods, Mona Bennett, Amu Puta, and Harry Simpson laid a path of sweat, blood, tears, and heartbreak so Black communities could survive and the next generation of Black harm reductionists and Black people would have an easier journey. I met Fred in Washington when he was the program director of Prevention Works!, a needle exchange organization. I was always involved in social justice work and engaged in formal and informal economies. Fred introduced me to my movement home. After spending years in prison, Fred became a leader in the harm reduction movement, including serving as executive director at harm reduction organizations in New York and Atlanta. He's transitioned from working in service-based and policy nonprofits to playing trumpet and performing in plays to bring light and visibility to people who are incarcerated, especially those in solitary confinement.

I was so deeply privileged to have Fred as a mentor to teach me how to be a harm reductionist and radical Black person, which allowed me to deepen my respect for everyone in my community.

Fred Johnson left school in the seventh grade, got his GED, and spent over a decade in prison. His street game and swagger were still fresh when I met him. After coming home from prison, Fred participated in groups where he saw people being treated with patience and kindness. He read and memorized everything about harm reduction and later joined Prevention Works!

in Washington, DC, where he created a peer program modeled after Philadelphia FIGHT, an early AIDS service organization that provided primary care. Fred transferred his skills from the streets to harm reduction. On the streets and in harm reduction, Fred saw people's strengths regardless of where they were at and reached out to other harm reductionists in other cities to learn and get support.

Fred introduced me to his mentor, Imani Woods. Imani, cofounder of Harm Reduction Coalition, was critical in helping the DC harm reduction movement grow. A fierce Black woman whose analysis on harm reduction focused on the intersecting struggles in the Black community, the hesitancy of Black people to believe in harm reduction, and paths to get the Black community to accept harm reduction, Imani was a force. She once wrote an article titled, "Bringing Harm Reduction to the Black Community: There's a Fire in My House and You're Telling Me to Rearrange My Furniture." In it, she describes the challenges with convincing the Black community that harm reduction would support the Black community. She says, "People look at me like I'm crazy when I go to the Black community and explain harm reduction. I am accused of supporting a policy that makes peace with genocide."

Fred and Imani invested in building relationships with everyone, including Black leaders, legislators, members of neighborhood associations, gatekeepers, families, drug users, and drug dealers in the city. There were so many people impacted by systemic racism who were angry at the thought of needle exchange, but Fred and Imani were humble, grounded, with an in-depth understanding of why Black folks in DC and other cities across the country felt this way, so they always led with compassion. Fred never demonized those who thought that giving out needles would further lead to killing Black people and increase drug use. He used harm reduction for our entire community, even for those who would dismiss it. They walked out the values of harm reduction. For example, training sessions were for everyone: program participants, community leaders, drug dealers, volunteers. They taught us that there isn't one person better than another, no matter the socioeconomic status, education level, level of drug use, where a person lived, how they made money, or gender.

Still, it was difficult for Imani and other Black harm reductionists to convince the Black community that harm reduction would save lives when community violence, incarceration rates, HIV and other blood-borne disease rates, separation of families, and unemployment were extremely high. Some of the barriers Black harm reductionists faced were the United States' long history of using Black bodies for research, huge disparities with drug and other sentencing processes, and the US intentionally putting crack cocaine in Black neighborhoods.

BIPOC Pushback

The pushback against harm reduction was not necessarily against harm reduction values and practices. Instead, it was a rejection of the co-opted version of harm reduction pushed by public health and social services. Harm reduction got watered down and became a public health intervention, devoid of the rich community values that came from the communities that originated it. Although BIPOC communities had been practicing harm reduction for centuries as a way to remain safe, Black harm reduction in the 1990s was rooted in public health, social service, policing, and/or the prison-industrial complex, because reducing drugs toward the goal of abstinence and completely ending drug dependence was assumed to be the answer to making Black communities safer. At the time, the majority of socioeconomic solutions for Black people were located in formalized systems such as the church, child and family services, nonprofits that held explicit goals of abstinence, social services, policing, and prison. This was during a time when Black people living in inner cities were being demonized as violent, crackheads, fatherless homes with mothers on welfare. With the help of Child and Family Services and law enforcement, the media reported untrue narratives about the Black family, and one of the most harmful narratives was "crack baby syndrome." At the time, "crack baby syndrome" was used to pejoratively describe children who were born malnourished to Black mothers who were often falsely accused of using crack cocaine during pregnancy. While advocates for people who used drugs fought against this narrative, it was not until numerous scientific studies over two decades identified zero conditions associated with infants born to a pregnant cocaine-addicted person. These studies watched infants grow to adulthood and found that there was no such thing as "crack baby syndrome." Instead, they found that pregnant people in inner cities often did not seek prenatal care for fear of social workers taking away their babies because the social workers thought they were using crack. Their babies were born malnourished because they did not receive prenatal care. Many families, including those with parents who used drugs and many more who were just afraid to seek care, lost custody of their children due to racial biases in social and medical care.

Harm Reduction as Organizing

Fred told me, "I can't ask people to pay me to free myself. They are not going to pay me for that. I grew up, got tired, and moved on." These words had been heard for centuries from Black ancestors, and were now heard from my mentor about the nonprofit-industrial complex, formalized public health harm reduction, the criminal system, policy, public health, and social work. Public health harm reduction as it related to giving out safer drug-using information and supplies, sex or overdose supplies, shouldn't be considered progressive or radical, because it is just lifesaving on a basic level. For Fred and Imani, it took hardcore compassion, love, kindness, and resolve to fight the system in spite of pushback from their communities, who were in the midst of the drug war, family separation, overdoses that weren't counted by the state, and extreme criminalization.

Fred taught us all to make no distinction between practice on the street and education. Everyone should have access to training and knowledge about harm reduction. Fred is a living example of harm reduction in practice and engages all of our community without expectations about where they will end up. He held patience for people without expectations of change for anyone coming to the needle exchange van.

Fred recalls, "All I did in harm reduction organizing work was the same thing I did every day on the street. I shot dope but I had a mother, father, brother, people in the community who knew me from the corner store, and my teachers. Harm reduction is about the community. When I was wrecking my community, everybody knew me, and I used those relationships to build something that I could feel good about and people could feel good about." This reminds me of Sunday dinner in Black homes. Everybody comes.

Liberatory Harm Reduction Looks Like Radical Justice

Fred taught me that Liberatory Harm Reduction looks like radical justice. It looks like when to breathe, when to walk through the fire, when to compromise; love; the importance of community creativity; walking out my own practice; and that while fighting wasn't always wrong, I should be compassionate and meet situations with grace and intention. Fred did this work so naturally that he forgot he created a space for all—a space where people who engage in street economies, sell drugs, use drugs, staff, leaders, volunteers, and a few allies could build relationships. We all had access to training to build up our skill sets. We deeply valued and invested in the expertise of those most impacted by drug use, the sex trade, and other street economies. While not explicitly saying it, he taught our community that knowledge is power and withholding knowledge is an extreme exertion of power. Sharing lifesaving information is part of how we get freer.

When I asked him about Liberatory Harm Reduction he said, "For Liberatory Harm Reduction to happen we minimally have to understand that the master's tools, in this case the public health system, social services, policy, and the criminal system, are not liberatory. Liberatory Harm Reduction must pull back from formal systems, listen, invest, and nurture the dreams of people of all ages in underground economies, without judgment about who they are and where they want to go. Always recognize and give them credit for their work." He said, most importantly, "People need to know when it is time for you to leave and move on to your next journey so new leadership has space to lead, cultivate new people, and help the next community's generation's dreams come true."

Liberatory Spaces of Glamorous, Queer Punk Rage

KELLY McGOWAN aka PATTI O'POSER

When Shira asked me to write about what punk has contributed to Liberatory Harm Reduction, my first thought was that it has something to do with the politics of resistance made more sustainable through the somatic release of irreverent, glamorous rage. Like the time we liberated trans artist and activist Chloe Dzubilo from mandated psych observation in Bellevue Hospital. By day two, her partner T De Long and I had convinced medical, social work, and psychiatric staff that she was in danger due to transphobia and medical neglect. Chloe had been assaulted by another patient, and a nurse had called her a "junkie." The nurse refused to treat infected sores on her arms that were caused by medication stents administered by the hospital's infectious disease ward earlier that week. Her "early" discharge was made official with constraints, of course. Chloe had to be released to the care of a mental health professional by midnight of the same day. So, Shira flew in from Chicago. Andrea J. Ritchie picked Shira up at the airport and delivered her to the doors of Bellevue's psych ward by 11:52 p.m., where she calmly signed forms releasing the hospital of liability.

The hilarity started immediately as Chloe began to art direct. First, she dropped her pants as the psych ward doors closed behind us and cackled, "Kiss my rashy ass," revealing bright red, untreated sores. As horrible as it sounds, this began the riotous laughter. Then she wrapped her white shirt around her body like a straitjacket and runway-walked the long narrow hallway, flipping unwashed hair and making supermodel faces for the camera as though the oral thrush around her mouth was fine lipstick. At the hospital's revolving exit doors, she borrowed Shira's sunglasses and directed multiple takes of an "avoiding-the-paparazzi" exit. We laughed until we cried and almost all of the toxicity, impotence, and rage at the medical-industrial complex (MIC) that had built up over the prior week was metabolized by glamorous punk irreverence.

This was 2010, less than a year before Chloe's death and fifteen years after her punk band Transisters released a song about an earlier experience at "Bellevue fucking Hospital":

> Where's your fucking sensitivity training?
> You're causing me a lot of stress!
> It's 1995! What the fuck?!
> I really need to talk to somebody now, right NOW!
> My friends need to be here, PLEASE!
> —Chloe Dzubilo, "Kaposi Koverstick"

Between releasing the song and the Bellevue liberation, Chloe had gone to college, served on mayoral commissions and New York State advisory boards, and spoken at international conferences advocating for compassionate care for trans people, people living with HIV/AIDS (PLWH/A), sex workers, and drug users. Even so, she was still being treated by the MIC as not worthy of basic care.

Radical Solidarity and Beyond

This book is about how we take care of each other without state support and, as the rise of mutual aid is demonstrating, how our capacity only grows when institutions fail us. When Chloe and I arrived in the mid-'80s (although we wouldn't meet for another decade) to the abandoned buildings, rubble-filled lots, and tent cities of the Lower East Side (LES) of NYC, mutual care was the body politic. Fragments of the architecture of the '60s and '70s liberation movements were still standing: elders and lessons from Black Panthers, Young Lords, Welfare Rights, American Indian Movement, and Weather Underground were part of community and grassroots organizing.*

Unlike the popularized punk culture of resisting middle-class suburban normalcy, a small group of anarchist punks were connected to working-class rage and LES solidarity politics. In 1984, they drew on the success of Rock Against Racism (RAR) UK† and formed the RAR US collective as a response to the police state, which provided endless examples of abuse and murder.‡ Unfortunately, US white supremacists were also taking cues from youth organizing successes in Europe, where skinheads (also known as

---

* Love for Wende Marshall and Frank Morales who taught us to build our strategies with an understanding of the shoulders we stood on.

† RAR UK formed from a groundswell of support for a letter written to music scene magazines calling out overt racism in the industry, specifically Eric Clapton's "keep Britain white" outburst during a concert at the height of his popularity. RAR UK continued to gain relevance as "cultural organizers" while working alongside the working-class political organization the Anti-Nazi League, in response to racist attacks by police and the political rise of the United Front, a far-right, fascist political party that was encouraging violence against working-class South Asian immigrants.

‡ Two police murders that had our attention: the 1983 killing of Black artist Michael Stewart during an arrest for graffitiing a subway wall and the 1984 killing of Eleanor Bumpurs, an elder Black grandmother with physical and mental disabilities, during a "routine eviction."

"skins") were becoming a neo-Nazi force.* In response, RAR leveraged concerts to politicize kids who were drawn to punks or skins for the fashion, music, and critique of mainstream biz as usual.† We also eagerly supported community organizing projects that continued the movement work of the Black Panthers and Young Lords. RAR's role was clear: scrappy young punks provided a mobile stage and high-end sound system to amplify the voices of movement organizers and artists. We secured NYC sound permits and interfaced with the police, who showed up in disbelief that, for instance, tenants on rent strike could be backed by so much volume.

In 1985, RAR joined an alliance of housing activists—including Harlem Fight Back and Fort Apache in the Bronx—by squatting a building to protect it from destruction or a gentrifying sale. LES squats were also practice spaces for being in community as and among drug users. The RAR house meetings often debated a "no needles/junkies" rule. Some argued that prohibition would protect us from police action and some referenced European squats that did so "to focus on activism."‡ Former Young Lord and President of the Union of the Homeless,§ Alfredo Gonzalez, would remind us of the Black Panthers' stance that *Drug users are our people*, not a threat to the movement. While we never reached consensus

---

* The skinhead movement started in Europe but was not originally aligned with white supremacist politics or culture. As Nazi movements recruited young skins in France, Germany, and the UK, the Autonomen squatter movement (prototype for what we now call Antifa in the US) began to organize in opposition.

† 1980s RAR US concerts combined punk bands like Reagan Youth—formed to critique the rise of the religious conservative movement—with reggae bands, Nuyorican Poets, Black Nationalists such as Amiri Baraka, and American Indian Movement activists and artists such as John Trudell.

‡ In 2012, a similar debate would surface in the Occupy Movement in NYC. "Are we a movement or a social service agency?" became a topic as Zuccotti Park became home to many poor and unhoused activists. This is not a viable question in movement building at any time and certainly not among the 99 percent, where solidarity, rather than unity, is a viable goal.

§ https://www.thenation.com/article/society/national-homeless-union/

on this debate, we also never agreed to police each other.

Even though we avoided adopting punitive policies, I kept it quiet that queer* punk sex worker† friends injected and nodded in my room. The other options were shooting galleries in abandoned buildings or Tompkins Square Park, where Nazi skinheads were bashing queers and Black and Brown punks. The movement elders who we had access to on the LES did not teach queer revolutionary history.‡ This, combined with the message from our families of origin that our lives were not precious§—we all got to the LES through some version of this story—left us queer kids to create sanctuaries for each other. One place where we could dance without watching our backs and experience the somatic release of irreverent, glamorous queer joy was the Pyramid Club on Avenue A, known for its commingling of drag, punk, and LES cultures. Years later, I would find out that the door person, who I snuck forty-ouncers past, was Chloe.

> Everything I know about community organizing I learned from nightlife.
>
> —Viva Ruiz, Thank God for Abortion

Jon Paul Hammond¶ was the first to invite the possibility of a *queer* punk politic when he came on the scene, embodying irreverent,

---

* Queer identity wasn't a thing then. We weren't strictly homo- or lesbo- or gay-culture-identified, so, other than an occasional European squatter passing through with a "Dyke" pin, I believe we preferred *punk* to any label referencing our sexuality.

† While the cash, food, or useful things that were "scored" while dancing in "topless bars" or "giving a hand/blow job" in the park were often named, no one called any of it *sex* or *work* then.

‡ This began to shift in the '90s, when Imani Henry brought Sylvia Rivera and her legacy as the spokesperson for the Young Lords Gay Lesbian Caucus into trans and harm reduction community organizing and the two-spirit group We'Wah Bar Che Ampe formed at the Native American Community House on Lafayette Street.

§ Referencing YWEP's message encapsulated at https://youarepriceless.org/.

¶ https://www.aaihs.org/locating-black-queer-pasts/.

wildly glamorous and prideful Black pansexuality.* In 1986 at the first national US Anarchist Gathering† in many decades, Jon Paul gathered a random group to do a theatrical anti-meat action during a chicken dinner. After, high on endorphins, flopped in a puppy pile on the floor of a church basement, we relished a found connection: we were all queer anarchist punks from San Francisco, Chicago, Philly, and New York City. Jon Paul continued to create life-affirming spaces at activist gatherings and, eventually, for queer and BIPOC drug users at National Harm Reduction Conferences. In the early '90s, he joined the original Harm Reduction Coalition Working Group and cofounded Prevention Point Philadelphia syringe exchange—with the support of his life partner, Wende Marshall—where he continued to bring his irreverent, endorphin-heightening, glamorous resistance to assimilation of any kind.

Soon after meeting Jon Paul, 13th Street squat momma Isabel "Isada" Dawson invited me and all my queerness, moving beyond solidarity, into her family. She taught so many of us that the art of being a big, messy, chosen family means going at the pace of mutual care, disappointment, healing, and joy *and* giving attention to local community needs. Within a few months of meeting, we were cohosting full-moon gatherings, co-organizing the Eviction Watch, and distributing clean syringes. As soon as HIV transmission through injecting became a threat to our friends and family, Isabel found a doctor who would supply us, years before Rod Sorge would launch ACT UP's syringe exchange in the LES.‡ Years later, when Chloe and I fell in love, Isabel and her family fully embraced us.

In 1991, radical queer harm reduction activist Keith Cylar§

---

* Jon Paul was the first person I knew to claim Pansexual as an identity.

† This anarchist gathering was two years before the 1988 Toronto Anarchist gathering where *Homocore* infamously started. Jon Paul and I were both there.

‡ https://www.villagevoice.com/1999/02/09/rod-sorge/.

§ Visual AIDS commissioned short about Keith Cylar: https://vimeo.com/372220515.

hired Isabel and me to implement what he called the Guerrilla Housing Program later known as Housing Works. We would gather peer workers,* cram into a two-seater van, collect donated furniture (mostly from the partners of gay men who had died of AIDS), pick up someone DOJ had released to a street corner, drive them to an apartment that Isabel had prepared, load in the furniture, and drive back to the office to start legal advocacy that would secure ongoing rent. The best part was when the Guerrilla-housed person met Keith. Within minutes, his love would help them metabolize the shame and despair that was triggered by years of systemic neglect and abuse by social service institutions. He knew exactly how to lead with the pleasure of a home-cooked meal and when to disclose that he was a "Black, HIV+, gay, S&M-loving, drug-using, dyslexic, cum laude–earning, co-CEO." Keith's irreverent glamour communicated that he, in his dreads and Armani suit, had their back and that they didn't need to pretend in order to be cared for.

> Peer support and learning in order to survive oppressive systems can be traced back to hush harbors during slavery when Africans gathered secretly and risked punishment and death to organize, heal, and connect with spirit. Movements and projects that continue this lineage through peer education have been shaped by the popular education movement in Latin America—catalyzed by Paulo Freire's *Pedagogy of the Oppressed*—that put feminist, Marxist, and anticolonial analysis into practice.
>
> —Wende Marshall, labor and community organizer and co-editor of *Insurrectionary Uprisings: A Reader in Revolutionary Nonviolence and Decolonization* (Daraja Press, 2022)

---

* Before launching its job-training program (to support the goal of majority of staff being former clients) and before HIV peer educator stipends were waived as income by HRA, Housing Works invited clients to volunteer as peer workers, which often led to full-time work.

Soon after federal Ryan White funding was secured for what became the first Independent Living Program for People Living with HIV, Isada and I left Housing Works, as our LES squatter style was not as useful to a well-funded housing program. A few years later, Chloe would become a client and provide the first transgender awareness training for staff. In 2011, at Chloe's ascension celebration,* Keith's partner, Charles, told mourners that she said, "You can do all the trainings you want, but nothing will change until trans people are running our own programs." These programs were eventually launched and led consecutively by two Black trans women, Arlene Hoffman and Bali White.

Glamorous, Reverent Spaces of Liberation

When you put together punk glamour, radical solidarity, queer family embrace, guerilla programming, and night club security, you get the Transgender Initiative at the Positive Health Project syringe exchange in midtown Manhattan.

On Thursday nights, starting in 1996, Arlene Hoffman,† Chloe Dzubilo, Richard Alvarez, and I cohosted a sanctuary for trans women who were sex workers or in the sex trade. I was the buffer between community and the requirements of the nonprofit-industrial complex and its white supremacy culture. Richard was our "bouncer," bringing his club kid with the House of Fields,‡ punk artist on the LES, red-rope nightclub doorman, "I love you, not-for-nothing NO!" energy. He embodied the possibility that the night could be both low-drama *and* fabulous. Our onsite MD provided hormone therapy and treated STDs, failed silicone injections, and other conditions for which trans-femmes

---

* See a slideshow of Chloe's memorial: https://vimeo.com/20986453.

† See Arlene's punk debut in Viva Ruiz's short film *There Is a Transolution*: https://vimeo.com/372220443.

‡ https://patriciafield.com/collections/house-of-field-x-martine.

were shamed and mistreated for seeking care. The evening was designed around the main attraction, Arlene and Chloe's cofacilitation of a multigenerational, drop-in, harm reduction peer group. They skillfully* created a loving environment where participants could connect with and support each other and, for those who chose, collaborate on advocacy efforts. The numbers grew and relationships deepened as word got out that we were comforting, fun, and for real. After two-plus years, Moshay Moses took leadership of the program and our crew moved on: Richard joined the Lower East Side syringe exchange; Arlene became the first director of Housing Works transgender programs; Chloe focused on art and advocacy; and I went back to school.

> Arlene and Chloe taught me that advocacy is self-care.
> —Kiara St. James, founding executive director, New York Transgender Advocacy Group

I met Shira in 1999 when she was facilitating peer harm reduction groups with youth in the street economy at the New York Peer AIDS Education Coalition (NYPAEC).† During one of my first days back in the office to implement the board's decision to close NYPAEC, Shira, wearing fabulous six-inch-tall platforms, handed me a booklet called *Building an Anti-Racist Board of Directors* and asked that I consider some of the suggestions. Her bold intervention stilled every irreverent punk cell in my body that wanted to *shut it down* as a way of avoiding the discomforts of governing a peer-driven, harm reduction youth program within the NYPAEC. Shira's calling in shook me into seeing that

---

* Arlene and Chloe met in the Gender Identity Project's transgender peer training program at the NYC LGBT Center.

† In 1993, I joined Edith Springer (whom Keith Cylar had brought to Housing Works to provide clinical supervision) at NYPAEC, which she had cocreated with Paula Santiago (who would go on to coordinate the National Harm Reduction Conferences for many years). We worked together with Rod Sorge and many others to establish NYPAEC as a not-for-profit organization.

she—the first staff with lived experience in the sex trade and street economy—had manifested genderless bathrooms, wound care kits, nap corners, not just as a checklist of harm reduction tools, but as care for her community. Shira invited me into radical solidarity so that "by us for us" peer-based harm reduction could be truly realized. This was the first of many times that my heart would say said yes to channeling our glamorous queer punk rage into creating reverent spaces of liberation.

The System Is Not Broken, but It Will Break Us if We Do Not Work Together to Dismantle It

Conversation with Kiara St. James

Kiara St. James: I first started hearing "harm reduction" when I came to New York City in 1994, when I was nineteen. If you're going to use a needle for anything—drugs, hormones—make sure that you always use a new needle.

I was from the South, so I believed in the kindness of everyone. This older femme was extremely nice to me and let me stay with her. Two weeks into me staying there, she took out a needle to give me a hormone shot. I remember being excited but also scared. And I'm like, "Is that a clean needle?" and she told me not to worry about it. Because I was nineteen, and just broken, I allowed her to use a used needle on me. That's how I acquired HIV.

I understood the importance of clean needles after that because of people educating me. So, I actually tried to apply it, because I knew that I wanted—no matter what I was going through at that time—to take care of my body.

ACT UP and all those different organizations were fighting but the government ignored them. So, they took it upon themselves to hold space for community. What I remember from that time is that there were always up to eight to ten people dying in Atlanta from AIDS every day. I remember that the main people who were paying for their funerals were the drag queens doing fundraising through their performances. They would raise money to bury community members whose families disowned them. They created spaces where the community members opened up their homes when their family or church family didn't want them. That's part of our ways of knowing: "Okay. I still see your humanity. I still see you as my brother or my sister, and I'm going to take care of you regardless." And that is the framework of harm reduction right there.

The people who had my back were the people who were most ostracized. They held me down.

There were Black trans women who saw my potential: Amanda Milan,* Arlene Hoffman, and Bali White. What I pulled from them is that the streets don't have to make you mean. By the end of the night, Amanda would say, "Girl, I know you didn't make no money. Here, take this," and she'd give me like a hundred dollars. Because Amanda was a moneymaker. Those nights when she like, "Girl, I know you didn't break even tonight. So, here." Or take us to the diner and order a big breakfast for us, and all.

Arlene Hoffman was the second Black trans woman I heard about that was not making a living through sex work. When I first met Arlene, I had just found out about Positive Health Project. I remember I went to the back, and here was this beautiful melanat-

* Amanda Milan was a transgender woman of color who was a sex worker living in New York City. She was murdered on June 20, 2000. Her murder led Sylvia Rivera to re-form STAR, and they worked to make sure her murder was investigated, and we held countless protests and memorials in her honor.

ed sister with glasses and this gorgeous hair, natural hair. I remember she was doing my assessment, intake, and all of that. And then I asked, "Are you trans?" She goes, "Yes, I am. Yes, I am." Very Arlene. And I'm like, "And you don't do sex work?" She's like, "No."

When I think of Arlene, I think about meeting a celebrity. That really inspired me and made me want to come back to find out more and really have her as a mentor. She had such a free spirit. I remember that she was very accomplished but at the same time very down to earth. I also picked up on a sadness that she didn't really go into details about. After talking with my friend Porsche, it made me realize that Arlene also had a history she didn't tell me about, including engaging in sex work and having her heart broken by men.

Arlene just really gave me hope. Arlene was kind of like that mother when I was finding my way in New York. I would come back like a proud child showing my certificate from a training, and she was like, "I knew you could do it." She showed me how to be a harm reductionist. Arlene and Bali taught me how to be clear with my "No." It helped me acknowledge my humanity.

I have Bali still in my life, thank God. Bali has really helped me to expect more from myself, because I don't think I really did. I think I was going through the motions. "You're not going to disrespect me." But at the same time, I was being disrespected. I was good at advocating for other people, but in my personal life I was just walking in fear, and scared.

Shira: I have been thinking about sex work as care work. Where are you on that?

Sex work is work, but it's also a whole lot of other things; it's so much more than a job. I found a whole community in sex work and a whole system of care. Sex work is more than transactional—there's many layers to it. I had days where I was on top of the clouds, but I had other days where I felt so drained. Because I am an empath, I grow to care about people, even my johns. Sex work gave me validation when nothing else did.

I know, especially for me, even when I wasn't engaging in sex work—this was before the internet and all of that—I knew the type of guys that, like me, I knew where they would be. They tended to be on the stroll. I've had johns who were professors and lawyers, and we didn't have sex. They just wanted to talk to me. They would pay me because we're kind of like therapists and sometimes there was no physical interaction at all.

How has public health impacted the practice of Liberatory Harm Reduction?

There's a problem with public health harm reduction. It is impatient, insincere, and clinical. I don't want to be in spaces that are clinical. I want to be in spaces where if I'm feeling a certain way, there's a connection and we talk about that. I think it's important to highlight that trauma-centered care has been really pushed by us: activists. And I think that we have to push and make sure that we're getting more funding into organizations that practice the real trauma-informed care—not what public health waters down and calls "trauma informed"—but actually centering trauma.

For example, I remember at Positive Health Project, there were some issues that were happening, and Arlene, Kelly, and other folks would keep the doors open past 9 p.m. because there was a lot of trauma going on. They would hold the space open until midnight and order pizza. That was how they centered us. That's what happens when you have people who really center the community.

Do you want to talk a little bit about harm reduction and New York Transgender Advocacy Group (NYTAG)?

If you're queer, if you're Black, if you're HIV positive, you are not allowed to the cool table. In order to be invited to the cool table, you have to be cis, white or racially ambiguous, very passable, and then you get invited. So, I founded NYTAG from being frustrated by going into spaces where they would have these cascades of graphics of Black trans women with the highest rate of HIV and violence toward Black trans women. Just being sick and tired of that, and understanding we don't get HIV because we're Black or trans. It's not because we're Black or trans that we're houseless. It's because of policy. It's because of systems of oppression. Working on policies has brought me so much joy.

I remember one of my speeches for World AIDS Day at Kings Theater a couple of years ago. I asked the audience to repeat after me: "The system is not broken, but it will break us if we do not work together to dismantle it."

I'm very excited, because one of the things that I'm working on with senator Kevin Parker, who's my senator here in Flatbush, is a Universal Basic Income.

Do you see Universal Basic Income as harm reduction?

Universal Basic Income is actually Liberatory Harm Reduction because people have access to housing, access to health care.

We're collecting data at NYTAG to educate community members, especially in New York City, because Black and Brown New Yorkers and residents of New York City pay the most taxes. Yet we have no say-so in how that money is being reallotted back into our communities. That money that they're playing with is our money. So, I want to get more traction and have Black and Brown folks say, "We want Universal Basic Income. This is our money, and this is how we want to see it spent."

We need to make sure that houseless people are housed. We need to make sure that, for people who struggle with mental health issues, that the police are not being called on them and they are not publicly executed by police. We're working on UBI with a lot of partners, like Defund the Police, which is another form of harm reduction. Police should not be called simply because you jaywalked. Don't we want to live in a nation where everyone is taken care of? We do, I think.

We need to not be sitting comfortably in our living rooms. We should be in the street shutting down things until Biden and Harris push through these legislations that we want.

Lincoln Detox Center: *The People's Drug Program*

Interview with VICENTE "PANAMA" ALBA

This excerpted interview with Vicente "Panama" Alba was originally published in full in The Abolitionist *(Issue 19, 2013), a radical political education publication of Critical Resistance. Molly Porzig, a Critical Resistance, Oakland, member and an editor for* The Abolitionist, *interviewed Panama about his experiences building the Lincoln Detox Center. Panama was a member of the Young Lords Party and counselor at Lincoln Detox Center in the South Bronx, New York, in the 1970s. This interview is essential to our understanding of the revolutionary work that seeded harm reduction. Panama helps us connect the dots between the War on Drugs, community organizing to push back on the MIC, and drug-user rights.*

Molly Porzig: What was the Lincoln Detox Center? How did it start and why?

Vicente "Panama" Alba: In the late 1960s and early 1970s in New York, we were living through a drug epidemic. In November of

1970, I was nineteen years old and had been a heroin addict for five years. I began using heroin when I was fourteen, which was very common for young men and young women of my generation. Fifteen percent of the population was addicted (communities in the South Bronx, Harlem, the Lower East Side, Bushwick in Brooklyn, including everyone from a newborn baby to an elderly person ready to pass on). The concentration of addiction was in teenagers and people in their early twenties and thirties. Addiction at that time was primarily to heroin.

In the 1960s, the US government engaged in a war in Southeast Asia commonly known as the Vietnam War, but the United States was involved in all of Southeast Asia. There was an airline that was an operation of the CIA, transporting heroin from Southeast Asia to the US. We see now in Hollywood movies "gangsters" importing heroin, but the bulk of heroin imported to the United States was a United States government operation, targeting poor communities of color, Black and Latino communities.

In New York, heroin devastated most of Harlem and the South Bronx. Young people utilized heroin very publicly, sniffing heroin at dance halls or in school bathrooms, which led to shooting up intravenously. This was an epidemic that Black Panther Michael "Cetewayo" Tabor, one of the New York 21, wrote a pamphlet on, called *Capitalism Plus Dope Equals Genocide*, which we used widely. In 1969, the Black Panther Party in New York City was decimated by the indictment of 21 Black Panthers (known as the Panther 21 or New York 21) and needed to focus on the trial, becoming inactive in other areas at that time. Because of the relationship the Black Panther Party and the Young Lords had, together we began looking at the heroin epidemic, the general health of our communities, and the public health positions of institutions against our communities.

Lincoln Hospital was built in 1839 to receive former slaves migrating from the South. By 1970, it was the only medical facility in the South Bronx. It was a dilapidated brick structure from the previous century that had never been upgraded. It was known as the "butcher shop of the South Bronx." In the old Lincoln Hospital (and even today) you walk down the hall and see blood everywhere—blood on the walls, the sheets, the gurneys, your shoes. Doctors were assigned there for internships and learned on Blacks, Puerto Ricans, and a very small diminishing white community in the South Bronx.

In early 1970, there was a woman by the name of Carmen Rodriguez who was butchered in the hospital and bled to death on a gurney.* Following that death, the Young Lords, with the participation of some Black Panthers, took over Lincoln Hospital for the first time and demanded better health care delivery for people in that community.

During the takeover, the Young Lords, Panthers, supporters, and translators set up tables where people came to document their experiences of the medical treatment. A major part of the takeover focused on how there were no translators at Lincoln Hospital. South Bronx is a predominantly Puerto Rican community, primarily of Spanish-speaking people newly arrived or second generation who spoke little to no English. People would walk in Lincoln Hospital for medical treatment and there was nobody there to understand your ailment or problem. The hospital administration had also been confronted about the lack of services for people with addictions, primarily heroin addiction. The community had told the hospital one of its shortcomings was that you come to the hospital and you get no treatment whatsoever. The hospital administration paid no mind to it.

Months later, on November 10, 1970, a group of the Young Lords, a South Bronx anti-drug coalition, and members of the

---

* According to *Filter Magazine*, in 1970, Carmen Rodriguez went to Lincoln Hospital for a routine abortion. The doctors failed to read her medical chart and gave her medications that caused a terrible allergic reaction that led to her death days later.

Health Revolutionary Unity Movement (a mass organization of health workers), with the support of the Lincoln Collective, took over the Nurses' Residence building of Lincoln Hospital and established a drug treatment program called The People's Drug Program, which became known as Lincoln Detox Center.

The police surrounded us, and we said we weren't leaving. By day two, the takeover had spread by word of mouth, and we had hundreds of people lined up wanting to get treatment for addiction. About a month later, the administration had to come to terms with the fact that we weren't leaving. They had been sitting on the proposal of some monies that had been earmarked for treatment that hadn't been implemented. The money was brought and staff was hired from the very volunteers of the Lincoln Detox program we started. We were very effective in doing so and kept our program running until 1979.

What was your involvement?

I joined the building of Lincoln Detox from day one. Before that, my primary objective was to go get drugs, until one time Cleo Silvers and I were sitting on a stoop and she pointed some important stuff out to me. She told me to look at the New York City police patrol car where two officers sat selling heroin. She said, "Look, those are cops. Look who you're giving your money to!" The climate in our communities at the time was very important. On the one hand we have the drug epidemic, but there was also revolution in the air—change was something that you could breathe, that you could taste, that you could feel, because the movement was very vibrant. Some days before October 30, there had been a massive demonstration called by the Young Lords, and I attended the demonstration even though I was still addicted.

Because of the way I felt that day, I told myself I couldn't continue to be a drug user. I couldn't be a heroin addict and a revolutionary, and I wanted to be a revolutionary. I made a decision to kick a dope habit. Coincidentally, that day I called Cleo, who told me to go to this place with these people. I met a couple of young brothers from the Puerto Rican Student Union, and they escorted me over to Cleo at Lincoln Hospital. It had just been taken over a half-hour before. As I was withdrawing from my addiction, I did not detoxify in Lincoln Detox, but detoxified on my own, cold turkey, a challenge I placed upon myself.

I was recruited out of that experience into the Young Lords Party, maybe a month after the first day of the program. The presence of the Latino movement within the revolutionary movement in the US hadn't occurred yet in New York. It had occurred in the Southwest with the Brown Berets, but the Latino community in New York was predominantly Puerto Rican. When I joined the Young Lords, I was assigned to Lincoln Detox, where I worked as a counselor.

What did the Lincoln Detox Center do? What approaches did it use?

We provided detoxification. We had support from medical doctors providing us with methadone, which we then provided to people in increasing dosages over ten days for people to withdraw, replacing the heroin with methadone and then decreasing it by milligrams every day. After the tenth day you would be physically clean.

This was also right around the time that Richard Nixon opened up relationships with China. A lot came out about the Chinese way of life and how health care was provided to the people of China. We heard about acupuncture. We read a magazine article about a situation in Thailand where an acupuncturist used acupuncture to treat someone with respiratory problems and an addiction to opium. We read that the stimulation of the lung point in the ear was the key of the treatment. We went down to Chinatown, got acupuncture needles and began experimenting on one another. We then developed the acupuncture collective within Lincoln Detox.

We also understood that an individual's addiction wasn't just a physical problem but a psychological problem. It was a widespread problem in our community, not because we as a community were psychologically deficient, but because oppression and brutal living conditions drove us to that. There was a book called *The Radical Therapist* by Jerome Agel that some of us read.

We developed therapy that integrated political education into therapeutic discussions. We held group sessions with overwhelmingly Black and Puerto Rican participants and engaged in conversations around what it felt like to be Black or Puerto Rican, what it meant for someone who was called a "spic" to not understand what Puerto Rican was. Puerto Rican people are colonial subjects of the United States. You ask a Puerto Rican generally, an unconscious Puerto Rican, and they'll say, "I'm a US citizen." Well, you are an unwelcomed US citizen, so what does that feel like and mean? The effects of colonialism and the treatment Puerto Ricans receive stateside are not understood because they become internalized. You have to start with what it means. How do you feel about your family's inability to provide for you? Why do the cops hate you? Why does the school hate you? I went to public school, didn't know English in fifth grade, and was placed in a class for the "mentally challenged." There are people who need that support, but I don't get it. What are the impacts of that kind of treatment by the institutions of society? What happens to a person who lives in those conditions, who gets beaten by police and called a "dirty spic" or who gets denied friendship because the person is white and you're of color? There is a cumulative impact of this kind of existence, and we would discuss it.

How did Lincoln Detox incorporate grassroots organizing into its ongoing work?

When you're consumed by chasing a bag of drugs, chasing the money to get the bag of drugs, being high, or being in an environment with other people you get high with, it becomes a way of life. When people want alternatives, you have to provide it for them. We did not have the resources to say: "Okay, you're seventeen, you can benefit from finishing school." Here's a school with caring teachers, caring counselors, and so on to bring people up to speed in education or to direct people to get employment, particularly people who had been out of the work force. Given the natural power of the therapeutic approach, this was all very important that it was voluntary, that it was people's will to do. If they learned things from our educational program and therapeutic sessions, they wanted to do something about those problems. We would direct them to get involved, to get engaged in campaigns that were going on in the community.

We had people advocating for people in welfare centers, training people on the rights of welfare recipients, and translators who would advocate for people who were Spanish speakers. We played a part in the founding of a coalition for minority construction workers, because construction work was a good paying job, and the industry excluded minorities. Those were a few things we did, in addition to political campaigns. Some people that came through our programs joined the Young Lords, Black Panther Party, or the Republic of New Afrika. Some became Muslims and got deeply involved. Some got involved in the campaign to free political prisoners or began building collectives.

We fought every day—we fought for the right to eat, the right to get paid, the right to be respected, the right not to be fucked with by the cops. We never asked for anything in return.

What were some of the strengths, successes, challenges, and weaknesses?

There were strengths and successes throughout, but it wasn't all glory. There were a lot of challenges and weaknesses. From the first day, November 10, 1970, we had a constant influx of people every day seeking help. Hundreds and hundreds came—I'm not talking about one or two dozen people—as the word spread about Lincoln Detox, the opportunity for people to walk in and get effective help from everyday people (not white professionals but their own people) who had a loving heart, developing an understanding of things they needed to articulate. People came from all over New York and Connecticut, Long Island, New Jersey, too. The Lincoln Detox program became so successful and effective that a United Nations delegation visited and gave us recognition for it.

At that point acupuncture became controversial because it was "nonmedical" people providing medical care. Laws then were passed about who could do acupuncture, making it so that it could only be done under supervision of a medical doctor who might not have a clue of what acupuncture is about. Those kinds of political struggles—to maintain funding for the program, to keep the program alive, against the local police as well as the hospital police, who continuously tried to make their way into the program (Lincoln Detox was a sanctuary where addicts could go and not be afraid of the police)—were big challenges. Then we struggled with the hospital to provide meal expenses for the program. People were coming off the streets, didn't have anything to eat and needed treatment. We struggled and eventually figured it out.

We also struggled with developing our skills in treatment, acupuncture, and detoxing. At the time we started the program, there was a big push to promote methadone maintenance as a treatment modality. Methadone is a scary drug, originally developed by Nazi scientists in order to furnish themselves with opioids. It's highly addictive, and the withdrawal is different from heroin. People slowly developed a protocol for detoxing off methadone. We could detox somebody from heroin in ten days and they'd be fine physically. Methadone was very painful for many months—three or four sometimes.

One morning in 1979, we went to work, and the Lincoln Hospital was surrounded by police checking the identification of everybody walking in. They had a list of names, and members of the Young Lords, Black Panther Party, and Republic of New Afrika, and other people were excluded from entering the facilities and were to be arrested if they tried to enter. They dismantled Lincoln Detox. One component they were very interested in was the acupuncture, because it was a money mill. Some people today say the Lincoln Detox still exists, but it doesn't. There's an acupuncture clinic at Lincoln Hospital but the program was dismantled.

Was the collaboration between different groups such as the Young Lords, the Black Panther Party, the Republic of New Afrika, and Muslim communities spontaneous, automatic, or a more intentional effort in developing the program?

That's a deep question. There's the overriding principle of unity and respect and there's the reality that we were all works in progress. *It's not like you go to sleep one night a junkie and wake up the next morning a revolutionary.* There's a process in growth and change. As products of today's society, we are not examples of the society we're building for tomorrow.

Collaboration and solidarity were very important to Lincoln Detox and there were a lot of struggles. We considered the Black Panther Party the vanguard of the revolutionary movement at that time, and there was the reality that the Black Panther Party was disintegrating. There were some people in the Black Panther Party and the Young Lords who were extremely arrogant. We had to struggle against and combat those tendencies. We would always go back to the principle of what is the best interest of the people. The outcome was very positive and we learned so much from each other. In 1973, when the American Indian Movement confronted the FBI at Wounded Knee on Pine Ridge Reservation in South Dakota, there was no question for us. It was automatically our responsibility to support and engage with that. We developed a philosophy, a practice that made it possible for us to do those things.

What lessons were learned that could strengthen work today?

I think that a lot of organizing that takes place today is funded. You don't hear about many initiatives that are independent efforts. One of the things that Lincoln Detox was very much a part of was support for the Attica brothers during the Attica Prison takeover in September 1971. We did twenty-something rallies in fifteen days throughout New York City. We didn't have the internet or cell phones, or institutions financing copy machines, or any of that. We hustled to type fliers, cut and pasted pictures, and burned stencils.

We built a movement and we looked for ways to make the movement survive without government funding. Nobody could tell us what we were going to do. Today a lot relies on foundation monies, and people focus on the money and don't engage in campaigns. Even though we forced the government for years to underwrite our work, eventually they had the power and took it out. We didn't have the power to continue that institution. If we were not in their facility could they have shut us down? I don't know, but it would have been different.

We need to recognize we can't have institutions within the institutions. I mean we eventually end up in one way or another in a place where Lincoln Detox ended. We need to think in terms of short range *and* longer-range efforts. How do you get rid of prisons under imperialism? You have to get rid of imperialism. In the meantime, you may take on some struggles that may take on some reforms and that needs to be studied and discussed.

We can look at it from the humanist viewpoint and see that we saved and changed a lot of lives, people who would have been dead from heroin. I'm one of them, one of a lot of people. A lot of people became contributors to progress, but in changing the world the obstacles change too. After heroin came crack. We did not stop the drug scourge in our community.

What are some of the legacies or long-term impacts of the Lincoln Detox Center?

Humbly, I don't think there would be the new Lincoln Hospital without our work. If it weren't for the struggles that we took on, the new Lincoln Hospital would never have been built, because all political interests had nothing to do with the interests of the people in the community. We had to fight to put the interests of the community at the forefront and demand that hospital be built. When they shut down the old and moved to the new Lincoln Hospital, they made space for every department except Lincoln Detox. The legacy spreads beyond that, too. If you go into any New York City public hospital, you see the Patient's Bill of Rights on the wall. That came out of the first takeover at Lincoln Hospital. We made it come alive at Lincoln Detox.

We Go Where Our People Are

Interview with
NATIVE YOUTH SEXUAL HEALTH NETWORK

I spoke with Iehente, Shane, Krysta Marie, and Emma at the Native Youth Sexual Health Network (NYSHN), an organization led by Indigenous youth that works across issues of sexual and reproductive health, rights, and justice throughout the United States and Canada.

NYSHN Mission Statement

Our values and what we believe in shape our relationships, decision-making processes, and our community work. They guide which relationships we engage and invest in and the ways in which we work together as a network, with our aunties, mentors, and youth leaders.

We, as well as our ancestors, have been keeping our communities safe and reducing harms long before the term "harm reduction" came into the English language. The thoughts we shared here are based on intergenerational learning, community organizing, the efforts and teachings of those most impacted, and sacred voices of those who we have lost.

Shira: Can you talk about the roles your elders' and ancestors' liberation work played in building the values and frameworks of harm reduction? What about the way you practice harm reduction comes uniquely from your practices of liberation and saving your own lives?

Krysta: Indigenous people have been practicing harm reduction for more than five hundred years. It was never supposed to be confined to injection drug use or substance use. It's been a way of looking at the world and practicing care where people are experiencing many forms of violence. If we think of harm reduction as this broad-based practice and Indigenous survival skill, then there's been many forms of it over the generations, even if we didn't call it that.

Within Indigenous feminisms, the practice is about staying alive—or trying to. Of course, we were not always successful, because our deaths have always been the intended outcome of colonization. When I think about the Land Back Movement, people speaking out about sexual violence, Bill C-31, women in our communities who have been disenfranchised through marriage and patriarchal social policy—that's harm reduction.

Colonizers said that the purpose of removing children into residential schools was because of "harm" happening to Indigenous children around a perceived lack of literacy or western education, which also conveniently removed people from lands that were deemed desirable. We didn't practice the same agricultural practices as Europeans, so that was deemed harmful to the economy. It's all bullshit, but that was one of the many justifications for the creation of reservations.

The anti-saviorship is a response to very public, prominent, Canadian and American founders talking about "Kill the Indian, save the child." It's such a glaringly public piece of the history in terms of the social policy justification and foundation of public health. It's this little doll inside of a doll of terribleness. That's what we're responding to.

Colonizers have told us what is harming us when, really, it's about what's harming the settler-colonial collective. Now we are asking ourselves, "How do we self-determine what is harmful and what isn't?" The colonizer narrative that substance use and addictions are the biggest problem in our communities is super hella racist and actually just an excuse to discount a lot of our relatives.

Shane: At NYSHN, we've had lots of mentors, aunties, and elders who are harm reduction rock stars. One of our community elders says, "We go where our people are."

Many of our people are incarcerated, and elders and traditional knowledge keepers fought their way into the prison system to provide them with culture, ceremony, and harm reduction tools; it's life-saving when you're existing in this terrible system that's trying to disappear you.

I learned about harm reduction from Indigenous people and value it because it aligns with my own Anishinaabe worldview. We have a common teaching about only taking what you need and leaving the rest. It can be applied to plant relatives, relationships, resources, everything! I was taught how to pick berries and lift the berry bush up. I can't just trample it and pick all the things because then it's not going to thrive for the next time that you need it. It's not just about your needs; it's about everyone else's needs and about the plant itself. By enacting this behavior, I am also reducing the harm to that plant and our relationship.

We don't have a word for harm reduction in Anishinaabemowin, but we have a lot of other words that describe the practice of reducing harm. One of our elders was talking about difficult relationships. I asked, “What in you made the decision to continue those relationships?” Her response was, “I’ve always built relationships with people that other people had a hard time being close to.” That’s a harm reduction approach.

I feel really grateful that our people have been carrying that legacy. It’s not about a specific person, but about the spirit of our teachings that we have carried through our existence in our bodies.

Emma: I came into harm reduction through Indigenous community organizing, through family. I came in knowing what harm reduction could mean and look like through the lives of my family members and bound community.

Harm reduction has become a place where we can meet with other cultures—even with public health—to communicate what we need for our communities. It’s a place, a term, to gather around. With the opiate crisis, harm reduction has become institutionalized or adopted by public health and social work institutions, which have watered down and co-opted it.

Harm reduction has always been about how we understand connection. Within the Anishinaabe worldview that I know, the word *bimaadiziwin* resonates. Some people say it means the good life, but that makes it sound like there’s a bad life and that someone has a right to tell you the difference between them. What I understood it to mean is practicing a way of being that’s all about maintaining respectful or harmonious relation, a balance in the world, and good relation with all of creation.

Harm reduction has often been the only term to explain why it’s important to be in right relation with our relatives who use substances or have been impacted by substance use, which is really pretty much our entire communities. Not just our human communities but our entire creation has been impacted by substances.

Not just in a negative way, too. I hold the truth of my relatives who have explained that substances have saved their lives and are a way of surviving trauma; you get trauma by living as an Indigenous person under colonial systems.

Haida harm reduction genius Andrea Medley taught me that connection is about recognizing who we are, what support looks like outside of the clinic. We can't just have individualized clinic models; we are part of whole communities, creations, and lands. We can't pretend that substance use is separate from colonization, land resource extraction, or everything that's impacting our community. It's all very much tied together.

Iehente: Harm reduction is ingrained in everything we do because it's a better way to care for each other that's been passed down. When it's institutionalized or a workshop, it's not enough. For example, like with many intense subjects, one "sensitivity" or "cultural sensitivity" workshop isn't going to solve racism. The same way that there isn't one "best practice" when it comes to harm reduction.

It's like the agreement that we have between the Anishinaabe and the Haudenosaunee called the Dish with One Spoon Treaty: take only what you need, and make sure there's enough to go around. The work we do—harm reduction, sexual health, full-spectrum doula care—is all connected because it's supporting everyone's different situations.

Marie: You mentioning the Dish with One Spoon made me think about how our communities have been reducing the harms of colonialism for the past five hundred-plus years. Before that, we were reducing harms in our communities and between our nations since time immemorial. Like everyone has said, it's part of our ways of being in the world.

Where do you look at how we practice harm reduction and see Indigenous culture incorporated that goes unrecognized by mainstream harm reduction movements?

Krysta: Hosting is a really good example, because it's coercive to do anything with somebody who hasn't eaten or is coming down. Food has to be part of the consent process if you want participation. If your basic needs haven't been met, it's too distracting to do any sort of programming or intervention.

Emma: NYSHN negotiates with communities to make sure that youth leaders will be fed well. "Yeah, pick whatever you want to eat and we'll cover it. You don't need to look at the prices." This is real grounding and centering of wellness that's about recognizing accessibility. Youth leadership doesn't mean throwing the youth into a sacrificial fire and telling them to figure it out. It's about recognizing that oftentimes honoraria gets spent on substances, rent, or picking up your cousins from school. By the time the gig rolls around, maybe they need a meal.

Krysta: I love that example because it is not that revolutionary. How is that not basic practice? It's so obvious, but in other funded programs, that's not the design.

Laverne, who I think cofounded or founded the Ontario Aboriginal HIV/AIDS Strategy, talked about how the fundamentals of harm reduction were based in Indigenous teachings of love. She talked about nonjudgmental care and meeting people where they're at. Love is one of our grandparent teachings.

Shane: A lot of community members have amazing, strong, caring values, but also carry the impacts of colonialism. That is a barrier to transforming trauma for themselves and to be able to see someone fully as they are and support them.

A lot of mainstream institutions that have Indigenous programs have different barriers and boundaries than us. When I see cultural responsibilities in action, I see our cultural teachings reflected. When I see the door shutting, time being shortened, deadlines happening, or punishing people for not fulfilling some weird-ass shit, I don't see our cultural teachings reflected. It doesn't matter if the place is plastered with medicine wheels.

Emma: I don't really notice my teachings in harm reduction because I'm using my teachings as harm reduction. Our practices are integrated extensions of our Indigenous ways of being. When we witness settler organizations missing or not doing those practices, it's very alarming! Sometimes you just have to disrupt it.

Our communities, collectives, individuals, lands, it's all one and we can't be separated from each other. That's a root teaching; harm reduction is about our practices and values of self-determination. It's about respecting somebody's bodily sovereignty and their expertise over their own life and meeting community where they're at.

Iehente: I would add gifting, which says, "We respect you. You are worthy. You deserve love." A good example is Indigenous Birth of Alberta's online webinars for labor, birth, lactation, and all kinds of things. The first certain number of people who sign up get a free care package. That's how you do it.

How is harm reduction an anticolonial practice? What does it center and what does it reclaim that reinforces those things?

Krysta: All of these instructions around *mino bimaadiziwin*, the Dish with One Spoon, grandparent teachings are passed down and very deliberately taught. There were systems put in place to teach future generations those same protocols.

Those things were also deliberately removed and disrupted in favor of capitalism, land theft, and genocide. There is a deliberate process of forgetting in terms of public health; they are not owning their ignorance. It's part of a larger discussion—complicated with communities who experience marginalization and violence as a result of arriving here [US]—that informs how we talk about ourselves and our community. How we talk about people who are trying to bring in progressive public health interventions, how we speak back to that and continue to have energy to talk amongst ourselves and figure out our own shit. How do we balance resistance work with reclamation work, not just talking about what you don't want, but enacting the future that you do want? This is the tension.

Shane: Harm reduction is an anticolonial practice because how could it not be? Everything colonial is harmful; the prison systems, the MIC, pathologizing trans people, the disappearing and removal of our people from our lands. Their response is, "Okay, we'll reform you," "We're kicking you out of housing," or, "You're in pain? No, I'm not going to give you a prescription for something that could help you." Harm reduction is an anticolonial practice because it responds back to those systems of violence.

Harm reduction is also a way to return to ourselves and our communities, to honor our experiences and heal from trauma, whether that's a neat box you can put a bow on or a lifelong journey. It's important to be explicit and say, "Someone I love is a drug user and they deserve to be in ceremony too," because people can remove themselves and never sit in the discomfort in order to see someone fully as they are. It's about reclaiming our own narratives. To have other approaches, practices, and people who can mirror back and create space for you to exist as you are is really powerful.

Iehente: I'm doing a lot of support for pregnant folks or folks who need an abortion: full-spectrum doula support. Everyone's still alive. Why do you think? Because we know how to heal. We know the medicines. The hospital wants you to do what's easy for them and their "normal" procedure. For the person it's happening to, it's a big life event. We are helping give people rights, power, and knowledge of their own bodies. Institutions are scared that they're not going to make money if you don't take their prescriptions or need their medical interventions.

Marie: The phrase "Meet them where they're at" makes me think of the Edge of the Woods ceremony. You stop at the edge, light a fire, and then folks see the smoke and come. You greet each other and have a conversation about why you're there, what you're bringing, what you want to get out of this visit or situation or relationship or whatever is happening at the time. It's about consent, which is inextricable from harm reduction.

When we support folks in our community, it's not only a responsibility to that person, it's to the community at large to make a place where folks are able to share their gifts with the rest of us. We all have so much wisdom and so many gifts, and colonialism and mainstream institutions prevent people from being able to share those gifts with one another.

Your article on indigenizing harm reduction breaks down harm reduction so freaking succinctly, but also the clarity of the Four Fires is such an enormous gift.

Krysta: There is this question "What would these fires look like on the ground while understanding the importance of the central home fire?" NYSHN has been using fire keeping as a reference point for community organizing and how to maintain our responsibilities. It's a really important role in our community that's weirdly gendered but doesn't need to be because it's a survival skill. Everybody should know how to make a fucking fire. It's one of the first skills that children are taught when coming into adulthood, when they can be responsible for something that could cause harm. That word choice, "are taught," carries a lot of value. It's also hella important, being able to light, heat and cook things. There's this idea of trying to maintain a central home fire—whether that's your own body, spirit, life—and then these other factors around it that either protect it or don't.

We named a few broad concepts that captured and went beyond the Four Pillars model, because pillars literally hold something up, and what is it holding up? Shocker, it's colonialism! Instead, we created a circular model that holds up whatever is put in the center. Those four things are cultural safety, reclamation, self-determination, and sovereignty. We've covered self-determination and sovereignty as central and important tenets. We talked less about cultural safety and reclamation because the idea is for people to map out what those tenets look like for them and their communities.

In recognizing this diversity of nations, peoples, and individuals, we struggle a lot with prescriptiveness. What do syringe/needle drop-off, distribution, and supply chains look like in various communities? It's all about presenting different options so that people with lived experience can decide.

Shane: We get asked all the time to build out practical examples and tell people, "This is what you do," but that's not our approach. Reclamation is really about reclaiming our own cultural and spiritual traditions. Sometimes people have a really hard time balancing the things they know are our teachings and still providing loving, generous care to someone who needs it. Often people are disconnected from culture or ceremony, and that's actually what they need the most. I would add more content around what those things look like and how they can be applied.

Visiting and greeting—the foundational hosting protocols that all of our nations carry—is important to us. We wouldn't leave someone to suffer by themselves outside alone because it's a core principle on how to be in relationship with each other. How do the home fires apply to supporting ourselves and people in our community?

Emma: There was an interview project with elders and relatives in the Downtown East Side where they gathered up their wisdom about harm reduction and substance use. It's beautiful and awesome, but there is tension between how much we tell what we do and what you need in your own community. It's that piece between empowerment versus instruction. That's part of what self-determination is about—recognizing what works here might not work there.

The skill of being in relation with each other and creating spaces where people can connect and figure out solutions based on their life is beautiful. The information, the support, the practical, putting out all of that stuff and then being like, "We'll help you figure it out together, but I'm not going to tell you what to do." That's also a very Indigenous way of teaching and learning.

There's not a lot of elders that'll be like, "You need to do XYZ." They'll be, "Here, I'm going to give you these teachings," or, "I'm going to tell you these stories over and over again, and then let you fucking figure it out, maybe let you know if you're not doing it right." That's often how traditional instruction has happened around me.

Chosen family, folks who have to build community outside of mainstream structures, blood ties, they watch and learn. We're a role model to each other about social norms. That's how people learn and practice. It's not through a how-to manual or workshop.

There's frustration and an uncomfortableness that we want people to sit with: Why can't people have all of the information that they need to make an informed decision for themselves and have that be enough?

Iehente, I'm really thinking about all of our pregnancy, substance use, and harm-reduction resources that are about breaking that down. It's not up to the OB, midwife or whoever to tell you what's safe or not. It is up to you—given the information in accessible ways—to decide for yourself where the risks and benefits are.

Emma: When Shane described that person out in the cold, responsibility to them isn't coming from a place of saviorship. It's coming from reciprocity. It's not about saying, "Oh, look at them. They have nothing. I have everything." It's about saying, "actually we're all in balance and this person has gifts." This is a principle of how we approach things from a nonjudgmental and peer-led space. That's also a harvesting practice; it's about that reciprocity of understanding that it's never just one way of relationality. If done right, you're always understanding that we are all coming into this world with gifts and our worlds benefit when we're able to share our gifts with each other.

Indigenizing Harm Reduction

NATIVE YOUTH SEXUAL HEALTH NETWORK

This guide was originally published by NYSHN in 2014.

With staggering rates of HIV, HCV, and IDU among Indigenous peoples, it is clear current mainstream models may not be meeting Indigenous peoples where they are at. What could harm reduction look like outside of urban centers in rural, northern, and remote communities?

Pillar Model

The 4 pillar model is familiar to many harm reduction workers, academics, and health policy analysts. While not the only theory on how to counteract harms caused by substance used, the interpretation and implementation of these pillars can sometimes uphold colonial ideals of health, power, and oppression.

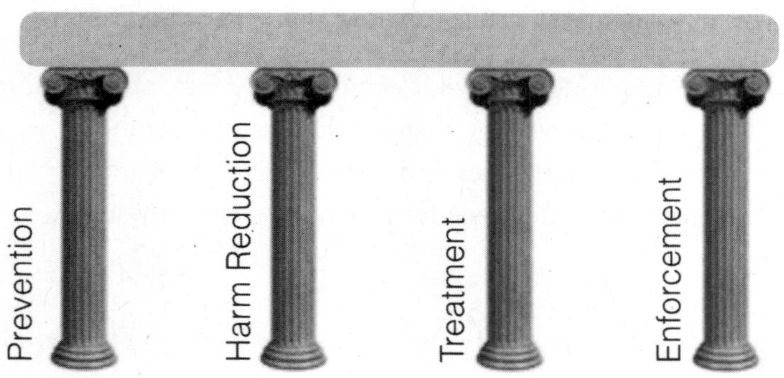

Moving Beyond 4 Pillars

Indigenous peoples have experience reducing harm in many ways, especially the violence of colonialism for the last 500 years. Mainstream harm reduction models and practices while certainly a step in the right direction, do not always fit in northern, rural, or remote communities. Indigenous peoples have many Nation-specific understandings, traditions and needs that mainstream services often ignore or interrupt.

By shifting our focus from interpretations of these pillars like policing, prisons, court mandated care and assuming "risk" is individual instead of systemic, we offer a critical analysis of what reducing the harm of colonialism can look like. This is not a "one size fits all" approach but an opportunity to reinterpret these ideas in community specific ways that recognize the diversity of Indigenous peoples.

Four Fire Model

By centering community wellbeing and the restoration of different Indigenous knowledge systems, life ways, ceremonies, culture and governance structures Indigenous peoples of many Nations and cultures can reduce the harm we experience in our lives.

"Acknowledge the power differences that exist between service provider and client/patient. Allowing and creating spaces for Indigenous peoples to feel safe to be our whole selves when receiving care."

Cultural Safety

"Colonialism uprooted and distorted many structures and ways of life within our communities, reclaiming cultural practices can strengthen us."

Sovereignty

"Principles like non-interference teach us to support and meet people where they're at, ie. not forcing treatment."

Reclamation

Self-determination

"Allowing individuals, communities and Nations decide specifically for ourselves what works best for us."

A practical guide to get you started...

Cultural Safety:

"Acknowledge the power differences that exist between service provider and client/patient. Allowing and creating spaces for Indigenous peoples to feel safe to be our whole selves when receiving care."

For non-Indigenous service providers and harm reduction advocates:
Good intentions are not always enough. Be aware that you are a part of the legacy of trauma and violence that well-meaning service providers, healthcare professionals and others have inflicted on Indigenous peoples. This means developing trust and relationship building while showing that you are making an effort to be different than that legacy. Actually say this to the people you are serving and be open to being held accountable for your actions or inactions.

- Ex: non-Indigenous practitioners complaining they are "just trying to help" or frustrated by low turnout in medical clinic settings

Utilize and leverage the power and privilege you do have for the benefit of Indigenous peoples. Be aware of tokenism in your workplace and advocate for meaningful involvement of communities and individuals. If Indigenous peoples are only frontline workers or temporary staff, but not management, challenge this and endeavor to change it.

For Indigenous community-based service providers and community members:
Indigenous youth may not always feel safe and at home with their culture for many reasons. Allow them to name who or what kinds of support they are interested in having, or learning more about, be it "traditional" or "allopathic/mainstream."

- Ex: Work directly with Elders, knowledge keepers and traditional supports in your community, build relationships and trust so you can refer with confidence, but be open to hesitation or concerns. Do not shame young people for choosing a mainstream method, or wanting to try multiple options.

Respectfully work with and gently challenge abstinence based programs that cite "traditional values" as a reason for not allowing people who are using substances to access ceremony or traditional medicines. Being 100% sober all of the time may be an extremely difficult task and if it is a minimum requirement for support, may turn many community members away from potential supports. Create options that meet people where they're at while respecting traditional and community protocol, like welcoming people into a space without active participation or having helpers who can work with people under the influence in respectful humanizing ways to deescalate any potentially harmful interactions.

Reclamation

"Colonialism uprooted and distorted many structures and ways of life within our communities, reclaiming cultural practices can strengthen us"

For Indigenous community-based service providers and community members:
Talk with each other and actively listen to each other's stories. Make a sincere effort to not judge, and be aware of your judgements when they come up. Involve all kinds of leaders, especially young people, in discussions about how best to support each other. It can be hard to piece apart our histories to understand what really is "traditional" or "Indigenous" especially when things like

religion, gender stereotypes and taking away our children all distorted how we pass on our culture and practice our values.

- Ex: Two-Spirit resistance and resurgence

For non-Indigenous service providers and harm reduction advocates:
Be comfortable with the uncomfortable. Know how to talk about colonialism and your complicity in it. Be willing to support cultural activities that don't fit into diseasecontrol models of what is 'effective' prevention or treatment.

Self-Determination:

"Allowing individuals, communities and Nations to decide specifically for ourselves what works best for us"

For Indigenous community-based service providers and community members:
Work with community members individually to find out what their needs are, and what works for them knowing it will probably be different from person to person. What you think is the main concern may not be for someone accessing services or looking for support. Maintain confidentiality and privacy as much as possible even when in a small community.

- Ex. often ensuring basic needs are met like food, clothing and safe housing are a first step to building trust and thinking about other issues that need addressing. People often develop their own coping mechanisms and strategies that should not be overlooked ("problem" substance use may be helping with anxiety or trauma).

For non-Indigenous service providers and harm reduction advocates:
Avoid a pan-Aboriginal approach to service provision. Don't

assume all Indigenous peoples are the same or have similar traditions. You don't need to be a cultural expert but you need to be aware of cultural appropriation, and whose territory specifically you are in, and the various communities you may share space with or serve.

- Ex. if you have more anthropological knowledge of cultural knowledge than a community member has access to culture look at the barriers influencing that disparity.

Sovereignty:

"Principles like noninterference teach us to support and meet people where they're at"

For everyone
Court mandated treatment is not the answer to everything especially if those treatments or supports are not meeting someone where they're at like requiring sobriety or nonuse all of the time. Harm reduction is not always about reducing the amount of substances used but identifying and knowing what behaviours or consequences are harmful and to whom and which can be reduced.

- Ex. drinking alcohol may seem like a problem, but being thrown out of the house for being under the influence is more dangerous, especially in the winter.

For Indigenous community-based service providers and community members:
By solely focus on substance use we miss the larger story, the systemic reasons why we as Indigenous Nations are in this mess in the first place. Trust that people know what is best for them in the

moment. Shaming our people for struggling will get us no closer to restoring what was taken.

For non-Indigenous service providers and harm reduction advocates: Be a respectful guest and visitor. Honouring original agreements is just as important to this work as clinical practices.

Understanding Harm Reduction

The history of harm reduction in this country is about the radical revolutionaries who believed that we, as all of those who were and still are disproportionately impacted by HIV and AIDS, deserved to survive. There are countless radical harm reduction groups in existence who take money from departments of public health and do some of the most life-affirming work—from putting naloxone in the hands of drug users to prevent overdose to giving out wound care kits to helping manage abscesses caused by injection or to address self-injury. This section is absolutely not about the radical harm reduction projects and activists who made syringe exchange possible in the United States. This section is about the unintended outcome of the incorporation of harm reduction into public health and the ways in which the state simultaneously liberalized and conservatized this precious practice.

I also want to name that the conditions in, say, Oregon, where so much drug use has been decriminalized, are vastly different than in municipalities where syringe exchange remains illegal and unfunded. The circumstances of place are not to be underestimated when it comes to our community's access to lifesaving information and supplies.

I want to explain the most common versions of harm reduction that I see play out in social services that are not grassroots or led by drug users, sex workers, or the people who are most impacted by criminalization. What makes these versions of harm reduction lack substance is they are not actively supporting self-determination or working toward true liberation from oppression by building our collective power as grassroots groups did in the 1980s and 1990s and some continue to do now.

Public Health Harm Reduction

The role of public health, which distorted and co-opted harm reduction strategies from the people who created it, has had a dangerous impact. First, let's break down how most people think about the basic concepts of harm reduction as an intervention that lives inside public health and social work. Throughout this section, I make the distinction between what I am calling "public health harm reduction" and what we are reclaiming as Liberatory Harm Reduction.

The basics of harm reduction, in both public health and in liberatory practices, are really quite simple and commonly practiced by most people as we take action to reduce harm in our daily lives. The best example is driving a car. Those who use seat belts in cars do so because research and common sense encourage us to make the dangerous act of driving less deadly. The act of driving is not shamed because of the risks associated with the activity—rather the focus is on making cars safer and more survivable. Driving is viewed as necessary and, at times, pleasurable. Even though it's a potentially harmful activity, it is still not stigmatized. This metaphor can help those of you without stigmatized life experiences to relate to the basic concepts of harm reduction.

Those who study this topic view harm reduction as something invented by Europeans during the AIDS epidemic. In fact, the European lineage of harm reduction is an important part of the overall picture, but it's not the entire picture. Maia Szalavitz, author of *Undoing Drugs: The Untold Story of Harm Reduction*, credits the coining of the term itself to a British researcher in 1986, who wrote about the need for a widespread reinvention of the ways drug users are treated and cared for by the United Kingdom's Health Ministry. After visiting Europe in the 1980s, Edith Springer, a white, antiracist, radical American social worker, brought the language and concepts of harm reduction to New York City. There she did hundreds of trainings, workshops, and lectures for public health officials, social workers, and activists on harm reduction practices. Subsequently, AIDS activists fought desperately for harm reduction to be incorporated into public health departments to stem the epidemic. Harm reduction, as a strategy to interrupt the spread of deadly viruses, offered an approach that was both pragmatic and effective. People on the ground, who were doing everything possible to stop the mass death of queer and trans people, drug users, and sex workers from HIV/AIDS and overdose, demanded that harm reduction solutions be included in public health strategies. The primary selling point that organizers made to officials is that HIV is a greater threat to public health than drug use and that users must have concrete tools to reduce the chances of getting a virus with no known treatment.

Many AIDS and harm reduction historians note that activists in New York City began running underground illegal exchanges as early as 1986. In reality, this is difficult to document because these efforts were illegal, and the only way to track who started what when is from flyers and zines, many of which have long since been destroyed. My own harm reduction lineage places the first syringe distribution in 1985 on the Lower East Side of New York, beginning with Isabel Dawson and Kelly McGowan—two women who remain chosen family to this day, and who are ignored in every accounting of harm reduction history except this book. Soon, activists both inside and outside of institutional structures began to fight for funding and laws that protected and supported access to clean syringes for drug users, and opportunities to dispose of dirty needles in efforts to keep neighborhoods free from used drug paraphernalia.

The result of this activism had both glorious and devastating outcomes. On the one hand, most states have free, funded, legal syringe exchange as of 2021. However, the cost is that public health departments that were not previously rooted in antiracist liberatory struggles claimed credit for our strategies, which erased the lineage of fifty years of community-based practices of struggle and survival in the process. Even more disturbing is how these institutions framed the bodies of drug users and people in the sex trade—*our bodies*—as sites of risk or contagion. The rebranding of our bodies as "high risk" for contracting a communicable and deadly disease that could have been less deadly and more controlled is as endemic to public health as the racism, ableism, and colonialism upon which the field of public health has been built.*

Recovery Readiness, Risk Reduction, and Public Health–Based Harm Reduction

When institutions cannibalize the people's practices, they take them wholesale and strip the concepts down into pithy parts that separate the values and intentions from the core rituals so they can be made palatable to the mainstream. This is usually done for a high price in the form of government grants and leaves behind singular interventions that look and sound like the original, but lack the intent, complexity, abundance, and love. When public health distilled harm reduction, it splintered into three parts: recovery readiness, risk reduction, and what I am calling "public health harm reduction."

* For a breakdown of the history of the MIC, please see Cara Page's and Erica Woodland's forthcoming book, *Healing Justice Lineages: Dreaming at the Crossroads of Liberation, Collective Care, and Safety* to be published in 2023 by North Atlantic Books.

Recovery readiness is the concept that drug users, people in the sex trade, and those of us struggling with activities that are deemed risky require an incentivized program to prepare us for what is considered the ultimate goal: abstinence and sobriety. The idea of recovery readiness is pervasive within social services and public health. It is an infuriating model because it is steeped in behavior-modification strategies that are often sneaky and involve invasive procedures such as urine tests as well as the trading out of coping strategies, for example, stopping drug use in exchange for basic survival needs like housing or therapy.

The need to use drugs to manage our mental health or to engage in the sex trade to financially support ourselves and children becomes baubles to trade in exchange for housing or healthcare. In short, the public health harm reduction application of recovery readiness is despicable. And yet, there is a time and a place for recovery readiness as one option for many drug users who may *want* (key word) more than cold-turkey, abstinence-only options, and for whom drug use has become chaotic and unmanageable from their own points of view. Recovery readiness offers a slower weaning process from substances and, unlike traditional treatment models, it does not expect someone to stop using immediately. Rather it offers a method to incrementally reduce substance use in exchange for more privileges and services within a particular social service program. What is critical to understand here is that recovery readiness is socially acceptable and plays on a politic of respectability. It is a public health intervention because it is steeped in the moral value that living life sober is better. It makes an *assumption* about someone's risk for HIV or hepatitis C based on their involvement in the sex trade or drug use and leverages behavior changes for resources.

One of the largest social services organizations in Chicago, Heartland Alliance, which positions itself as an anti-poverty, human rights organization, has been enticing people involved in the sex trade and street economy for decades with its lure of housing as a reward for maintaining sobriety. Harm reduction for Heartland Alliance, which also operates five detention centers for migrant youth, involves using the patronizing catchphrase, "preparing people for change," as they engage in coaching work with clients to move along the pathway toward sobriety. The program that Heartland Alliance offers has more opportunities than most social services—which is simply stopping drugs overnight. The program asks people to slowly stop using drugs over a period of time through a slow reduction in use. In this way, recovery readiness slowly halts use of whatever substance of choice was viewed by the social service as being "in the way" of getting life-changing social services.

The linking of social services to behavior change creates a hierarchy in our basic needs and forces us to lie to get help. We have to say that we are not using drugs to get pain management from a doctor, we have to say that we went to the Twelve-Step meeting to get the bus card from the social worker, we have to say that we were late coming back into our housing program because we were delayed by our boss rather than smoking the last blunt before having to appear sober for the night—and so on.

The phrase, which many of you have heard, *Meeting people where they are at*, has become the anthem of recovery readiness and, I would argue, of the entire world of public health harm reduction. On the surface, this phrase means that social service, medical, and public health workers should start with the facts of a person's life and understand the world that person lives in, their values, and their goals. In reality, this term looks like *Meeting people where they are at—so we can move them to where we think they should be*. There is an implication that even though you can get a clean syringe or condom from an outreach worker, over time you will become abstinent or sober.

Risk reduction is another approach that is often confused with harm reduction. Because of the supplying of services and resources to those of us who are deemed "high risk," risk reduction is based on the idea that people can and should mitigate the chances of disease, pregnancy, and overdose with simple acts like utilizing condoms, clean syringes, and naloxone. Risk reduction has been made both separate from harm reduction and synonymous with it. It's a curious contradiction that grew out of the need to be less threatening to institutions that could embrace pieces of the philosophy of harm reduction but not the whole.

Risk reduction is not the only part of harm reduction, but it is one of the central ideas that runs throughout Liberatory Harm Reduction and public health harm reduction alike. Largely based on the idea of individual behavior change, risk reduction is the idea that one can choose safety by making "any positive change," a catchphrase that Chicago Recovery Alliance popularized by educating people on which actions carry greater risk.

When I was first coming of age in harm reduction projects in the late 1990s, almost every place I went relied on peer-to-peer engagement. Sometimes this looked like hiring "people with life experience" in the street economy, with drugs or in the sex trade or sex work to do front-line outreach work. But more commonly it was people who had lived experience starting their own organizations, outreach projects, and nonprofits. Because the work at the National Harm Reduction Coalition (NHRC) was led by people with stigmatized life experiences, the harm reduction principles that NHRC wrote are still radical to this day. One of the most important principles is that harm reduction is a peer-to-peer model led by those of us with stigmatized life experience. We are considered experts in our lives, and social workers, doctors, or employees of a health center, for example, should be in a horizontal relationship with us. Liberatory Harm Reduction means that we are all teachers and learners.

HARM REDUCTION COALITION
HARM REDUCTION VALUES

ACCEPTS THAT LICIT & ILLICIT DRUG USE IS PART OF OUR WORLD

↓

MINIMIZES HARMFUL EFFECTS RATHER THAN CONDEMNS OR IGNORES

UNDERSTANDS DRUG USE AS A COMPLEX, MULTI-FACETED PHENOMENON → A CONTINUUM OF BEHAVIORS

TOTAL ABSTINENCE

SEVERE USE

→ SOME WAYS OF USING ARE SAFER THAN OTHERS

ESTABLISHES QUALITY OF INDIVIDUAL & COMMUNITY LIFE & WELL-BEING - NOT NECCESSARILY CESSATION OF ALL DRUG USE – AS THE CRITERIA FOR SUCCESSFUL INTERVENTIONS & POLICIES

CALLS FOR NONJUDGEMENTAL, NON-COERCIVE SERVICES & RESOURCES TO PEOPLE WHO USE DRUGS & THEIR COMMUNITIES

ENSURES THAT PEOPLE WHO USE/USED DRUGS ROUTINELY HAVE A REAL VOICE IN THE CREATION OF PROGRAMS & POLICIES DESIGNED TO SERVE THEM

AFFIRMS PEOPLE WHO USE DRUGS (PWUD) AS THE PRIMARY AGENTS OF REDUCING HARMS OF USE & SEEKS TO EMPOWER PWUD TO SHARE INFORMATION & SUPPORT EACH OTHER IN STRATEGIES THAT MEET ACTUAL CONDITIONS OF USE

BAN THE BOX!!

RECOGNIZES THAT THE REALITIES OF POVERTY, CLASS, RACISM, SOCIAL ISOLATION, TRAUMA, SEX-BASED DISCRIMINATION, & OTHER SOCIAL INEQUALITIES AFFECT PEOPLE'S VULNERABILITY TO & CAPACITY FOR EFFECTIVELY DEALING WITH DRUG-RELATED HARM

DOES NOT ATTEMPT TO MINIMIZE OR IGNORE THE REAL & TRAGIC HARM & DANGER THAT CAN BE ASSOCIATED WITH ILLICIT DRUG USE

Peer-based work, which relies on what we now call mutual aid, allows us to rebuild trust in our intuitions by trusting ourselves with one tiny step at a time and seeing the realities of our lives reflected in others around us so that we break isolation and remember we are not the only ones in struggle. This is one of the many reasons why the most radical harm reduction formations are peer-based. Someone who is in the life knows the life, and witnessing someone who has walked in your shoes taking action through leadership reminds us of who we are. This helps us trust ourselves just a little bit more. As we said in YWEP, "When we play leadership roles in organizations, we get the chance to show ourselves that we are the solution—not the problem."

Public health harm reduction often removes this value altogether for many reasons. It may be because a grant requires someone with an advanced degree to supervise the program, or it may be because liability insurance requires the nonprofit to be a drug-free workplace under employment law, so it cannot legally hire active drug users. The professionalization of harm reduction has led to such an enormous disconnect between the original values and practices that this style of work should now be considered a different field. It has become "public health harm reduction" and does not view us as whole people living whole lives. It views us as an assemblage of risks to be managed and is primarily concerned with its own liability at the expense of the self-determination, body autonomy, and liberation of BIPOC who are sex workers, queer, transgender, using drugs, people with disabilities and chronic illness, street-based, and sometimes houseless.

Sarah Daoud says:

> One easy way to know for sure that corporate nonprofits aren't practicing Liberatory Harm Reduction: they're the same ones doling out punishments that keep people unsafe and unwell, that force you into compliance over self-determination. That

> take away your resources you were using to practice harm reduction in the first place. Kicking you out of the shelter for missing curfew, refusing to fill your prescription until you stop using or until you lose weight, taking away your kids because your domestic partner hurts you, locking you up in psych if you resist a medical intervention that you don't want or need. Calling the cops on you, forcibly medicating you or sterilizing you, and on and on and on. They're supposed to be where you get help, but often they're actually sites of violence. It creates a culture where young folks are afraid to ask for help, because help usually comes with harm and control. The best social workers I know are at constant risk of losing their jobs, because they're trying to practice Liberatory Harm Reduction in a system that wasn't built for it. These systems seek to control us, punish us for being "defiant," and then toss us out when we can't function as they demand.

Public health harm reduction often separates us from the community context we are a part of by not addressing the root causes of harm like the MIC, the War on Drugs, land rematriation, and structural oppression. Moreover, it often causes institutional violence through its relationship to the police, to transphobia, to constant pathologizing, and its ongoing role in the criminalization of the very people that originated harm reduction.

Fuck the Concept of "High-Risk"

Let's talk about the term "high-risk behavior" and why I only use it with quotations. "High-risk behavior" is a stigmatized way of talking about the gorgeous and varied coping strategies we reach for when we are trying to heal from trauma or just survive day to day. Laura Janine Mintz, MD, PhD, my chosen family, YWEP cofounder, a practicing physician in Cleveland, notes, "I think 'high-risk' comes from people expanding a medical term, about how a particular action is more statistically likely to result in disease transmission/harm in general and does not consider what is applicable to a specific individual. It is a limited understanding of risk that's based in stigma."

We become, to the outside world, reduced to the label of our "high-risk behaviors": we are junkies, hoes, crackheads. In other words, we are disposable. And while many of us have spent years reclaiming these words and use them with pride at times, summarizing us with labels only makes it easier for us to be killed by institutions and by the media, which erases us, makes us flat victims, and hypersexualizes us simultaneously.

Liberatory Harm Reduction believes that we should have all the information and education we want and need to make the choices that work best for us: *it doesn't label people or drug use itself as inherently risky and it doesn't prioritize behavior change.* Liberatory Harm Reduction deepens the idea of risk reduction because it recognizes that, for example, capitalism, racism, police, and misogyny are the biggest dangers for those involved in the sex trade. In this way, the sex trade and its dangers do not exist because of what one worker does or does not do while participating in it.

It is my argument that the term "high-risk behaviors" has become code in public health and social work. It is code for racist beliefs, for transphobia, for whorephobia, and for a general fear of those of us who take our healing so seriously we are willing to do *what we have to do to survive*—YWEP's tagline. Emi Koyama describes "negative survivorship" and the way we are blamed, shamed, and labeled for our coping strategies. Victim blaming is implicit in the phrase "high-risk behavior," and for many of us, our tools and strategies are criminalized. Let me say it again: *our survival is criminalized.*

Liberatory Harm Reduction does not allow public health and social work to organize us by which possible blood-borne pathogens we may contract. Public health and social work have created harm and exacerbated trauma in the lives of people who are criminalized for their survival. We are turned away from doctors, hospitals, and care settings for moralistic reasons and because we present "poor outcomes" for their statistics and are viewed as throwing money away on people who "will not or cannot change their behaviors." For instance, the fear of COVID-19 in my community is not only the fear of contracting and passing the virus to others, but also the fear of going to the hospital only to be uncared for and allowed to die. With cause, we fear we will be judged unworthy of a ventilator due to drug use, eating disorders, maps of self-injuries on our bodies, houselessness, pre-existing health conditions, because we are fat, or other factors that make us less of a "societal loss."* Dr. Laura Janine Mintz says, "We are considered unreliable in our account of our own experiences and what is happening in our bodies. I'm thinking about all of the people that have been turned away and told that their oxygenation was fine when it wasn't."

Risk Is a Relationship

> *An addictive relationship that develops is one in which the addictive object is invested with the magical belief that the substance can provide a soothing, caring or healing that people cannot.*
>
> –G. Alan Marlatt†

I say over and over that harm reduction is about relationships at its core. It is a mutual aid model that places all activities, from drinking coffee to violence to drug use, on a spectrum of harm.

---

* I am including eating disorders and self-injury here because I do see these behaviors as criminalized by public health and the medical-industrial complex.

† Please see G. Alan Marlatt, Mary E. Larimer, Katie Witkiewitz, eds., *Harm Reduction: Pragmatic Strategies for Managing High-Risk Behaviors*, second edition (New York: Guilford Press, 2011).

It recognizes that drug use can become chaotic and dangerous for some people, and in that moment, someone may choose abstinence to stay alive. It also recognizes that drugs are used for pleasure, to regulate trauma, or for a myriad of reasons that cause little to no harm to anyone.

The same activities under the same circumstances will carry different risks based on your relationship to them. The relationship that each person has to being involved in the sex trade is very individual; what may be a validating opportunity to control my own schedule and make more than minimum wage may be violent and terrifying for someone else. For example, trading sex for money as teenager for me was considered "high risk" to the outside world because of my age and gender presentation. However, I felt mostly safe. Now, as an older person with disabilities, my ability to negotiate my safety feels much less secure, even though as an adult it is assumed that I have more control and power to navigate risk.

When I first read the Alan Marlatt quote above, I thought about myself and about people I've loved who use substances for survival and to gain a sense of control and safety. When I reached this understanding, after years of sitting in Twelve-Step circles and being in harm reduction projects, it really surprised me. All my life, I had been told that people who use substances are "out of control." But I started to realize that many of us who have survived trauma have endured a lack of safety and secure attachments in most parts of our lives. *When there is nowhere safe to go, the predictability and dependability of drugs or alcohol can be a place of safety.* This is a very different message from what we usually hear about using substances as a self-harming act, or that using substances harms others so much that they must intervene, shame, or wholly reject us to keep themselves safe, forcing us into abstinence or into a Twelve-Step recovery model.

Public health and social work have predetermined what the functions of drug use are and prescribed the average person's optimal functions, regardless of the actual level of harm or harmlessness of the activity. Consequently, we radically undervalue the importance of our relationship to substances and how much we count on them. The consistency of waking up and knowing the pattern of your day because it is determined by drug use can be relieving and pleasurable, or it may be overwhelming and oppressive; in fact, it can be all of these things at once. Being able to view drug use as an act that creates safety, as a secure attachment, is profound and transformational. Thinking about drug use and addiction on an elastic continuum from pleasure to chaos and everything in between creates an opportunity to reconsider addiction. It gives us permission to think of our presumed "high-risk" behaviors as brave.

We Heal in Relationship

> *It is part of our task as revolutionary people, people who want deep-rooted, radical change, to be as whole as it is possible for us to be. This can only be done if we face the reality of what oppression really means in our lives, not as abstract systems subject to analysis, but as an avalanche of traumas leaving a wake of devastation in the lives of real people who nevertheless remain human, unquenchable, complex and full of possibility.*
>
> —Aurora Levins Morales, *Medicine Stories*

In 2009, YWEP conducted a groundbreaking participatory action research study titled *Girls Do What We Have to Do to Survive: Illuminating Methods Used by Girls in the Sex Trade to Fight Back and Heal.* This study was coordinated by our former youth staff Jazeera Iman and Naima Paz with adult ally support from Catlin Fullwood. More than sixty-five members participated in creating, implementing, and documenting the research report. Young People of Color in the sex trade and street economy found that institutional violence made individual violence worse. When we experience violence, harm, or loss and reach out to hospitals and social services, even those that say they are offering harm reduction options, we are often turned away or criminalized for our survival. The research points to countless experiences of young people going to the hospital for an original complaint of something such as flu symptoms and ending up in the psychiatric ward because of old self-injury scars. We found, time and again, that even the assumption based on our appearances that we were involved in the sex trade or street economy made workers in whatever agency we were seeking help from deny us. "High-risk" is not about us—it's about the systems of oppression that work together to kill us.

In the same study, YWEP found that one of the most important methods that young people used to slow the wounds caused by institutional violence was breaking isolation. Coming together for big or small events meant that we were able to experience connections and interrupt the shame that comes with being targeted for our identities and/or activities. Researcher Brené Brown's influential work on shame identified findings similar to YWEP's. Brown identified the four parts of building resilience to shame as: a) recognizing shame and its triggers; b) practicing critical awareness; c) reaching out; d) and speaking to shame. Brown states, importantly, that this is not a linear process and that people go through each of these parts at different times. YWEP's study identified that young people in the sex trade and street economy used all of the strategies Brown described to heal and fight back—so much so that for a while we joked that she stole our research (she totally didn't!). Brown's study gave national recognition and validity to something that harm reduction practitioners and young people in the sex trade have always known: shame kills, and we can heal from shame through connection with others like us. In this way, harm reduction philosophy is more than trauma-*informed*: it is a trauma-*centered* practice and a communal medicine for generational shame.

Liberatory Harm Reduction is not only about our relationships to our stigmatized behaviors or identities. It is also about how we save each other by breaking isolation, being present, and accompanying each other's journeys. The social stigma that we experience because of how and what we do to survive creates shame and separation from the world. At times, it is even best for our mental health to disconnect from others and focus inward.

Twelve-Step programs also interrupt isolation through peer-based support. But they send contradictory messages though the popular program slogan, "People, places, and things," which refers to the patterns and relationships that are negatively associated with drug use and other stigmatized behaviors. "People, places, and things" seems similar to Brown's findings on recognizing triggers and practicing critical awareness and prioritizing abstinence. Meaning, if we are seeking sobriety then we must remove ourselves from the "people, places, and things" associated with our use, and break the predictability of our patterns. Using this logic, it's not just your mom, or the walk from the train to your house where you used to buy drugs, or the cartoon that you watched while high after school, or something else that triggers you. It's more than that—almost a patterned trance or body memory. It's the acknowledgment that your body carries information and knowledge of which you are not always conscious. So, "people, places, and things" trigger you back to that body memory, to the relationship you have with whatever activity you are seeking to stop through the adoption of a Twelve-Step program. Creating space to explore these profound, impactful relationships is how harm reduction works and how Twelve-Step programs function.

The main difference between harm reduction and Twelve-Step programs is that harm reduction disconnects the concepts of recovery and sobriety. While it doesn't privilege abstinence or value it above other relationships to drugs or stigmatized behaviors, it does include abstinence as an option that people *may* choose if it works for them. The magic that is generated by peer-to-peer relationships and the healing that Twelve-Step programs can bring is central to harm reduction. Many will find this shocking, as Twelve-Step and harm reduction appear to be at odds. For example, harm reduction practitioners will never ask someone to admit powerlessness over a behavior. Instead, a harm reductionist will ask people to step into their power and to take control of their choices. Harm reduction rejects the idea that someone steals their mom's TV or their kids' coats because of addiction; instead, if you take your kids' coats and sell them for drugs, you're an asshole—thousands of people use drugs every day and would never dream of doing this. It challenges Twelve-Step ideology by asking the real question, "When have you ever made change from a powerless place?" Harm reduction says the path to healing is charted by living into our power through taking control of our choices and being responsible to ourselves and others in the process.

Liberatory Harm Reduction is also about not becoming dogmatic, and that it is a gift—retaining or developing an ability to examine different situations, think outside the box for a solution, and rely on the people who have the lived experience as experts is powerful. Rather than viewing people who use drugs or are involved in the sex trade as broken, harm reduction views us as the best possible resources to change ourselves and the world. It allows us to be present in our creativity and our imaginations, dreaming of options together. In this narrative, there is room for everyone.

THE *Political Framework* OF LIBERATORY HARM REDUCTION

ANTICAPITALIST

HEALING JUSTICE

END THE MEDICAL-INDUSTRIAL COMPLEX!

PRO-INDIGENOUS SOVEREIGNTY

NO BORDERS!

disability JUSTICE

BODY *autonomy*

TRANS JUSTICE

REPRODUCTIVE JUSTICE

EMPOWERMENT THEORY

CRIMINALIZED SURVIVORS ARE IN CONTROL OF ALL BIG & SMALL CHOICES IN OUR OWN LIVES

The Invisible Mechanics of Liberatory Harm Reduction: Risk, Set, Setting

In 1984, Norman Zinberg gave public health and Liberatory Harm Reductionists more to work with in his book *Drug, Set, and Setting*. This book, which has also become known within the world of behavior change for its critical theory, gave academic support to things that activists have been saying for decades. In his theory, Zinberg uses the term *drug* to mean to any substance—from caffeine to cocaine—someone uses for mood- or mind-altering experiences. *Mindset*, or *set*, describes the mood and state of the person prior to using a drug. *Setting* refers to both the social location and the physical location of the person during use. For example, a gay person sitting on a gay beach with friends during a butterfly migration using LSD will have a radically different drug experience compared to an isolated teenager in a dark bedroom using LSD alone. Zinberg also used this theory to explain why some people can use drugs without becoming addicted to them, whereas others become dependent quickly.

This succinct theory allowed us to begin thinking about how an individual's mind, body, spirit, and emotional state, in combination with their physical or social location, impacts their drug experiences and sets them on a spectrum spanning from recreational to chaotic use. It provides a framework to manipulate our environments and patterns of use to create the safest and most positive outcomes for those practicing supposed "high-risk" behaviors.

Risk, set, setting (RSS) is what we more commonly use to make safer decisions inside Liberatory Harm Reduction communities. RSS accounts for the fact that harm reduction applies to more than drug use and can be modified to apply to any risk that people face, from policing to sexual harassment to ordering off the dollar menu at McDonald's.

In popular culture and traditional drug treatment, the drug itself is centered and emphasized as the only problem that deserves focus. Many people who use substances have had the experiences of being turned away from therapy or housing programs because those programs fear liability laws that prevent them from working with active users. Sometimes the therapist or social worker may even believe that substance use must be treated and the person completely sober before working with someone at all, even if that person is experiencing a crisis unrelated to their drug use. These ideas are in fact central to most mainstream medical and social services and run counter to both liberatory and public health harm reduction alike.*

Risk, set, setting challenges these antiquated and discriminatory practices. The theory breaks down the components of how someone experiences risk and demonstrates that the person's mindset is as critical as the drug they are using, as is where or how the drug is used. All of these factors together work to create a safer versus riskier, enjoyable versus scary drug experience.

In the hundreds of workshops, trainings, and classes I have taught, I have found RSS to be the simplest introduction to the pragmatics of all forms of harm reduction. For example, someone in a violent relationship (risk, set) who is sharing drugs (risk) with their partner come into contact with blood-borne viruses because pressure may be placed on them to shoot up after their partner and to share injection equipment. The setting is also a factor in the risk if they are using in public and rushing to avoid the possibilities of violence and arrest (setting).

Applying RSS: Overdose

I am choosing the example of overdose for two reasons. First, the harm reduction response to overdose through putting naloxone di-

* There is also something important to name about the thinking of addiction as a brain disease. The disease model is both compatible with and runs in opposition to ideas of all forms of harm reduction. I strongly encourage reading all of Carl Hart's writing—Hart is a neuroscientist who has successfully unraveled many misunderstandings about chemical dependence.

rectly in the hands of drug users is one of the most elegant examples of Transformative Justice in our movement work today. And second, without naloxone and RSS, I would not be here. When we understand RSS, we can begin to play with this triangle and address common outcomes. We can use Zinberg's idea to challenge everything from overdose to criminal targeting. We can rethink this model and apply it to intimate partner violence, police violence, self-injury, medication management, disability, chronic illness, houselessness, and more.

Once the components are broken down, we can begin to create harm reduction solutions. Let's take *setting* and think about the widely known fact among drug users that bathrooms are a common place where people overdose. Many harm reduction programs have responded by placing syringe disposal units, naloxone to reverse the effect of opioids, literature, and even buddy systems in bathrooms. One of my favorite cafes in Olympia, WA, had a set of overdose prevention tips done in embroidery and framed on the wall inside their bathroom, which was popular among people who injected and had no other private place to do so.

Understanding how to manipulate the factors in situations to avoid danger or make situations safer means you can begin to expand the RSS model for other situations. I use the activity below in my workshops and classes:

> Imagine you have a superpower that allows you to freeze time. The key descriptors that cannot be changed are the age of the person, the drug or situation, and the location of the activity or event. You do not have the ability to stop someone from doing something or change anything about them (like their age). Yet you do have the ability to freeze time, and to add a useful tool or idea that will increase the likelihood of someone staying safer.

What do you do? For example, in the mid-2000s, during the rise of heroin laced with fentanyl—a much more powerful and deadly opioid—overdose prevention activists and syringe exchange outreach workers went through parks with naloxone and waited outside public bathrooms, watching for people who might be using and who were not coming out of the bathrooms. Trainings and workshops took place outside of park bathrooms on how to reduce overdose, use naloxone, and avoid police. Bathrooms, or the setting, were identified as the place where harm reduction strategies could be the most effective. Other syringe exchanges chose to build relationships with drug dealers—addressing the risk itself to reduce the harm. Contrary to popular belief, many dealers prefer living customers and are invested in community safety. Some dealers chose to label their products when they discovered it had been laced while others stopped selling it altogether.

My first experience of overdose predated naloxone distribution to drug users. As a teenager, I used the overdose prevention strategy of injecting slowly and "tasting"* the drug as it moved through my veins, and I realized that it was too strong for me. I had a bad drug experience that night but did not overdose. The second time, in my late twenties, the person I was dating at the time received naloxone from Chicago Recovery Alliance and saved my life by injecting it into my thigh. What we know about overdose is that anyone—even the most experienced user—can overdose. We know that people are most likely to overdose after a period of abstinence—for instance, when exiting rehab programs, hospitals, or prison. We also know that drug quality and what drugs are cut with can contribute to overdose. When heroin, an opiate, is cut with fentanyl, a much stronger opioid, the drug becomes stronger and more deadly.

* "Tasting" is an overdose prevention strategy and a common term among injection drug users. When you inject a drug through your veins, a flavor fills your mouth and you can, sometimes, discern the power of the drug and if it is laced with something. This isn't a foolproof strategy, however, and the best intervention will always be using naloxone.

Example of *Risk, Set, Setting* Applied to Reducing Opioid Overdose (OD)*

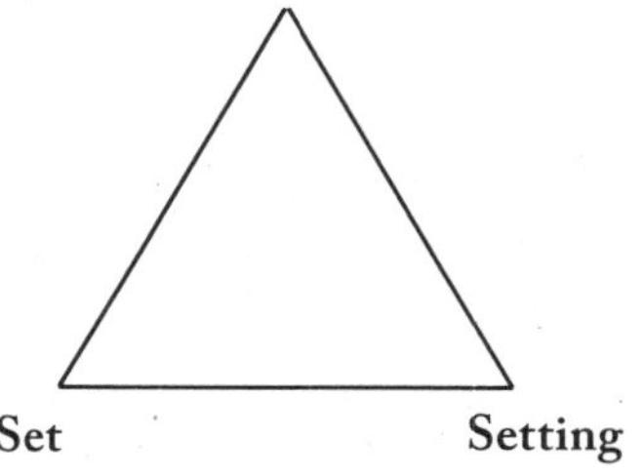

- Know your dealer/supplier and have a relationship with that person.
- Taste your shot and learn to identify the flavor that fills your mouth when you inject heroin. For example, fentanyl can taste sweeter and have a different rush.
- *Snorting or smoking opioids reduces overdose risk. Combining other drugs (like alcohol or cocaine) with opioids makes overdose trickier to reverse.*

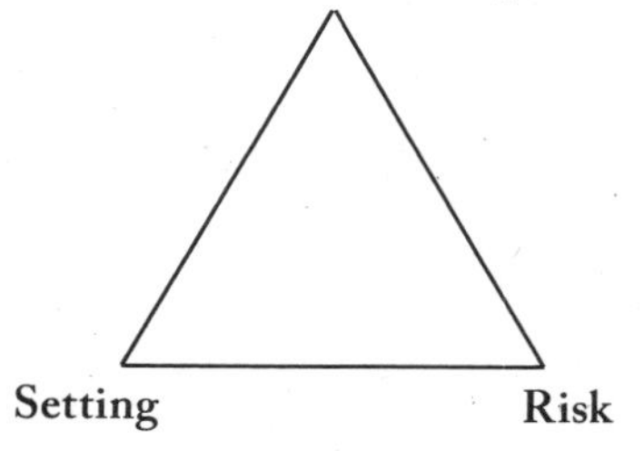

- Use with a friend who has some idea of how to detect overdose, knows how to do rescue breathing and/or has naloxone handy—the drug that reverses opioid overdose.
- *Make an OD contract with a trusted friend, family member, or using buddy. An OD contract spells out what you want to happen in the event of overdose. Examples include: "If I overdose do not call 911, use 1 dose of naloxone only"; or "Call 911 immediately and do not leave me alone." OD contracts can also include childcare information and hospital preferences.*

* Thank you, Maya Doe Simpkins, for your thought partnership on this chart.

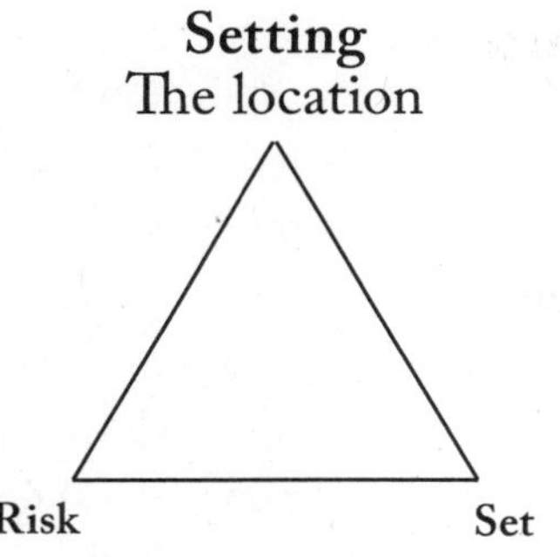

- If you are using in a room with a door, consider leaving the door unlocked so that someone can get to you.
- *If you have a public bathroom because you run a café, coffee shop, church, or other establishment, consider keeping free naloxone in the bathroom. Put overdose prevention information on the walls or handouts. Consider installing a pull cord in case of emergencies.*

All Change Is Loss

Liberatory Harm Reduction approaches decrease the risk of incarceration and death while improving the quality of life. They build individual and community power simultaneously. Abstinence, while meaningful and important to some people, is not wholly achievable for everyone all the time. And when we offer only a one-size-fits-all solution, we are making illness (including HIV), incarceration, and death inevitable for those who cannot be aided by that solution. We would not ever offer only one intervention in many other areas of care work, but this is rarely the case for drug users, people in the sex trade, street economy, or in the midst of a stigmatized life experience. It is one of the many ways that our lives as criminalized survivors are systematically devalued.

The dominant narrative that we have constructed about drugs and drug use has distorted ideas about innocence and guilt. We think that people "aren't ready" to change, are "in denial" about change, or "don't know how" to make change. We repeat expressions like "If you know better, you'll do better!" This kind of thinking has warped our ideas of culpability and responsibility, namely, who can't be held responsible (*the addict*), who can be held accountable (*the sober*), and why we believe this to be true. In Liberatory Harm Reduction, there is room for people who do cause harm to be self-reflective and accountable to those they have harmed, because harm reduction does not idealize health or wellness as white, able-bodied, and free of behaviors that the world deems unwanted. There is room in harm reduction for people who have used their whole lives, who would never dream of stopping their drug use, *and* who also never dream of hurting the people closest to them. Liberatory Harm Reduction is about practical strategies rather than exiling people until they are able to achieve a standard that may or may not be realistic.

Moreover, Liberatory Harm Reduction recognizes that all change involves loss—even positive change can be predicated on loss. Models that preach behavior change never name this reality. If we expect our friends, family, community members, or clients to always approach change as if it's rewarding, and as if their inability to change is due to lack of skills or resolve, we are missing out on opportunities to have genuine and honest conversations about the losses that always come with change. Even basic and commonplace changes—like moving, changing jobs, switching shelters, or even having a child—can produce feelings of fear and dreaded "what if" thinking.

Recognizing that loss is part of change also helps us understand why change is often so slow. Many health advocates often posit education as the solution to behavior change. But the emphasis on education ignores the emotional toll of the loss and fear involved with grieving change. For me, my drug use, my self-injury, and my involvement in the sex trade have been among the longest and most reliable relationships in my life. Ignoring the mourning process that changes in relationships bring on is a form of institutional violence. Liberatory Harm Reduction acknowledges loss and supports you to figure out what fills that space. From Dr. Laura Janine Mintz:

> When you quit smoking, if you decide that you want to sustain it being a non-smoker, then you need to think about why you're

> smoking and what it is doing for you (I would suggest cigarettes are self-care a lot of the time) and what else you're going to do with those feelings, that experience. You have to say that smoking is great and I am going to miss it.

I have taken the example even further in my own change work and thought of "cigarettes" as a relationship in and of itself. One participant in my workshops contacted me to tell me they had written a letter to "cigarettes" as part of their exploration of quitting. I encouraged them to write one back to themselves as though cigarettes were the speaker.

Our fear of loss can cause us to fall into anxiety spirals at the thought of change. That's how powerful the trigger of loss is. Yet we talk about change as though only good things will come from it, and as if grief isn't a factor. I have five new babies in my life right now and, as much as the parents love and are grateful for their babies, they are absolutely mourning the loss of their former lives. They are simultaneously carrying joy and shame around this change, and only tiny corners of the internet offer solace for parents struggling with these contradictions. The more we recognize and validate and honor the importance of loss, the more we are making room for people to come through with authentic processes. Liberatory Harm Reduction, in addition, must always value and acknowledge that not changing behavior is just as valid as making a shift.

Many of the first research and science-based studies about harm-reduction interventions that have created more possibilities for institutional care (for example, Andrew Tatarsky and Alan Marlatt's work has changed minds at the American Medical Association) have not integrated a systemic understanding of the PIC. Prisons represent an enormous risk to the public, as has been made increasingly evident to those who denied it before the COVID-19 pandemic. Prisons are sites of both violence and death. For departments of public health to not recognize the need for prison abolition is willful ignorance.

Those of us who have been saving each other's lives in community understand that addressing the relationship between the PIC, HIV, disability and chronic illness, trauma, and all forms of systemic oppression is absolutely essential to reducing harm in our neighborhoods and families (chosen and not) and sets us up for the long-term work of collectively addressing the root causes of oppression with no one left out.

Letting Go of the Language of Loss: Twelve-Step Terminology and Pop Culture

I want to honor the complicated impact of Twelve-Step programs in my life and the lives of so many people I love. I have moved in and out of Twelve-Step groups since I was a very young teen and have both hated and craved the entirety of the program. With harm reduction as my spiritual practice and life partner, I have valued the ability to use the tools of Twelve-Step programs when I have needed them.

The Twelve-Step meetings that really changed me were started by queer and trans BIPOC life-long harm reductionists. They created spaces that challenged one of the guiding principles in the tenth tradition of Twelve-Step programs, called "outside issues." This term means that nothing "controversial," such as politics, religion, or drug and alcohol reform, should be discussed in Twelve-Step. This impacts BIPOC and anyone who does not fit a colonialist, cis-heteropatriarchal ideal by relegating us to the sidelines. Our ability to be seen and struggle with the realities and the value of our lives is pushed aside in favor of not disturbing whiteness.

At its best, Twelve-Step provides nonjudgmental peer-to-peer support with a clear formula and set of strategies that have significant impact to those who are seeking difficult and life-affirming change. These spaces can be places of reclamation for queer, trans, and BIPOC people that are nurturing and allow them to be whole. They can be spaces where the practice of Liberatory Harm Reduction dismantles the oppression that is embedded in other Twelve-Step spaces and treatment programs.

At its worst, Twelve-Step exists in carceral spaces whose language has been infiltrated by the treatment industry with deadly consequences. The treatment industry has caused irreparable damage to Twelve-Step in many ways, including co-opting language and practice that are now a part of pop psychology. The distortion of Twelve-Step has unfortunately become ingrained in our popular culture, and it largely serves the function to create distance from and to "other" people with stigmatized life experiences.

This co-optation of Twelve-Step is why my favorite meetings are those started by harm reductionists. When harm reductionists practice Twelve-Step, it feels like "loving anarchy," as Viva Ruiz, founder of Thank God for Abortion, describes:

> Twelve-Step works for me because it was modeled by people like Chloe [Dzubilo] who were harm reduction people, or I would not have stayed. I was lucky. I came in through sex workers who Twelve-Stepped me from the bars I was working at so it already implied there's room for me here because there are people like me here. I take to heart this Twelve-Step slogan: take what you like and leave the rest. But I took, "Come in and get loved." I heard, "The war is over, come in, relax." I would not have stayed if I hadn't been taught through the people who brought me into the rooms that love and acceptance of who I am in the moment—no matter what—is how anything changes, not the other way. Come in, be loved right now as you *are* for change to happen, instead of changing everything to deserve love.

Treatment programs seek to create a system that is "all or nothing." For example, in treatment settings and most nonprofits that offer Twelve-Step or recovery-oriented programming, there is an expectation that everyone is sober. In fact, people are regularly asked to leave programs and meetings—potentially losing their housing or other material needs—because there is a suspicion that they are using substances. Harm reduction knows that we cannot be separated from who we are and how the impact of structural violence plays out in our lives.

I am often asked, *How can people who want to be sober and others who are still actively using drugs share community space?* The answer is with clear communication and boundaries and through the Disability Justice practice of building spaces that incorporate everyone's access needs. ***Harm reduction lives in the tension and the space between people and relationships.*** Liberatory Harm Reduction gives us permission to live with "both and." As a practice of self-possession, harm reduction wants us to have boundaries that keep us safe and for us to live into the tension that everyone has different boundaries and they all must be honored.

One meeting I facilitated always had participants who were high and others who were abstinent. To start, we generated a list of our individual access needs. Then, through a collective consensus process, we created practice agreements for all meetings and updated them as our access needs shifted. The agreements stated that people could be in the meeting high; we all agreed to not use in the meeting space or building. We also asked that people respect those who were sober by not offering to share drugs before, during, or after the meeting, and that people do their best to not allow the smell of their preferred substance into the meeting space. We asked that those who sought abstinence not judge anyone's use, not label people, and allow people to show up and participate—even if that included times when people were nodding out from their high. We asked that the pace of the meeting respect everyone. We agreed that moving slowly was better than leaving people behind.

The irony is that while the vast majority of Twelve-Step wholly rejects all forms of harm reduction because it does not prioritize sobriety, harm reductionists recognize there is a time and a place for abstinence and views Twelve-Step as a tool that can be successful for some. Where harm reduction differs dramatically is that it does not place "sober living" at the top of the hierarchy and does not believe that remaining abstinent from drug use, alcohol, sex work (yes, there is a Prostitution Anonymous group—I was required to go for several months and it was not a good time), self-harming, or engaging in disordered eating can or should be the goal for everyone. I remember a dear friend who decided to stop using cocaine after about five years of daily use. When they told me they quit coke we were sitting in a bar drinking whisky and we toasted to their six-month period of killing that habit. Now, twenty years later, they still haven't touched cocaine, but do casually use other substances. In non–harm reductionist Twelve-Step thinking, this would *not* be considered a success. My friend would be thought of as "replacing one addiction for another" or not "fully on the road to recovery." But within a harm reduction model, my friend made the change they wanted to make and maintained it. Period.

Liberatory Harm Reduction wants us to celebrate us exactly as we are. It asks us to make no behavior changes at all—only to be in connection with others. As an introvert, my connection to my people has been gently coaxed and never chased. I have been invited and honored for the times I can show up, and never shamed. One of the most enraging parts of Twelve-Step language that upholds abstinence as the ultimate goal/success is how we internalize it and how it's portrayed in pop culture. We are told we are "dirty," so we begin to believe we aren't "clean," and, worse, not worthy of being loved.

Somewhere along the line, the treatment industry version of Twelve-Step thinking just became a part of how much of the world's population thinks about drug use. And while some of the language can be useful to consider when people are voluntarily participating in Twelve-Step programs, most of it has become dangerous because it has left the Twelve-Step program container. Without the Twelve-Step container, this language is at best useless and at worst used to justify violence.

The misuse, overuse, and general obsession with pathologizing language has leaked into pop culture, making the "othering" of us even more alarming as it encourages loss, fuels the idea that we are disposable, and gives people permission to annihilate stigmatized survivors and encourage criminalization. It is for this reason that harm reductionists become incensed by the misuse of these terms and the conflation of concepts like "recovery readiness" and "risk reduction" with any kind of harm reduction approach. These words are used to distance people and make us monsters.

So much Twelve-Step language and practice are rooted in white, ableist, and cisheteropatriarchal dogma and have shaped how we devalue people's coping strategies and life experiences. I ask you to think with your peers, comrades, and community about language that feels shaming. What words would you like to replace with words that keep us whole and loving? That allow us to show up as complicated people who live in relationship to all the parts of ourselves?

I lasted fewer than nine months working in a public health–based harm reduction setting that was an alternative to incarceration (ATI) program offered through the Manhattan court system. As a condition of people's participation in the ATI program, they had to submit to weekly urine tests to ensure that they were not using illegal or illicit drugs. Each week, the courts faxed my supervisor the names of people whose urine samples tested positive for drugs. One day, I saw my supervisor file the fax in a red folder she labeled in large, marker letters, "Toxic." I was shocked. I asked her why it was okay to label people who use drugs as "toxic." She sent me home early for the day.

The words that follow are never used within Liberatory Harm Reduction networks, settings, programs, meetings, or anywhere at all. Each of these words can become weaponized against people. Because the true definition of these words varies among Twelve-Step programs—the definition and application of the word "enabling" may look different in Gamblers Anonymous compared to Prostitution Anonymous—I have chosen not to offer the verbatim definition from Twelve-Step literature. In truth, for the purposes of this book, the meaning that you probably already know from pop culture is the meaning that matters the most. It is useful to ask yourself about the meaning of these words and how you have applied them.

Letting Go of Twelve-Step Language

When words like the ones mentioned here are used in a harm reduction environment, it's a red flag that there is disconnect between politics and practice. This use of Twelve-Step language works to create violence and to pathologize people and relationships.

Terms such as *codependency* and *enabling* should be able to describe relationships that we all deserve; relationships that have empathy and a healing influence on each other. Instead, using these words causes confusion around solutions and tools that keep people alive and conflates the difference between saving each other and harming each other. In Liberatory Harm Reduction practice, boundaries are highly valued. Labeling relationships as *codependent* or *enabling* removes the possibility of negotiating boundaries that can work for both people. It removes the possibility for mutual understanding of needs and an intimacy that could be based in reciprocity.

Referring to people as *the addict* or calling people *clean* is dehumanizing, limiting, and stigmatizing. It implies that we are "dirty" unless we are separate from whatever life experience the outside world views as unacceptable.

The word *relapse* suggests that there is one desired state—abstinent—from which we can fall instead of being in a long-term and negotiated relationship to our coping strategies and survival practices. These words don't create room to integrate learning into our lives because when a person *relapses*, the implication in Twelve-Step programs is that they haven't gained any skills. The context-changing work and healing work they have done is erased, and they are at zero. In Liberatory Harm Reduction, change is not linear, and we do not consider "abstinence" to be the ultimate state of being; we don't use the word *relapse*. We value every moment of our lives; not just the moments where we are abstaining from doing something.

The language of *denial* is particularly enraging to me. As a lifelong antiviolence activist, this term is gaslighting. If someone is viewed as "unwilling, unable, not ready, or not interested" to stop doing a particular activity, *denial* is applied to negate their experiences. *Denial* comes out of social work, therapy, and medicine. It is similar to the label *resistant*, which social workers use to describe someone who is not showing up for services rather than acknowledging that the services or interventions don't fit. The use of *denial* is really just systems defending themselves when they're failing.

The phrases *rock bottom* and *tough love* are also violent. These words are used as excuses for when the abstinence model isn't working and directly implies that trauma is necessary for people to become *sober*. Rather than acknowledging structural oppression, *tough love* blames people for simply being in a struggle. It is particularly chilling, as *tough love* gained traction as a concept for parents who struggle with raising their children. The concept gave way to a rise in structural violence as they reframed young people's coping mechanisms, survival strategies, and whole identities as individual "moral failings," which often looks like kicking young people out of their family, school, or foster care setting. This is especially true for young people who are queer, transgender, drug-using, or living *any other life* that is considered unacceptable by society.

As much as we can, I urge us to release this language. My mentor and lifetime chosen family member, Kelly McGowan, says:

> When the [preceding] words are said to you, come into your head, or leave your lips, remember that it's a part of the dominant carceral culture and that it takes constant attention to build our practice of shared, liberatory language. First, thank yourself/each

other for noticing that these words do not reflect our liberatory vision and, when you can, disarm them by asking yourself/selves how am I/are we saving our own lives right now? Because you are.

We Deserve More than the Myth of Trauma-Informed Care

It's important to stop and address the concept of *trauma-informed care* (TIC), which simply means that system representatives, such as doctors, social workers, teachers, and others need to recognize that the person they are treating or teaching may have had a traumatic experience in the past. In movement spaces, we use the term TIC to indicate a certain analysis about the layered impact that interpersonal, institutional, and generational violence have on our lives.

Throughout this book, we have been thinking about trauma and the importance of understanding and respecting all ways that survivors cope, heal, and weave complex communities together.* The truth is that, at minimum, many of our strategies as survivors are viewed as negative, as Emi Koyama wisely describes, and are too often criminalized. I tried to think of examples of people who use illegal or illicit drugs or who live and work as a part of the street economy who are not criminalized. While it's true that BIPOC are violently and intentionally targeted by the War on Drugs and the War on People in the Sex Trade and Sex Workers, all people who use illegal or illicit drugs are actually in a complicated relationship with the law.

When I expand my thinking to people who self-injure, who decide to go off their psychiatric meds, or who have eating disorders, I realize that almost all coping strategies are stigmatized. Depending

* The book *The Courage to Heal*, written by Ellen Bass and Laura Davis was forever in my backpack throughout the 1990s and helped me make critical connections between my own healing work and the thinking I would later do on community accountability.

on a person's age, race, and/or gender presentation, the judgments of institutional representatives can have carceral implications.

I remember when a close friend who was experiencing severe flu symptoms went to the emergency room to get care. Their arms, like the body parts of so many people I love, had raised, but long-healed scars from self-injuries created both through burning and the use of razors. When the scars revealed themselves as my loved one rolled up the sleeves of their hoodie to get relief from their fever, the triage nurse, who by definition had medical training and should have certainly realized that the scars were decades old, decided that my dear person required an immediate psychiatric evaluation. The nurse asked them no questions, not one. She placed them on a forty-eight-hour hold and transferred them to the on-site psych ward. As the emergency contact, I got the call at one o'clock in the morning to come to the unit as soon as visiting hours began. I was confused and enraged. After being held against their will for two days, they were released by the attending psychiatrist, who told me plainly that my friend should have never been admitted. They never received treatment for their flu symptoms. We left the hospital and went directly to one of our local clinics, where they were diagnosed with walking pneumonia.

As we walked through the hospital corridors to get to the exit, we passed no less than a dozen signs that stated the hospital values included offering trauma-informed care. This story outlines the hypocrisy of the TIC model. The dilemma is that currently we have no better language to describe the mandate we need, because the poster campaign that so many institutions use has made these words a faint echo. We need organizations and institutions to understand the real causes, meanings, and daily impacts of trauma in our interpersonal and collective lives. Part of our work, as Liberatory Harm Reductionists, is to recognize that the state and systems set up to care for us actually cause harm in our lives. Our work is to invent and imagine healing that increases both individual options and interrupts systemic harms. It is this combined approach that will get us closer to a world where we are able to always heal on our own terms.

The lack of a complex trauma analysis leaves all of us vulnerable, especially people whose survival strategies have been named morally wrong or criminal. More than vulnerable, we have become targets of a system that cannot make sense of us and instead seeks only to control us. Sometimes I think these systems have little help to offer, and at other times I think these systems hoard resources from our communities intentionally and force us to fight each other for what little access we have. To get minimal assistance, we are forced to lie to our health care providers about our drug use, sex work, medication adherence, and more to cover our tracks as much as we can. Even when we want to stop using drugs and seek out rehab or other forms of assistance, we are subject to humiliation and monitoring of our bodies that is designed to reduce caseloads and keep costs down.

When seeking medication-assisted treatment (MAT) like methadone or Suboxone, the treatment from doctors is frankly subhuman. The average person can wait months or even years to get into a MAT program, and then must be free of other drugs to stay in the program. I have had several friends who intentionally became pregnant for the sole purpose of getting into rehab or onto methadone because pregnant people have access to priority placement. If you noticed shock or judgment come up when you read that statement, I invite you to answer it with curiosity and compassion. What is life like when becoming pregnant is the best option for someone who wants to get off drugs? What does it mean when the system is so targeting and traumatizing that options for support are limited to the point where we can only think in extremes?

When I was finally able to find a doctor who prescribed me Suboxone, which is how I effectively stopped using heroin (but not all opioids) in my thirties, I was able to get into a program at my local syringe exchange. The program itself required few hoops because it was in a harm reduction setting. This is far from a common experience, and I know that my community relationships are what kept me alive while I waited for the waiting list to clear a path for me to get the life-changing appointment I needed. At the time, I got support from my community at YWEP, including Dr. Laura Janine Mintz, who was not yet in medical school. Over a decade later, when she established her own clinic working with drug users, sex workers, and people of all ages who identify across the gender spectrum, she focused her PhD studies (in addition to her medical degree) on chronic pain and trauma because she had firsthand experience with what it takes to survive and to try to access the MIC for help. She shared an experience with me that she had when she was getting certified to offer MAT to drug users:

> Public health–driven harm reduction has been a useful tool in some ways. I'm so happy that these meds are widely available to people (note: PLEASE someone come up with an effective medication support for stimulant users) and that syringe exchange is easier to access, but the thinking remains constrained by moralizing feelings about drugs that may or may not be relevant for people's lives. Public health harm reduction means, "meeting people where they're at . . . kind of." One of the people leading my training talked about "a harm reduction approach" as being in contrast to a "really taking action" approach, meaning stopping all opioid use. It's so easy to tell that most of the people that go to medical school have never been around drug users (even cigarette smokers!) in their lives. And they've never been face to face with how hard it is to come into the medical system and ask for help when you're marginalized in any way. Nor do they know how incredibly humiliating most drug treatment is and that many have made the decision to internalize that humiliation and shame as a part of the process. That the operating value is that drug users don't know themselves, have no insight into their lives, and need to be instructed exactly about every move they

make. It's so tremendously depressing. If a person has money, they can potentially end up in something that is less humiliating. Most people I'm around don't have that kind of cash.

When doctors (and doctor-types) say "harm reduction" to mean "some activity that is slightly less reprehensible to me than what they are currently doing," it breaks my heart. It's an insult to all the people in this book, all the people that we've lost who have fought for the community-centered practices that have saved so many people's lives. It's a dilution of the real radical and difficult work to figure out *with the person* what will reduce harm to them, to their families, and to their communities. It includes addressing the harm of all the carceral systems (medicine, prison, social services) in its analysis. That asking for help and providing help can get messy and unclear. That real work is sometimes so complicated and so difficult, and also it's the place where I am clear that I'm in my purpose, doing what I need to do, and sometimes really helping to support people in changing their lives.

Every time I run into a trainee, I try to explain that there's a different way. I'm not the only person that practices like this; I'm in community with others, thankfully. My doctoring is radical because I figure that anybody, including fat people, people in pain, BIPOC people, trans and gender-diverse people, queer people, drug users, intersex people, disabled people, undocumented people, absolutely everyone, are the best experts of their own bodies, and what they are thinking should drive the bus of what their medical management should be.

And that is the heart of it right there: the MIC does not ever allow people to be in control of their bodies and choices, which in itself is retraumatizing and a form of violence. To allow anybody to determine their own care is considered radical inside of healthcare, social work, and adjacent systems. How can these systems even begin to claim that they are trauma informed? To help me think through the limits of the concept of trauma-informed care, I turned to my thought partner Erica Woodland, who is the founding director of the National Queer and Trans Therapists of Color Network. An interview with him and Cara Page is featured later in this section, but I have chosen to present pieces of our conversation here, too, because I think it's essential that we spend time thinking about trauma and healing, simultaneously, from a multi-dimensional framework:

> The truth is that the medical system is set up to profit from, not heal, trauma. Trauma is both monetized and weaponized by the state, by social work, by the MIC, by care workers. Trauma has become a business. The term *trauma informed*—which is a term that so many of us have pushed institutional representatives, nonprofit leaders, and movement organizers alike to embrace—is frankly the bare minimum. The term *trauma-informed care* comes out of the MIC. It's their best attempt at trying to treat people like humans in the context of all kinds of violence and abuse connected to that system. It's really rooted in a charity model and a service model, which is not getting at the things that harm reduction or Healing Justice are all about. We don't have the language or analysis around how trauma from state violence is shaping our responses to everything all the time.
>
> The basics around what TIC is offering, I think is useful. But giving that useful information to people in the medical system will ensure it will be misused. The way I was trained, I learned about how to be trauma informed through my initial work in harm reduction. Then, every job I've ever had since then in social work, I was like, "Oh my God, what are you doing?!" Just from simple things like "You don't just touch people when you don't know them," I found that the basics are ignored. And even in movement work, we move too fast and ask practitioners and healers to helicopter in so that then organizers don't have to be accountable. It's kind of like, we're just going to hand trauma to these specific people and not deal with the fact that it's everywhere all the time and the way that you're doing the organizing is reactivating people's trauma. And also, as medical providers, organizers, and social workers, you're experiencing vicarious trauma that you're not tending to.

We need to start considering trauma as a macro concept, thinking through how living in the constant reality of repeated and daily trauma impacts people on an individual level. For example, the experience of houselessness is not a singular event but, for many, is an experience of trauma that repeats each day and night. TIC reinforces the idea that trauma is only individual and that it is caused by a particular and specific event or set of events that is uniquely experienced by the individual alone. This way of thinking places the responsibility on the individual. I can't tell you how many calls I get from social service organizations that want a training on trauma or self-care but are not willing to look at their organizations as sites of institutional harm.

Woodland describes how Liberatory Harm Reduction considers historical trauma, collective trauma, and intergenerational trauma and asks people to think about what their personal and collective trauma responses are inside of those formations.

> I don't want to say there is no personal trauma, but everything is always situated inside of the collective. Nobody's experiencing trauma outside of relationship. There's something about that context that feels really important. It's not as simple as the individual or the personal by itself. It's like that individual or personal trauma is in a broader context that is shaping the experience of the trauma itself. The very basic definition of trauma is an experience that overwhelms you on a physical, emotional, spiritual, psychological, psychic level—all the levels of the human experience. Everybody has a very unique experience of trauma. We need to land on something that better describes how we collectively experience each other's trauma. In Maria Yellow Horse Braveheart's work, I could imagine she would argue that in an Indigenous context, what happens to one person is happening to everyone, but that's not the context that any of us really are living in. And yet, even though that's not the context that any of us acknowledge we are living in, that is the actual reality. I don't know if that makes sense.

Yes, it does make sense. And it's a truth we ignore.

Our Beautiful Mess: The Practice Values of Liberatory Harm Reduction

Every Liberatory Harm Reduction project I have been a part of, be it mutual aid or organizing, has also been a space that actively worked to interrupt, respond to, and transform the daily experience of trauma through carefully cultivated emphasis on both individual and collective resilience. It is my personal belief that every traumatic experience has a simultaneous experience of resilience embedded in it. Every time I have gotten up from an experience of violence, even taken a breath after an attack, it is my body and spirit gathering their resilience and propelling me toward the next breath again. Sometimes my resilience has simply looked like taking the next breath and putting those breaths slowly together into an entire day. The popular Twelve-Step slogan "One day at a time" has often felt impossible, when one second at a time was all I could possibly manage.

Somewhere along the way, I realized that what Liberatory Harm Reduction does is give us our power back through the daily practice of both big and small resilience strategies. I do not believe it is possible to empower someone else. The definition of empowerment is to be in control of one's choices. That is something that comes from knowing and feeling like your choices are yours to make. That feeling does not come from the mythical concept of "self-esteem." We have sadly conflated the notion of self-esteem with the endlessly important concept of empowerment. Self-esteem would have us believe we are involved in the sex trade, afraid of public speaking, or struggle to eat because we don't believe in ourselves. Self-esteem individualizes systemic power indifference and blames us for how we respond. Empowerment, in contrast, helps us take charge of our own lives and is a practice of healing in the face of oppression and trauma. The "beautiful mess" is a concept that we started to use in

Chicago during a time when we had regular meetings of harm reduction practitioners. We were all working as part of social services that had an understanding of institutional violence and interrupting the reach of carceral systems in the lives of people who were using drugs or involved in the sex trade, street economy, and sex work. I don't remember exactly who coined this term, but I recall when Lara Brooks, one of the co-founders and the first coordinator of the Broadway Youth Center's drop-in program in Chicago, said it to me.* We were driving on a mission to pick up someone who had experienced a violent attack, to figure out what care we could offer. Our hearts were hurting for this person and for all the pain and suffering. I said something like, "Why is it that survivors are always the ones who show up to help even when they are also the ones who are often hurting the most?" Lara said, "I am not sure. I think it's the beauty in the mess." From that moment on, whenever we noticed an experience of trauma and resilience that was happening simultaneously, we named it a beautiful mess. We used it several times a day and began to realize that the beautiful mess, also known as holding contradictions, recognizing the limits and limitlessness of a particular moment, was part of the practice we were building.

The political values of Liberatory Harm Reduction are something that people can intellectually grasp. We can see why creating housing for all people is a part of ending prisons. We can understand how ending the medical-industrial complex connects to Reproductive Justice. It is harder, I've noticed, for people to practice the values of Liberatory Harm Reduction in a daily way. Fortunately, embracing mistakes and not being afraid to try new things are part of our belief systems. It is never too late to start again, be in our humanity, and embrace as much of ourselves as we can.

* The Broadway Youth Center began as a harm-reduction project and centers LGBTQIATSGNC and BIPOC houseless and street-based young people in Chicago.

PRACTICE VALUES

WE ACCEPT THAT DRUG USE, SEX WORK, EATING DISORDERS, SELF-INJURY & OTHER COMPLEX EXAMPLES NAMED IN THIS BOOK ARE A REALITY IN PEOPLE'S LIVES. WE DON'T PRESSURE PEOPLE TO STOP, LEAVE, OR CHANGE.

People ARE MORE IMPORTANT THAN RULES

BALLROOM

CHOSEN

STREET

...AND OUR ANIMAL COMPANIONS ARE ALWAYS WELCOME

WE HONOR ALL FORMS OF FAMILY

WE ARE NOT DEFINED BY OUR DRUG USE OR ANY OTHER BEHAVIOR. (UNLESS WE DECIDE WE ARE.)

Self-Determination

OUR BODIES BELONG TO US.

NO ZERO TOLERANCE POLICIES!

EVER.

DON'T BE AFRAID TO TRY

SUPPORTS ALL FORMS OF ECONOMIC RESILIENCE (INCLUDING SELLING DRUGS & SEX)

healing is not LINEAR

MISTAKES & MISSTEPS ARE PART OF THE PROCES

PERSONAL ACCOUNTABILITY

WHAT ARE YOUR COMMUNITY'S VALUES?

TRUE SOLIDARITY

WE ACCOMPANY EACH OTHER THROUGH OUR ROUGHEST MOMENTS

practice NOT PERFECTION

PERSON IS EXPERT (NOT JUST WHEN YOU LIKE THEIR ANSWERS)

CREATIVITY

IF THERE IS NO SOLUTION, MAKE ONE UP!

OUTCOMES ARE NOT PRE-DETERMINED BY OTHERS, WE MAKE OUR OWN PATHS

Led by US for US

US = CRIMINALIZED SURVIVORS

NO POWER OVER
WE BUILD POWER
TOGETHERNESS
(GROUPS, MEETINGS, CIRCLES, CONSENSUS)

KEEP IT COMPLICATED

embrace the beautiful mess

RADICAL ACCEPTANCE

ALL CHANGE IS LOSS

interdependence

RELATIONSHIP IS EVERYTHING

MAKE BOUNDARIES AS YOU NEED THEM & RESPECT YOUR OWN & OTHERS' BOUNDARIES

Moving Away from Public Health Harm Reduction

Harm reduction as a public health strategy relies heavily on a 1982 study, "Transtheoretical Model of Behavior Change" by psychologists James Prochaska and Carlo O. DiClemente.

Prochaska and DiClemente explain that behavior change, like healing, is not a linear process. Their experiments, which began in the 1970s, demonstrate that people move through multiple stages, often in a circular pattern, known as the "wheel of change," when attempting to make a shift in their patterns—especially patterns as ingrained as addiction. The publication of this study provided those care workers pushing harm reduction into the public health sphere a solid framework, because this "discovery" underscored that the long-term, elusive, internal, and psychic processes that humans naturally take when making even the smallest of changes are different for everyone, and they do not have clear timelines.

This gave public health activists an evidence-based argument when advocating for the necessity of syringe exchange, because people need to make incremental changes in order to make bigger changes. And the threat of HIV yielded the saying "You can't get clean if you die from HIV first," which was used to persuade institutions to offer alternatives to abstinence-only programming.

One of the critical differences in Liberatory Harm Reduction philosophy, as opposed to a public health strategy, is that it doesn't rank the outcome of "making a change" above the outcome of "not making a change." In other words, as Dan Bigg from Chicago Recovery Alliance used to say, harm reduction sets a menu of options. I would add that it doesn't value the salad over the mashed potatoes; it places no inherent value in the options themselves. This reflects harm reduction's loving practice of reinforcing self-determination and body autonomy through a truly non-condemning and anti-shaming approach. It is one of the reasons that harm reduction is not only a trauma-centered practice but also an empowerment model.

As a survivor, harm reduction allowed me to reclaim my power in small ways every day, because the philosophy reflects back every choice I made as an example of my own power—regardless of what that choice may be. Just the act of making the choice is me taking my power back. As a community practice, we affirm each other's right to make the decisions we need to make to take care of ourselves to 1) show love for one another and 2) enact the belief that survivors should always be able to choose their own paths, even when you personally disagree with what's chosen.

Recently, I had a conversation with comrade and friend Emi Koyama. Emi and I met about 15 years ago, but we knew of each other through mutual connections and activism years before we were formally introduced. Emi is a multi-issue social justice activist and writer, who synthesizes feminist, Asian, survivor, dyke, queer, sex worker, intersex, genderqueer, and crip politics. These identities, while not a complete descriptor of who she is, all impact her life. Emi's website, Eminism, and her many zines on disability, queerness, fat liberation, the sex trade, trauma, harm reduction, and survivorship have saved me many times over. Emi is also the founder of the Intersex Initiative, a national activist and advocacy organization for people born with intersex conditions started in

2001. With other sex workers, Emi has formed a harm reduction project called Aileen's, a peer-centered organizing and hospitality space led by and for people in the sex trade working along South Seattle's Pacific Highway.

I talked to Emi about this "no change" behavior model, and she reminded me of an old story. The sun and the north wind are in a battle to determine which one is more powerful. They decide to make a bet about a passing traveler to see who can make the traveler take off their jacket first. No matter how hard the wind blows, the traveler just pulls their coat tighter around their body, but when the sun blazes, the traveler takes off their jacket and places it on the ground. The moral of this story is that persuasion is better than force—and it serves as an allegory for the difference between traditional treatment models and harm reduction. Traditional treatment models, which explicitly work to "break the addict" and "rebuild the addict," have abused the Twelve-Step program model in so many respects. One important way is that Twelve-Step fellowship honors that the evolution of change is cyclical, and that people do not make any change before they are ready. The treatment industry and other models, which are too often mandated by courts, make the false and frustrating claim that Twelve-Step programs* are their backbone. This type of harm reduction, as a public health model, would be the sun, shining brightly and present for the moment when the traveler decides, on their own turf and timetable, to take off their jacket.

But this is a limited view. Harm reduction is a liberatory philosophy steeped in the values of self-determination, body autonomy, Disability Justice, Healing Justice, Reproductive Justice, and Transformative Justice that is survivor-centered and survivor-

---

* There are countless studies that show the ineffectiveness of the treatment industry and Twelve-Step programs—too many to list or even quote. It's curious how we have accepted that treatment models work when studies consistently reveal that people do not have the desired outcome (meaning sobriety) after going through a twenty-eight-day program.

created. The Liberatory Harm Reductionist understands the moral of the story to be "How dare you fuck with the traveler?", and the traveler's community members would offer shelter, shade, and support to overcome these oppressive forces. To respect that the traveler has inherent wisdom is core to the beliefs of not only harm reduction but all survivor-centered work.* If the traveler was on a path without a community, the traveler would practice harm reduction by searching for their own creative solutions. Maybe the traveler would seek shade under a tree. Or maybe if the cold north wind was blowing, the traveler would use heroin to keep warm and rest until the storm was over.

Harm Reduction: A Survivor-Led Strategy

> *No coping mechanism is "maladaptive" or "unhealthy" in itself unless and until the survivor themselves decides it is.*
>
> —Emi Koyama

I think that I became a harm-reduction activist as child, maybe by the time I was five or six years old, as I would strategize plans for staying safer in my own body. Like many survivors, I learned the patterns and cycles of mood swings and cascades of painful trouble that would come out of nowhere; they became ingrained in me, and I believe that hypervigilance kept me alive. When the words "harm reduction" were first said to me, I was seventeen; it was like a missing puzzle piece landed, and my world became organized at last.

A few days ago, a professional researcher said to me that it was "incredibly rare" for someone to inject drugs at fifteen and that this was an indicator of early trauma. For a moment,

* It is often called the strengths perspective in social work or the belief that individuals all have internal resources and mirroring those back to those seeking help is essential.

I was confused by her comment; I know many survivors who use drugs, but not all of us do. Yet most people I know injected drugs for the first time around the same age that I did. I found myself wondering why she said this to me. Was it personally important to this researcher that my story be "rare"? What peace did it give her to think that my tale was that of a misfit? I began to think about all the other parts of my story that would probably be called rare: I started to self-injure when I was four years old, and the list goes on.

One of the most comforting aspects of harm reduction is the validation of what Emi brilliantly terms "negative coping" or "negative survivorship." Although I didn't come across her writings on the topic until about ten years ago, Emi named something about harm reduction that has always been true for me. "Negative survivorship" is a resilience model that celebrates our ability to show up in whatever forms we can. In my case, I showed up with torn skin to manage my dissociation; I showed up in and out of sobriety to manage my ongoing chronic pain, nightmares, and intrusive thoughts and images—plus, being high was just a fucking relief compared to everything else in my life.

The weaving together of the survivor-centered framework with harm reduction principles was instinctual for me—as it has been with so many other antiviolence activists I know—because we know how difficult it is to leave abusers and to survive abuse. It is important to pause here to say that I am using the word *survivor* to describe my experience with childhood sexual and physical violence because it fits how I see myself currently. It took me a long time to understand myself as a survivor, and I have struggled with the simultaneous truths of feeling like a victim of harm—harm that shouldn't have happened, harm that started early in my life and continued uninterrupted for years—where I felt powerless and overwhelmed and as someone who also survived. I also want to say that I now use the term *survivor* because I did survive it and can see the track marks of the harm and resilience across my life. I use the word *survivor* with full knowledge that there are so many of us who do not make it and are no longer with us. As a resilience model, harm reduction should never leave out those who do not survive, nor should it set up a false binary that survivors are the "strong" ones.

Disability Justice helps us understand how dehumanizing it is to overvalue "strength" and asks us to rethink our ideas of "health" and "weakness." In Emi's article "The Uses of Negativity: Survival and Coping Strategies for Those of Us Who Are Exasperated by the Empty Promise of 'It' Getting 'Better,'" she writes:

> Blaming of people experiencing negative feelings is closely connected to the popular ideology of positive psychology. Positive psychology, or at least its popular versions, announces that we all "have the power" to change our lives through transforming our attitudes, neglecting how our power is constantly being weakened, undermined, and stolen by violence and societal injustices in our lives. If we all "have the power" to be happy simply by changing our minds rather than material reality of our everyday struggles, it reasons that those of us who are unhappy are to blame for our own misery.
>
> The society prescribes "healthy" ways for us to cope with difficulties in our lives and admonishes us for using "unhealthy" ones. "Healthy" coping strategies include exercise, consistent eating and sleeping schedule, accessing support (but not too much, or you will become a "whiner"), hot bath. "Unhealthy" ones involve substance use, eating "disorder," self-injury, and other "negative" things that push away our support system. When we engage in these "unhealthy" coping strategies, we are blamed for causing more problems to ourselves.

The Icarus Project, now known as the Fireweed Collective, a network of people living with experiences that are labeled "psychiatric illnesses" but who reject the conventional medical model of "mental health" and "mental illness," published a handbook about the use of self-injurious behaviors to cope with difficulties in our lives. In it, the authors identify a long list of actions that might be described as self-injury, but often are not, including*:

- working very hard
- dieting
- exercising excessively, or not at all
- piercing
- getting tattoos
- playing football
- mountaineering
- skateboarding
- ballet
- working in a job you hate

Each of these acts may cause pain, injury, and other undesirable consequences, but they are generally considered "normal." What are the differences between socially appropriate and inappropriate self-injury? There may be many factors, but one of the tendencies I observe is that self-injurious behaviors that are compatible with capitalism and uphold societal hierarchies (conforms to cisheteropatriarchal values) are generally considered socially appropriate, while those that undermine our ability to be productive workers and happy consumers are considered inappropriate.

I believe that "unhealthy" or negative coping strategies that we use some or most of the time must be validated and supported. It does not necessarily mean that every coping strategy is equally

---

* To read the entire Icarus Project handbook, go to yumpu.com/en/document/read/6714401/hurting-yourself-the-icarus-project.

valid all the time, but the validity and desirability of coping strategies need to be evaluated by the person experiencing it, rather than externally imposed on them by society. This includes suicidal thoughts. I have long struggled with thoughts about suicide and self-harm, but I have since come to accept suicidal ideation as a coping strategy rather than merely a symptom or a warning sign. After all, every time I contemplated suicide, it helped me survive. The failure to recognize our resilience in suicidality makes it difficult to have honest conversations about how we truly feel.

Liberatory Harm Reduction gives us the space to be in pain, to acknowledge that all change—even positive change—is loss, and that we deserve to be a part of a community of people who can hold the complexity of all that we are, and all that we are processing.

Harm Reduction Principles in Survivor Advocacy

My journey to abolition of police and prisons has evolved. I started from a "fuck the police" stance. I was forced to perform a cop's favorite sexual favors under the threat of arrest. He first caught me with a lot of drugs in my pocket on my way back to the park after leaving a club on West 14th Street. At this time in New York City, the area called the Meatpacking District was known to be an outdoor workplace for many people trading sex for money, drugs, and survival needs. He saw me walking down the street, my all-black clothes clinging to my fat body, my make-up streaked from the heat of the dance floor, where I would sleep in the corners on as many weekend nights as the doorperson*

* I later learned that the bouncer was the queer Latinx artist Richard Alvarez, who also worked the door at the first syringe exchange by and for trans people led by Bali White at Positive Health Project in 1997. Replicating the night club scene and to keep the predators away, the outside of the syringe program operated with the glamorous intervention of a velvet rope and depended for its safety on Richard's vast relationships in the community and his kind but firm voice.

would allow. No matter how careful I was, that cop found me in the lower parts of Manhattan at least a half a dozen times. I did not know how to escape him without doing exactly what he asked of me.

I have often had conversations with other people who have life experience as sex workers or involvement in the sex trade and street economy in which we discuss our bodies as the actual physical site, the actual geographical location, where the intersection of racism, misogyny, transphobia, capitalism, and violence plays out. Because of this, my journey to politicization from "fuck the police" to prison abolition as an adult was not about theory. It was about being a witness. A witness to the violence in my own life and the lives of people I loved and cared for.

After my experiences with the cop, the connections between sexual violence and policing were made clear to me on a different level. The people incarcerated in the minimum-security prison where I worked had almost all been arrested for breaking the law for income-generating purposes. They were in the sex trade, stealing, or participating in some other form of the street economy, like hiding drugs in their bodies for dealers or providing some other nontaxable services. I began to understand that our survival was criminalized, and that the size and damage of the penalties depended on what we were doing, in what neighborhood, and what we looked like. As I made the connections between racism, capitalism, misogyny, transphobia, and criminalization, I began to understand that for those whose lives are criminalized, fighting off an individual officer's sexual predation was only one small part of the picture of the PIC.

At the same time, I was volunteering for the local syringe exchange while some of my chronic pain and disabilities were getting diagnosed slowly and often incorrectly. My access to health care was shit. I had no real health insurance to speak of, and I was so busy lying to my doctors (and nearly everyone I knew) about my life that I started to see the connections between the medical model, prisons, the War on Drugs, and the cops. Lying helped me to understand that hiding was an essential part of navigating systems, because to be transparent about my whole life meant denial of treatment and facing possible criminalization. If I told a doctor I was opioid dependent, I would not get the critical medications and care for my chronic illnesses and disabilities. The MIC and PIC were, and are, interlocking systems, benefiting from the exploitation of nearly everybody I have ever intimately interacted with.

I believe that survivors of sexual violence have a secret stash of power; we grow our insight out of a need for protection, out of needs to anticipate a violent swipe or someone grabbing us off the street. Some people also form this sixth sense out of generational understanding and awareness of how to escape white racist predators, and they hone psychic practices that allow us to apprehend danger. The survivors I met during this time formed underground networks of safe houses that ignored traditional social service models, including domestic violence shelters, because so few people got help from those places. From where I sat, drug users, people in the sex trade, transgender people, and LGBTI people were thrown out or refused help by shelters, hospitals, police stations, and even soup kitchens every single day—all the places we were socialized to believe would help and protect us only criminalized us further and trained us to lie to get our needs met.

I began to see that all the shelters where I worked or stayed were not reducing problems but making them worse. I saw the shelters fight to expand carceral strategies, from mandated reporting* laws to sentencing for people who purchase sex to the

* Mandatory reporting, which on the surface appears to be a strategy to end violence in families, actually dramatically increases state violence and interpersonal harm. See Dorothy Roberts's article on the family regulation system, "Abolish Family Policing, Too," *Dissent Magazine*, https://www.dissentmagazine.org/article/abolish-family-policing-too.

expansion of domestic violence courts. It was the mid-1990s, mass incarceration and drug arrests were rampant, and I could not wrap my head around how to be a feminist who did not believe in the state or institutions supported by the state. I was experiencing what Emi Koyama describes in her essay, "Disloyal to Feminism: Abuse of Survivors Within the Domestic Violence Shelter System." Emi writes:

> Feminist movements have struggled to confront abuse of power and control within our very movements, even as we critique and resist the abuse within this sexist society. On a theoretical level, at least, we now know that not all of our experiences are the same nor necessarily similar, that claiming universality of experiences inherently functions to privilege white, middle-class, and otherwise already privileged by making their participation in these systems of oppression invisible. We now know, for example, that fighting racism requires not only the obliteration of personal prejudices against people of different races, but also the active disloyalty to white supremacy and all of the structures that perpetuate systems of oppression and privilege.

Emi's foundational essay shows the deep flaws in the ways that the state and the nonprofit-industrial complex address sexual violence and purport to support survivors. It is clear that a person's identities are surveilled, policed, and punished in the person's attempts, simply, to live. Emi's own thoughts helped me to understand my struggles reconciling my feminist ideas and the stated feminist goals of the shelter. My feminism is rooted in Transformative Justice, harm reduction, and abolition; it is clearly anti-carceral, pro-BIPOC, pro-trans, pro-queer, pro-sex work/pro-ho, and anti-colonialist/pro-rematriation. The shelter's ideas of feminism were based on perfect, passive, submissive victims needing help from the state; they subscribed to carceral feminism. In my own practice, and in key collaborations, I've attempted to take to heart many of the lessons and methods Emi lays out.

Emi Koyama's zines were some of the first writings I found that linked the antiviolence work and violent world I was living in with harm reduction. The National Harm Reduction Coalition gave us the principles for US harm-reduction practice (see image on page 120), which are still radical and rarely fully practiced in public health settings. Emi took the principles from NHRC and updated them to reflect the trauma-based work being done by those of us who identified as survivors. Focused primarily on intimate partner violence, domestic violence, and violence in the sex trade, in sex work, and in the street economy, the image we created for this book is taken word for word from her zine written in the late 1990s. When I reread what she wrote then, I am painfully aware of how relevant it is, how little has changed, and how necessary it is for us to have a clear understanding of the role of violence, trauma, and survivorship in our harm reduction practice.

SURVIVOR-CENTERED HARM REDUCTION VALUES

ACCEPTS THAT SURVIVORS LEARN TO COPE IN WHATEVER WAYS THAT REDUCE THEIR PAIN & INCREASE THEIR SENSE OF CONTROL, INCLUDING THOSE TRADITIONALLY VIEWED AS "UNHEALTHY"

↓

MINIMIZES HARMFUL EFFECTS RATHER THAN CONDEMNS OR IGNORES

IRREGULAR EATING & SLEEPING PATTERNS

03:19

ESTABLISHES QUALITY OF INDIVIDUAL & COMMUNITY LIFE & WELL-BEING - NOT NECESSARILY CESSATION OF ALL ACTIVITIES DEEMED "UNHEALTHY" OR "UNSAFE" – AS THE CRITERIA FOR SUCCESSFUL INTERVENTIONS & POLICIES

UNDERSTANDS EACH METHOD OF COPING AS A COMPLEX, MULTI-FACETED PHENOMENON

SOME WAYS OF DOING IT ARE SAFER THAN OTHERS

A CONTINUUM OF BEHAVIORS

NO ACTION — RECKLESSLY EXTREME

CALLS FOR NON-JUDGMENTAL, NON-COERCIVE SERVICES & RESOURCES TO PEOPLE WHO ARE COPING WITH THE EFFECTS & AFTERMATH OF ABUSE & THEIR COMMUNITIES

ENSURES THAT SURVIVORS ROUTINELY HAVE A REAL VOICE IN THE CREATION OF PROGRAMS & POLICIES DESIGNED TO SERVE THEM

AFFIRMS SURVIVORS AS THE PRIMARY AGENTS OF REDUCING THE HARMS OF VARIOUS COPING METHODS AS WELL AS THE AUTHORITIES ON THEIR OWN EXPERIENCES & SEEKS TO EMPOWER THEM TO SHARE INFORMATION & SUPPORT EACH OTHER IN STRATEGIES THAT MEET ACTUAL CONDITIONS OF SURVIVAL & COPING

RECOGNIZES THAT THE REALITIES OF POVERTY, CLASS, RACISM, SOCIAL ISOLATION, TRAUMA, SEX-BASED DISCRIMINATION, & OTHER SOCIAL INEQUALITIES AFFECT SURVIVORS' VULNERABILITY TO & CAPACITY FOR DEALING WITH THE EFFECTS & AFTERMATH OF ABUSE

WE ARE EXPERTS IN OUR OWN LIVES

DOES NOT ATTEMPT TO MINIMIZE OR IGNORE THE REAL & TRAGIC HARM & DANGER THAT CAN BE ASSOCIATED WITH CERTAIN COPING METHODS SURVIVORS MAY EMPLOY

—EMI KOYAMA—

Drugs, Alcohol, and Accountability

A few years ago, I was at a conference and heard Shannon Perez-Darby talking about her first experience learning what true accountability looked like by witnessing her family member go through a Twelve-Step program. Shannon's speaking to the connection between addiction and accountability as a practice was one of those moments when I felt my whole world come into focus.

My first experience in a Twelve-Step program was when I was thirteen years old. I was in ninth grade and was required to attend a group called "Rainbow Kids," which was an Alateen program for young people whose families were impacted by addiction and whose parents were divorced.* I hated this meeting. It was filled with clichés and corny positive-thinking mantras; I was existential, depressed, actively plotting to leave home, coming out as queer, and furiously fantasizing about revenge against every adult that I knew.

I later had a conversation with Ejeris Dixon, a leading Black, queer Transformative Justice organizer who has also struggled with addiction in their family. They noted:

> I got all of my analysis of the police as violent from my father, who was an alcoholic, because we had some different points where either I called 911 or I thought about it, knowing that whenever that happens, they could kill my dad, and then also thinking about, well, what are the other options? What else can we do? This is where Transformative Justice as harm reduction is also just me trying to stay alive, trying to help us keep our apartment. Right? So, let's not be so loud that the landlord comes. Let's see what we can do to alleviate the situation. Let's see how everyone gets their needs met. Also, let's see how the cops don't show up. Right?

---

* Alateen is a Twelve-Step program for people ages 13-18 who have been affected by someone else's addiction.

When Shannon Perez-Darby reminded me that Twelve-Step programs were a place where many of my (more functional) family members may have learned about taking responsibility for their behavior, I went through a process in my mind about whether or not this was something I experienced, both in my personal and professional life. I remembered so many times where I strategized about how to stay safe and alive and avoid more systems intervention.

Remember, harm reduction is a high-accountability and high-responsibility model. This means that, for instance, users are responsible for their own behavior and not given permission to blame their addiction as an explanation for their behavior. It means that if your roommate behaved irresponsibly, then your roommate cannot explain their behavior by saying they are/were "powerless over their addiction," a required refrain in Twelve-Step programs. While in both harm reduction and Twelve-Step practice amends are encouraged and a personal inventory and self-reflection process would begin, it is only in harm reduction that we learn to separate accountability from sobriety. Harm reduction demands that everyone take responsibility for their own behavior whether drunk, high, withdrawing, or sober.

I cannot tell you how many times we have been asked at Just Practice Collaborative (JPC) how people can be held responsible for harm they have caused if they are still actively using drugs or alcohol. In a conversation with another Transformative Justice organizer, they remembered calling JPC and telling us the story of "someone who is sweet until they are drunk," and then "all these unsafe behaviors come up." They asked us,

> What is the accountability mechanism that also recognizes, is it ever fair in a process to say, 'You must be sober'? Because demanding sobriety is taking so many choices away from people—drinking could be the only thing holding that person together. But, speaking as someone who has done things that are completely fucked up and outside of myself and outside of my

> values, what do we do about that situation, and what's the best way to approach it?

It took some time for me to come up with the simplest answer: the same way you would hold anyone else accountable. In fact, many people who use function better when drunk or high than when sober. There are other people who do not remember their actions when they are using and have a hard time connecting the dots between events or behavior. The consequences for someone who is violent or harmful when drunk should be the same as for someone who does not drink: securing safety for the people that person is harming by setting boundaries. As a diehard harm reductionist, I am a boundary queen. In fact, half of my friends don't even have my address, and even though I have had the same phone number for over fifteen years, I turn it off for large portions of the evening.

Harm reduction is an empowerment theory. This means that everyone should be in control of their choices. Violence or the threat of violence is the opposite of empowerment because it takes choices away from other people. If we can build our communities, activist organizations, and mutual aid groups on a Liberatory Harm Reduction philosophy, then we can have shared practices for interrupting and transforming violence.

> I believe that people who've survived violence as children and also people who struggled with addiction, that we are natural strategists. I was thinking about how I create tools. And most of the toolkits, safety tips, things I would say are written partially based on my body, almost. So, I will either think about scenarios I've been in and have saved myself from or gotten people to help me save myself. And that becomes a tip, a part of a toolkit. So, I was just like, oh, there is this part of the tool generation process for me that is like, yep, tried that. Didn't work. Yep, tried that—but it needed something. In this way, harm reduction has been embedded in our lives and communities for a really long

time because it's like "Oh, you mean living? Living in this body and surviving?" Harm reduction is about saving our own lives because so many people don't care if we live or die. But for harm reduction I'm grateful, because I think there are lessons that we bring from being close to death and from witnessing and supporting others who are, and for being and living within the communities that people either actively or tacitly discard.

—Ejeris Dixon, Vision Change Win

Disability Justice and Harm Reduction

As syringe exchange activists in the mid-1980s built on the existing "survivor centered" frameworks that were co-evolving in the antiviolence movement, they also built on existing ideas of Disability Justice.

According to the second edition of the Disability Justice primer, *Skin, Tooth, and Bone*, published by Sins Invalid in 2020:

> In 2005, disabled queers and activists of color began discussing a "second wave" of disability rights. Many of these first conversations happened between Patty Berne and Mia Mingus, two queer disabled women of color who were incubated in progressive and radical movements which had failed to address ableism in their politics. Their visioning soon expanded to include others including Leroy Moore, Stacey Park Milbern, Eli Clare and Sebastian Margaret. These conversations evolved over time, at conferences, over the phone, formal and informal, one-on-one and in groups. While every conversation is built on those that came before it, and it's possible that there were others who were thinking and talking this way, it is our historical memory that these were the conversations that launched the framework we call disability justice. This group named and made clear that "ableism helps make racism, Christian supremacy, sexism, and queer- and transpho-

> bia possible" and that all those systems of oppression are intertwined.
>
> - All bodies are unique and essential.
> - All bodies have strengths and needs that must be met.
> - We are powerful, not despite the complexities of our bodies, but because of them.
> - All bodies are confined by ability, race, gender, sexuality, class, nation state, religion, and more, and we cannot separate them.
>
> Disability justice activists, organizers, and cultural workers understand that able-bodied supremacy has been formed in relation to other systems of domination and exploitation. The histories of white supremacy and ableism are inextricably entwined, created in the context of colonial conquest and capitalist domination. One cannot look at the history of US slavery, the stealing of Indigenous lands, and US imperialism without seeing the way that white supremacy uses ableism to create a lesser/"other" group of people that is deemed less worthy/abled/smart/capable. A single-issue civil rights framework is not enough to explain the full extent of ableism and how it operates in society. We can only truly understand ableism by tracing its connections to cis-hetero-patriarchy, white supremacy, colonialism, and capitalism. The same oppressive systems that inflicted violence upon Black and brown communities for five hundred-plus years also inflicted five hundred-plus years of violence on bodies and minds deemed outside the norm and therefore "dangerous."

As anti-police and prison abolitionists, many members of the Disability Justice Collective were also present for harm reduction conversations and organization building during the late '80s and early '90s. Just as it is not accidental that harm reduction is a space safe for sex workers (because we were there to bring it to fruition), harm reduction must also be grounded in anti-ableism because it is essential to understanding how able-bodied and able-minded supremacy drives the stigmatization and criminalization of so many survivors' experiences.

I was first diagnosed with a chronic illness—endometriosis—when I was sixteen. By the time I was twenty-one, I was diagnosed with rheumatoid arthritis, fibromyalgia, interstitial cystitis, vitiligo, and some long-term kidney issues. By this point, I understood that I was disabled, and I had enough harm reduction practice in me to know how to get through my day with creative problem solving—like the years when I wore a helmet all the time, because I kept falling from a combination of physical pain, exhaustion, and the effects of pain management medication.

I had many conversations with Nomy Lamm, who brilliantly linked disability with fat oppression in her zine, *I'm so fucking beautiful.* But it wasn't until I had a conversation with Mia Mingus, in 2004, that I was able to speak with another person of color about the layers of racism embedded in ableism and in notions of health. Mingus, a longtime Reproductive Justice activist, harm reductionist, and Transformative Justice practitioner who cofounded the Bay Area Transformative Justice Collective and the Disability Justice Collective, writes about the importance of breaking isolation—something that survivors of violence, people with disabilities, and those with criminalized identities struggle to do. At the intersections of Disability Justice and harm reduction, she says, "Harm reduction is the only way we know how to survive." She continues:

> Harm reduction has always been a part of disabled people's survival, long before there were words for it. We have always had to learn how to survive on our own, either as disabled communities who have been segregated and pushed to the edges of the margins of society, or as isolated individual disabled people who do not have connection to disabled communities.
>
> The latter is especially common, as the overwhelming majority of disabled people are not born with their disabilities, but instead acquire them at some point in their life due to

violence, oppression, or trauma. Conditions such as dangerous working environments, poverty, pollution, incarceration, war, and lack of access to adequate healthcare, clean water and healthy food are often what create disability.

The intense segregation of disability in society often means that disabled people's lives are hidden away, either literally or hidden in plain sight. We are often forgotten, with no social nets, and forced to live with devastating conditions—such as lack of access to housing, employment and education; inadequate state financial support with cruel arbitrary rules which intentionally lead to forced poverty; rationed state provision of care that often does not meet the needs of the few who are granted it; institutionalization and incarceration; and overwhelming isolation.

We find each other out of necessity and create bonds to not only combat isolation and stigma, but to help keep us alive. This is disabled community, and it forms as a lifeline for our survival. Disabled community in and of itself is a form of harm reduction in a world that seeks to keep us apart and oppressed. The very act of finding each other and banding together—even if it is connecting online across borders or as neighbors, or whether it is inside of a group home or prison or disabled classroom—is a form of harm reduction. This is especially true because one of the most defining parts of being disabled is isolation, and denial of access to connections, communities, family, relationships, love, affection, and intimacy.

This kind of isolation is even more heightened when other systems of oppression and violence are layered on top of disability and ableism. Because most disability is acquired through harmful social conditions, many of the people who become disabled are those who, because of oppression, are most impacted by these conditions: poor black and brown communities who are forced to work dangerous jobs, or undocumented communities who do not have access to healthcare or who are subjected to routine violent raids.

> This understanding of interdependence can permeate and fundamentally shape our lives. Those disabled people who have attendants who grocery shop and cook for them may have their attendants cook large meals that can be shared with fellow disabled loves ones or always make sure to share grocery runs. Disabled communities have been practicing collective care for generations, creating community care collectives to support them with their access needs or doing the work to build and maintain relationships in order to get access.
>
> For many disabled communities, we have forged our own paths on our own terms in a world that would rather see us dead. Our roots are in freak shows, mental institutions, medical experiments, orphanages, and being locked in the back rooms of our own homes by our own kin. We have worked to define ourselves outside of the medical industrial complex and ableism, outside of disgust and fear. We have used harm reduction without even knowing that was what we were doing. We have done what we needed to do to survive by reducing harm wherever and whenever we can, together, and worked to seed dignity, love and pride along the way, fundamentally shaping disability culture and legacy forever.

Harm reduction invites us to heal in relationships, to be witnessed, to be unashamed, and to struggle against the MIC, together.

revolutionary love notes

The love notes left here tie together the ideas of trauma, Disability Justice, and the pushback on public health harm reduction. Liberatory Harm Reduction cannot exist without us—the rebels, the crips, the survivors. Harm reduction is an intricate ecosystem, as Bonsai Bermúdez and La Tony Alvarado-Rivera discuss after this chapter, and it's one that cannot be taken apart from radical accessibility.

Harm Reduction Is Disability Justice: *It's Not Out There, It's in Here*

LEAH LAKSHMI PIEPZNA-SAMARASINHA

Leah Lakshmi Piepzna-Samarasinha is the author of Care Work: Dreaming Disability Justice *and co-editor with Ejeris Dixon of* Beyond Survival: Stories and Strategies from the Transformative Justice Movement, *as well as seven other books. A long-time Disability and Transformative Justice movement worker, their new book,* The Future Is Disabled: Prophecies, Love Notes and Mourning Songs *is forthcoming October 2022.*

When Shira asked me to write about the intersections of Disability Justice and harm reduction for this book, I balked. I thought, *Am I qualified to write this? I'm not someone who's been in the middle of the harm reduction movement. I'm more like a cousin.* Then I thought, *Well, a lot of people in my life from teenagerhood on are people who've used drugs, and a lot of my friends, lovers, and extended community have been or are sex workers. I'm the child of two alcoholics and of a multigenerational trauma–holding, abusive birth family, who grew up to make chosen family and community with a lot of people who are also trauma-surviving weirdos. I'm someone who lives with chronic pain and uses different practices to deal with it, including substances, and has been gate-kept from pain meds because of being seen as "drug seeking" . . .*

Huh. Maybe I do have something to say about Disability Justice and harm reduction after all? And I guess this is the point: that both harm reduction and Disability Justice are for everyone.

Another thought was, *Well, most people I know who use drugs or alcohol and/or are in harm-reduction communities in some way are disabled.* Let's start there.

Let me explain this by providing something that's the first slide in every "What Is Disability Justice?" training I've done: a definition, or two, of disability.

> *When we speak of disability, we are celebrating the brilliance and vitality of a vast community of peoples with non-normative bodies and minds, whether a disability is visible or not. This includes, though is not limited to, folks who identify as disabled, chronically ill, Deaf, mad, neurodivergent, and more.*
>
> —Showing Up For Racial Justice Disability Justice Caucus*

* "Disability Justice Home Manners," SURJ Disability Justice Caucus, https://surj.org/resources/disability-and-access/, accessed April 29, 2022.

I always think this definition will get old, and it never does. People are fascinated to see a definition of disability that is a fuckton larger than the narrow slice they might know. *You mean asthma counts? You mean anxiety counts? What about my Tourette's? You mean trauma? Chronic pain? You mean I can be disabled even if I don't have an Official Diagnosis?* Yup, yup, yup. Disabled is anyone who has a body or a mind that is not "the norm," according to the medical-industrial complex. Using UN stats, 40 percent of the world is disabled. The reality is that probably most people are disabled, Deaf, neurodivergent, Mad, chronically ill, or more than one of the above. (And then people go, *Wow, I've never seen a definition of disability that talks about disabled people as having a community. Or mentions being brilliant and vibrant, not just a bunch of defects.*) People use drugs for all kinds of reasons, but one primary reason is because of pain: to kill, reduce, or manage pain that is physical, emotional, spiritual, or all three, in order to have experiences of pleasure, intimacy, connection, and spirituality. Those experiences—of being a survivor with anxiety, depression, complex post-traumatic stress disorder (CPTSD), BPD, and more, or someone with chronic pain who self-medicates—are disabled experiences.

I believe harm reduction is already a Disability Justice practice, led by disabled people of all kinds, even though it might not always think of itself that way. Because when it comes to the presence of disability in movement spaces, it's not out there, it's in here.

People I have met who do harm reduction work may or may not use the D-word to refer to ourselves, but, in my experience, harm reduction is a movement filled with and led by people who have disabilities—physical, chronic illness, hep B, AIDS, mental health disabilities and differences, and neurodivergence. Harm reduction is also a movement that believes in and tries to practice some of the central principles of Disability Justice. Namely: that we, people with lived experiences of disability and substance use, are the authorities on our lives, not the doctors, the lawyers, the prison guards, or the social workers. We're not just a set of defects to be corrected into normality—we have communities, skills, and wisdom. We have a vision of living our best lives that does not always mean sobriety or living a "straight life." We meet people where they're at and ask what they need, without trying to fix them into normality. And, most importantly, we keep each other alive so much more than the state or the medical-industrial complex do (even though, of course, many of us navigate using the state or the medical industrial complex for a Medicaid-funded surgery or a monthly check).

But what is Disability Justice?

Disability Justice (DJ) is a movement created by Black and Brown and poor white and queer and trans revolutionary disabled people in 2005. They wanted a movement shaped by someone other than the white disabled people in leadership in much of the disability rights movement, which had often led to racism and white supremacy in both the organizing and the strategy, focusing on a single-issue, legal/civil-rights approach. They also wanted a movement that would be an alternative to Black and Brown nondisabled activist and community spaces perpetually "forgetting" about disability, disabled people, and ableism. They wanted to create a revolutionary movement that centered Black and Brown, queer, and trans disabled experiences, wisdom, and ways of organizing and building community.

To see more, you can read Sins Invalid's "10 Principles of Disability Justice" or check out their Disability Justice primer, *Skin, Tooth and Bone*.* But to hit some key points, Disability Justice is

* Sins Invalid, *Skin, Tooth and Bone: A Disability Justice Primer,* https://www.sinsinvalid.org/disability-justice-primer, second edition, 2019.

an anticapitalist and anticolonialist movement. We don't think disabled liberation will happen if a handful of white disabled people get rich and powerful, and we see colonization as being a birthplace of ableism. We talk about and try to practice cross-disability solidarity and collective access—learning each other's languages and experiences as different kinds of disabled people. We show up for each other and build access collectively for everyone in a group or community, instead of as a one-off, fix-it model.

One of the primary offerings of Disability Justice is that there is no one right or wrong way to have a body or a mind. Disabled queer Puerto Rican/Jewish writer Aurora Levins Morales writes, "There is no neutral body from which our bodies deviate."* In Disability Justice communities, cure and becoming able/ normatively bodied or minded is not the primary goal. Living better, on our own (disabled) terms, with autonomy is the goal. So is changing society so that it doesn't make our lives miserable while actively and passively working to kill us. Disabled white trans writer Eli Clare has written about the concept of "brilliant imperfection,"† about the particular gifts that disabled bodies and minds bring to the world, that "cure" would erase—what disabled queer poet Laura Hershey calls "the miracle of error."‡

DJ is practiced a lot of different ways. The primary place I've seen DJ community is in disabled peer networks of information and support sharing—on social media, at someone's house, in friend groups, and in the corner of the food stamps office. We talk about what the real deal is, like when your catheter comes out during sex or you're in a particular kind of DID activation. We

---

* Aurora Levins Morales, "Mountain Moving Day," in *Kindling: Writings on the Body*, Palabra Press, 2013.

† Clare, Eli, *Brilliant Imperfection: Grappling With Cure* (Durham, NC: Duke University Press, 2017).

‡ Laura Hershey, "Translating the Crip," https://poets.org/poem/translating-crip, November 2010, accessed April 29, 2022

share pills, and info about pills, and tricks for getting off the pills, and stuff that isn't about pills. We pool money, share strategies for surviving everything from suicidal ideation to how to limit CP tremors during an MRI. We listen to what people say they need instead of telling them what they should need. We work to help others take control of their lives and survive on their own terms, instead of focusing on "fixing it." That sounds like harm reduction to me—the harm reduction I know that sets up safer injection sites whether or not there's a permit, feeds people and insists that drug users do not need a social worker or authority to speak for them: they are their own authorities.

I am not aware of a ton of overt movement linkages between harm reduction and Disability Justice—yet. But I can't help but think that if harm reduction and Disability Justice movements joined together and built coalitions, there's so much we could win. On the legislative front, we have so much in common when it comes to fighting to decriminalize and end the gatekeeping of drugs—all drugs, but in particular drugs used to manage pain—decriminalize Narcan and overdose reversal and remove the gatekeeping barriers to pain medication access (including criminalized drugs), barriers that impact BIPOC disabled people the most. We're both fighting against denials of vaccines and care to people seen as "bad risks," including drug-using, disabled, and imprisoned people. We're both fighting against the weaponizing of psychiatry and the proposal of social workers and "wellness checks" as replacements for policing—insisting instead on what we know would help us live well: affordable, non-gross housing, control over our bodies and lives, economic justice, community, pleasure, joy, and easy access to respectful health care that we choose. Most of all, though, we have communities of love and support and real talk to build with each other and learn from each other.

To do so will mean many things, but a big part of it may mean engaging in an ongoing practice of working to undo our internalized ableism. So many of us have survived by being tough, not admitting we need help, and managing our pain on our own. We minimize our disabilities because it's not fucking safe to let them show—from the most visible to the ones that are easier to squeeze in a corner. We've been taught that having needs is to be entitled: that's for some rich someone someplace else. Often, we've learned to distance ourselves from other people with disabilities like ours or not like ours—to be the one special one in a system of scarcity that says there's room for only one cripple who doesn't have any needs, really.

However, if there's one thing that working in the Disability Justice community has taught me, it's about how both hard and extremely life-giving it is to learn to love myself and the other disabled people who are, and are not, like me. It's not easy. In fact, it's really fucking hard and it's an ongoing practice. Nobody taught us how to love ourselves or each other. But when we fumble our way toward undoing internalized ableism, the kind of acceptance and relaxation into power and relationships we build are like nothing else. They create crip friendship and comradeship. They make room for access stuff to be easy and for disabled brilliance to shine. They undo toxic shame. Our disabled love for ourselves can heal us in the places where we've been the most thrown away. And that is the biggest reduction of harm there is.

Conversation with La Tony Alvarado-Rivera and Bonsai Bermúdez

La Tony Alvarado-Rivera is a Chicago-based, Latin-e, queer organizer who has been working with young people in harm-reduction projects for nearly two decades. Now the executive director of the Chicago Freedom School, a project founded by Mariame Kaba that teaches education for liberation and organizing to young People of Color, La Tony was an essential part of the making of the Broadway Youth Center as the Mentor Program Coordinator and worked with the groundbreaking About Face Youth Theatre.

Bonsai Bermúdez is the cofounder and executive artistic director of the Youth Empowerment Performance Project (YEPP). Bonsai completed a master's degree in guidance and counseling from the University of Puerto Rico with a concentration on LGBTQI+ issues. Bonsai has been working in the social justice service field for more than twenty years, focusing on trauma, Transformative Justice, and harm reduction practices. With a bachelor's degree in theatre and dance, they have worked professionally as a ballet/modern dancer and actor.

La Tony: I started learning about harm reduction at the Broadway Youth Center (BYC) around 2005. I worked with young people who were LGBTQI experiencing houselessness, and it was like, oh, this harm reduction is actually a tool for our community. Liberatory Harm Reduction frames it well because it's about our survival. It isn't about pathologizing a certain group of folks. It was, hey, young people are here to build new as they experience trauma, harm, hurts.

Learning it in my midtwenties, while I was also using substances, has allowed me to actually practice it in my daily life and see what it would look like. There's something about being rooted in anti-oppression frameworks as a Brown, queer person who would engage with Black people, with folks with disability, throughout my work in community organizing. The idea of solidarity makes me understand meeting people where they're at, learning about people's experiences, processes. The beauty of harm reduction is that it's relationship building as solidarity building because I have the opportunity to engage with folks and then go back and think with an anti-oppression framework about where I have my own biases—what did I grow up thinking about drug use, substance use, sex work?

We know that folks create a plan, and then it shifts so there's no perfect answer. I love that harm reduction is individualized, it is a process, it is a love for your community, it's about understanding. The core frameworks that I'm working from and that are here at Chicago Freedom School are anti-oppression, Transformative Justice, and Healing Justice frameworks.

Bonsai: I was raised in an environment in Puerto Rico with sex work, drug use, lack of housing, mental health issues, colonized bodies and minds, in a household where my father was a Vietnam War veteran with all the PTSD and physical damage. How many times my mother had to run with all of us because my father was getting physical, so domestic violence is another one. What we currently are calling [Liberatory] Harm Reduction was the thing to do to keep ourselves safe and my mother to keep us safe.

When we were sick, we were sent to the *comadrona/santiguadora*, the person with *unguentos* and plants to bring levels of healthiness and not necessarily to go to the hospital. I was submerged in community-driven, trauma-centered, harm reduction practices. When I moved to Chicago, it was like, whoa, there is a theory and a philosophy behind this, and I remember being thirsty to gain all that language to understand what happened in my family's history.

What makes the difference between Liberatory Harm Reduction versus public health applications is being trauma centered. The state and the public health field have not developed wisdom and understanding about how trauma works and manifests in people's bodies and do not allow the deeper work. Because Liberatory Harm Reduction is community centered, I feel we have better wisdom about how trauma works in people's minds and bodies, and we are able to bring strategies that are more impactful into our practice of harm reduction.

La Tony: Coming from it as a community organizer, as a youth worker, it's, *Let's strategize with the folks being impacted.* If I don't know the experience of a young person using sex as a survival mechanism or have that experience, being able to share this harm reduction framework as a way of existing, of living, is really empowering for a lot of young folks. It's allowing young people to feel respected, acknowledged, like, *Hey, let's work together to build strategies.*

What I've always appreciated about BYC is we were able to process strategies rooted in a Transformative Justice model where we're not going to call the cops, we're not going to rely on the state, because we know that these systems are just going to further criminalize young people. It takes thought partners to be able to challenge each other, saying, *Hey, I'm thinking of this, young folks have offered this, what are other options for strategies that you have used?* As much as we work to not involve institutionalizing young people, there were moments that forced us to look at institutionalization so that we could push away from it.

Bonsai: It's like a community-centered ecosystem. We are always sharing and growing with each other: practicing, mastering, passing on so many powerful things that these young people taught us. La Tony, you named about you learning from people; I have been learning from you. That's part of the ecosystem—we have created a community-learning dynamic.

La Tony: I love what you said about the ecosystem. Learning in community is like this fragile, almost subversive, almost queer framework. It was such a blessing for not just my work but my life.

Bonsai: The public health field is packed with people that have not had the experiences that can help them to understand how trauma works, that teach them to strategize, to meet people where they're at and have Liberatory Harm Reduction come to life. We are actively strategizing how to do this work.

La Tony: It sounds watered down, but [a key component of this work is] relationship building that includes nonjudgmental solidarity building. The relationship building allows us to see everyone as deserving, beautiful, gifted human beings in a system.

The other piece is acknowledging that these systems have demonized drug use and created a mental health crisis, generational trauma. Systems of colonization, racism, misogyny are telling us that these people are bad, and we're countering that narrative by saying, *Actually, I believe in you, I see you, I welcome you.* But also understanding that if we are trying to create system change, then what is my social responsibility to also fight against those systems that have told me sex work and drug use is bad, that people with mental health issues should either deal with it or find therapy.

The relationship-building piece, the systems-change piece, is where we have to ensure that the folks who are practicing harm reduction are a part of the solutions. It is essential that we are learning from each other, we are practicing putting strategy together.

For folks building solidarity who aren't drug users, haven't engaged in street economies or the sex trade, or don't identify as using harm reduction specifically in their life, then the question for you is, *What is your social responsibility to build solidarity and fight against these systems that are harming folks?*

Bonsai: Yeah, relationships, I think that's the heart, the core, the engine, really what moves Liberatory Harm Reduction work. Without it, I don't know how the hell harm reduction really happens. It is community driven. Once those relationships are being nurtured, being built, being developed, being in progress, then we exist in a community-driven space.

Being trauma centered is so essential to really activate, nurture, navigate life through a harm reduction lens, especially for people impacted by many injustices. Generational trauma is part of it. I'm still unpacking the generational trauma of my own family, and I am like, fuck, this is really something that has been instrumental in how I see the world through a harm reduction lens.

La Tony: I would also add if there's no understanding of harm reduction within Healing Justice, then Healing Justice feels not as complete. If we're not talking about harm reduction, then we are missing something huge. Linear is not the way we achieve healing; it's a process, and part of that is thinking about how harm reduction can actually be introduced to folks, to young people, to ourselves as part of the healing strategy. Let's say we're trying to reduce our drug use—the goal isn't to necessarily have it to end, but to understand how drug use may actually be a tool for my healing.

WHAT IS *Healing Justice?*

A DIRECT CONFRONTATION AGAINST: RACISM, EUGENICS, ABLEISM, ENVIRONMENTAL INJUSTICE, ANTI-IMMIGRATION POLICIES, MISOGYNY, & TRANSPHOBIA. IT IS PRO-SEX WORK & STREET ECONOMY.

a Black Southern Resistance Model

an anticapitalist & anti-state political strategy

collective care for our movements

Led by Black, Brown, Indigenous People of Color as both healers & organizers

IT IS NOT...

- AN INDIVIDUAL ACT OF SELF-CARE
- A BUSINESS MODEL
- AN INDIVIDUAL PLATFORM
- AN OPPORTUNITY TO BLAME INDIVIDUALS FOR NOT TAKING CARE OF THEMSELVES
- A MOVEMENT

The Beautiful Mess: *Justice in Our Healing*

Healing Justice is at the core of Liberatory Harm Reduction. The lifeblood of each philosophy is the belief in self-determination, the belief that healing and growth happen best inside long-term relationships, the right for people to choose how and when they engage the allopathic medical model, and a demand that healers fight the systems of power that interrupt our ability to get care on our own terms. Liberatory Harm Reduction and Healing Justice both are largely ignored by mainstream activists because their tenets are uncomfortable. These models require doctors and other health care workers, social workers, legislative policy makers, healers, and organizers to make room for the fact that their ideas about bodies, safety, and health leave out enormous swaths of our communities. They require us to make room for the reality of what it means to show up in our bodies exactly as we are, without anyone asking us to leave, change, or conform.

Healing Justice and Liberatory Harm Reduction are inextricably tied together because they are both about the active strategies that people use to collectively heal and push back on the medical-industrial complex. Healing Justice is not personal "self-care," singularly focused, and it is different from what is offered by health insurers, doctors, and the MIC, which tells people that the only way to have an acceptable body is to be non-sick, non-disabled, non-fat, and non-drug-using. The MIC also tells us that we cannot have a normative body if we use it to make money selling sex or use our bodies to regulate our trauma via self-harm. We cannot have normative bodies if we decide not to take our psychiatric medication, accept (or struggle with) our eating disorders, or do not buy whatever supplement or prescription we are told to without being called "noncompliant," in "denial," or "resistant to care."

At this point, the concepts of health, wellness, and self-care, ideas that initially existed outside the MIC, are now so intertwined with capitalism that they have become lost to those of us who are committed to dismantling the MIC and disconnecting it from carceral thinking and systems. Cara Page notes that

> The Medical Industrial Complex, like the Prison Industrial Complex, relies on state dependencies and constructs of care and safety that are based on containment, control, and behavioral conditioning versus looking at the impact of colonization, slavery, imprisonment, detainment, and capitalism on the collective well being of our communities. Both systems were created to further harm and heal under the guise of curative models that shame, blame, and pathologize communities and our collective bodies.

Similarly, Dr. Laura Janine Mintz, who practices medicine from a harm reduction framework, said to me,

> The contemporary "wellness and self-care" industry is a billion-dollar enterprise that is mostly apart from the MIC and focuses on individual strategies about buying stuff, and is also apart from practices of "community care." It is invested in a colonial extractive process. At least to me, the relentless bullshit fake garbage comes at me through "healing" social media accounts trying to sell me whatever supplement/miracle cure is supposed to make my body normative again.

Healers, activists, and practitioners of all kinds are flummoxed by the multitude of creative ways that we, as survivors, queer and transgender people, people with disabilities, drug users, and sex workers, live in the body on our own terms. We have long demanded body autonomy, and we will not stop until we have reclaimed the right to be in our bodies and make decisions for ourselves at all times.

Digging into Healing Justice

Healing Justice teaches us that we, by virtue of being alive, deserve access to any and all medical and healing interventions, from herbs to surgeries. It also teaches us that we, as healers, have a responsibility to organize when we, or our communities, are blocked from these resources as a part of institutional and structural violence. Healing Justice is based on the political value of total body sovereignty. Because the belief in body autonomy is essential to harm reduction, those of us who are practicing both of these lifesaving strategies interweave harm reduction and Healing Justice seamlessly. I would argue that when we separate Liberatory Harm Reduction from Healing Justice, or vice versa, we are left with public health risk reduction steps or "self-care" interventions, devoid of liberatory politics and practices that truly improve our collective well-being.

Kindred Southern Healing Justice Collective defines Healing Justice as "a political strategy conceived in 2005, and formally launched in 2006 by the Kindred Southern Healing Justice Collective, to intervene and respond on generational trauma and systemic oppression. Healing Justice also builds community/survivor led responses rooted in southern traditions of resiliency to sustain our emotional/physical/spiritual/psychic and environmental wellbeing."

One critical misunderstanding about Healing Justice and Liberatory Harm Reduction is the idea that they are only individually based interactions, a set of interventions you can do with yourself or someone else to practice self-care. On the contrary—

both Healing Justice and Liberatory Harm Reduction are deeply communal, not only in the way we center community and people with lived experience as experts, but also because we believe in addressing the root causes and conditions that create the harm we live with.

More than just the combination of the words *healing* and *justice*, Healing Justice is an anticolonialist practice that must be steeped in Disability Justice, Reproductive Justice, environmental justice, harm reduction, and Transformative Justice to be true to its founding principles. In this way, Healing Justice is not about affordable yoga classes; it's about challenging the roots of the MIC and reclaiming land-based healing and care practices—including the right to give birth outside of a hospital, the right to access care while using drugs or involved in the sex trade, and the rights of people with disabilities to heal on their own terms.

Fuck Your Healthy. Fuck Your Wellness.

The idea of *wellness*, especially individual consumer practices of self-care (like massages), is often confused with Healing Justice. Healing Justice is inherently anticapitalist. Full disclosure: I feel partially responsible for how the term *wellness* became something that you can buy at a Walgreens. Like most poorly thought-out, shitty strategies, this particular moment in conversations about wellness* started out with good intentions. Around the mid to late 1990s, we used it to push back on the MIC view of health and to challenge *healthism*, the idea that there is one ideal, able body,

* Dr. Laura Janine Mintz notes, "I agree with your general sentiment—*wellness* can suck a dick, and capitalist notions of wellness are fucking garbage. The history of the word began around the 1940s and the concept of a wellness spa is way older—most prominently, here in the US with John Harvey Kellogg in the early twentieth century, and with the earlier natural healing ideas internationally for . . . forever. The wellness/natural living concept also has a huge history in the right-wing world, as in 'Be a natural Nordic Nazi,' et cetera."

and that body has certain test scores that account for everything from cholesterol to IQ to levels of physical activity. From *ideal body weight* to ideas about sobriety and medication adherence, healthism permeates the social service field from health clinics to rehabs and is the foundation of the entire allopathic medical system. Harm reduction and Healing Justice counter healthism because they embrace the idea that, as Glenn Marla says, "There is no wrong way to have a body."

Liberatory Harm Reductionists and radical healers began to use the word *wellness* as a response to the use of the word *healthy*. Everywhere we went there was the looming judgment from *healthy choices*, *healthy food*, or *healthy habits*. While the word *health* was predetermined—you had to be born with it or buy it—the word *wellness* felt broader at the time. We put it on zines, named activist projects, and generally plastered the word *wellness* everywhere we could.

Through more conversations with Dr. Laura Janine Mintz, I learned about Robert Crawford's 1980 article defining *healthism* as a "preoccupation with personal health as a primary—often the primary—focus for the definition and achievement of well-being." This stands in contrast to both Healing Justice and Liberatory Harm Reduction, which are grounded not only in ideas of collective care but also in the thinking that physical and mental health cannot be "achieved" and does not have a singular destination or representation, which is inherently ableist and not trauma centered.

At this point, I *hate* both the terms *wellness* and *healthy*. Every time I hear these words I hear codes for weight loss, sobriety, and general bullying that says we are supposed to look, feel, and pawn our parts to serve capitalism. I particularly hate how corporate health care took over naming my experience in my body. How, when I call to get my prescriptions, they say, "Have a well day," or, "We hope you're well." In reality, businesses would prefer that I am unwell. Drug stores feign care to keep me as a customer because they don't want to lose the thousands of dollars per month Medicaid has spent on my prescriptions. While I cannot prove that corporate drug stores directly stole our language, I can say that I know marketers pay attention to what we do on the streets (heroin chic in the '90s certainly showed us that), and while we were training everyone from other service providers to medical students to departments of public health on our harm reduction strategies, we began to see an overall increase in daytime television and yoga studios using the language of wellness. Co-optation was inevitable, and before we knew it, *wellness* was a prominent marketing strategy all over drugstores and health insurance logos and taglines.

This whole conversation forces people with chronic illness and disabilities into a dichotomy of *healthy* versus *unhealthy*. I have multiple chronic illnesses, disabilities, and addictions, a life-long committed self-injury practice, and CPTSD. I have been participating in the sex trade on and off for thirty years. I have had health insurance less than ten years cumulatively in my life. I have been considered fat since I was seven years old and was forced on each diet that medical doctors were legally permitted to prescribe for children.* This yielded a life of eating dysregulation, disorders, and dysmorphia. As a survivor, my mental health has vacillated between extreme dissociation, leading to a diagnosis of dissociative identity disorder, and panic attacks that leave me frozen in my tracks, requiring friends, partners, and chosen family to move me back into safety. I will never be *healthy*.

In a conversation I had with my comrade Elliott Fukui, a member of the education team at Fireweed Collective and a Mad

* Dr. Laura Janine Mintz told me that "doctors are now actively pressured to place children on diets as a part of regulations for healthcare 'quality,' despite the negative impact of dieting on children. There are now recommendations in favor of bariatric surgery in kids! Fat stigma and phobia is real within the medical world because these tactics are being pushed even as the statistics for bariatric surgery and dieting are appalling for both adults and children." An analysis of fat oppression is a critical Healing Justice concept.

Queer organizer, we talked about the inextricable connection between Healing Justice and Liberatory Harm Reduction, the impact of colonialism and capitalism, and how they impact ideas of mental health and wellness. Elliott is a longtime organizer I met when we both lived in New York City in the early 2000s. At the time, Elliott was working with the Audre Lorde Project* and was a member of Icarus Project, the first harm reduction organization to address mental health. The Icarus Project first made visible the reinforcing connections between the MIC and the PIC, along with their discussion of the intersection of madness and oppression. The Icarus Project "navigated the space between brilliance and madness" and created a guide with the Freedom Center called *Harm Reduction Guide to Coming Off Psychiatric Drugs* that has been truly transformational among people who both work in and seek services from psychiatric health care providers (see reprinted excerpt from this guide on pages 241–47). Their zines made the world livable for so many of us living with mental health shame and stigma because they provided real-world strategies steeped in intimacy, relationships, and healing.

The next generation of the Icarus Project was founded in 2017 and called the Fireweed Collective, defined as

> a crew of Mad, Disabled, Neurodivergent, & Atypical QTBIPOC who center healing justice and social justice in our peer support groups and monthly webinars. Our work seeks to disrupt the harm of systems of abuse and oppression, often reproduced by the mental health system. Our model for understanding "severe mental illness" is community and relationship-based and divests from the prison industrial complex and psych wards.

---

* The mission of the Audre Lorde Project from their website: The Audre Lorde Project is a Lesbian, Gay, Bisexual, Two Spirit, Trans and Gender Non Conforming People of Color center for community organizing, focusing on the New York City area. Through mobilization, education and capacity-building, we work for community wellness and progressive social and economic justice. Committed to struggling across differences, we seek to responsibly reflect, represent and serve our various communities.

Elliott makes the connection to colonialism, capitalism, the MIC, and the PIC explicit by stating:

> All of these ideas of prisons, policing, psychiatric hospitals are built from the same punitive framework that we inherited from England and colonization back in 1492. They are all punitive models with the intention of controlling bodies. And when I started thinking about the history of how psychiatry has been utilized to justify putting away survivors, putting away veterans, putting away people who had experienced immense trauma, going after People of Color and Black and Indigenous people . . . and then, whatever their response or reaction was to being diagnosed or forcibly medicated, restrained or locked in cages, was then pathologized and frequently criminalized. Is it mad for a child who survived childhood sexual abuse to overly react to touch on a playground? Is that actually madness? Is it actually madness for someone who experienced sexual violence to want to control their environment or to move into hypervigilance?
>
> In a lot of ways, I started recognizing that our survival was being punished. When you think about dissociation, when you think about people who move into manic phases, when you think about depression, all of those things are actually the things that kept us alive in a lot of ways, the ability to remove yourself, your mind, from something traumatic that was happening. . . . This is where harm reduction is really important and powerful.
>
> When I started in psychiatric care, a lot of it was around my mood stabilization. So, I was consistently rapid-cycling between mania and depression. And I would hallucinate, but I was also experiencing pretty frequent and consistent violence at school. I was surviving childhood sexual abuse and I was surviving all these other things, too. So, for me, it came to the point where when I was in psychiatric treatment, the whole goal of the "treatment" was *You need to be functional.* The goal is for you to be able to work forty hours a week. The goal is for you to be able to sit in class.

> The goal, it wasn't to heal. It wasn't to examine what I was experiencing in the world that would make me react that way. And even as a child at twelve, and I'm a very tiny person, and back then I weighed probably eighty pounds—if I would have an episode, you would have five security guards on top of me in a second. And I would get a shot of Ativan, and I would be left in a room alone. At some point I had the realization that I was being punished for expressing emotion for what had happened to me and was happening to me.
>
> My madness does impact me. Some people would say their madness is a gift. I'm like, *Yeah. It's a mixed bag depending on what you're going through.* I started seeing my depression, seeing my mania, seeing my dissociation as survival strategies and tools that as a small child. . . . And think about how resilient children are, everywhere, experiencing horrific fucking shit. How brilliant I created alters, so I didn't have to carry the weight of trauma alone. I figured out how to stay in bed to rest my body through depression. In those moments, as a young person, I was being punished for it. And so, I developed shame around it, and developed shame around my depression, shame around my mania, and around my dissociation. But as I got older, and more involved in movements for liberation, and started building more with other survivors, recognizing that cutting can sometimes mean not killing yourself, straight up. Burning can sometimes mean not killing yourself. And this whole idea of a normal level of mental health cannot make sense under these conditions.

So, when we started using the word *wellness* in harm reduction projects, we were pushing back on the idea that healing is something you can buy, and that there is only one way to live fully embodied lives. We were pushing back on the MIC, which either dismisses people with addiction as *drug seeking* or labels us as *noncompliant* when we aren't sober. We were pushing back on the view of us as *crazy* or *criminals*. We were claiming our survivorship—even our negative survivorship—as Emi Koyama explains.

We started herbal programs and cooked together while high or between sex work clients. Meal cooking became parties—eating, talking about foods we love and where we learned this recipe or that preparation skill. Dr. Laura Janine Mintz observes,

> The racialized wellness shit around food is especially disgusting in the context of medicalized fatphobia—the fact that most people get the message that bland food is somehow better for everyone is both racist and incorrect. The spices and seasoning and contrast of foods from one and other, AND the fact that food is meant to be a source of connection and community, THOSE are the things that improve health and life, and the research on long-lived groups of people confirms that it's not the molecule in the wine, it's sharing the wine with someone who you love, eating food that you cooked together and shared with everyone.

We crocheted ourselves together, building our power and control over our lives through reflecting back our small successes and praising the glow of the sweat it took for us each to make it through the day. We continued our resilience practice by offering ear point acupuncture for people in our spaces, often called community acupuncture or detox acupuncture. We created opportunities to study the Lincoln Detox acupuncture method that was started by Dr. Mutulu Shakur in the South Bronx in the 1970s.* We built on the work started by the Young Lords and Black Panther Party and collectivized and reclaimed ideas of care for drug users, people in the sex trade and street economy, and BIPOC.

Community acupuncture is distinct from the acupuncture

* For more about this, see the interview in this book about the Lincoln Hospital takeover and the politically radical work of Dr. Mutulu Shakur of the New Afrikan Independence Movement. Shakur, who is currently incarcerated as a result of a COINTELPRO operation, created new options for detoxing from drugs using acupuncture that are still taught and practiced today and whose work became the basis for the National Acupuncture Detoxification Association or NADA practice.

practiced in most of the United States because it's practiced by laypeople and peers, and two to twenty (or even more) people receive a treatment at the same time. I have distinct memories of learning ear point acupuncture at Lincoln Detox in the South Bronx from one of the original founders of the practice and from someone who was present at the time of the takeover. While we learned about the size and shape of the ear, which needles to use, and how to insert the needles without causing pain yet achieving maximum precision, we also learned the story of how Latinx, Black, Indigenous, and other People of Color united in the South Bronx to demand health care for drug users. Every day for a month, I traveled from Brooklyn to the Lincoln Detox Center and sat with a group of ten harm reduction practitioners while we learned about health care disparities, discrimination against drug users by the medical system, and how to carefully twist a small needle in such a way that it mellowed a craving for drugs and alcohol. We practiced on each other and on community members who came to the clinic for free treatments in exchange for letting us learn on their ears.

When I returned back to the youth programs I was a part of, I worked with other drug users who had trained in ear point acupuncture at Lincoln to establish Community acupuncture drop-ins. We filled our small spaces with as many lawn chairs as we could fit and offered free treatments for young people who used drugs. Those spaces were opportunities to disclose depression, for instance, because we could ask for a needle placed in the center of our foreheads just below the hairline and in line with our noses that would help us—not only because of the power of acupuncture itself but also because the communal space allowed us to show each other our vulnerabilities through where our needles were placed.

When I talked to Tanuja Jagernauth, a long-time YWEP adult ally and cofounder of Sage Community Health Collective, about the importance of harm reduction analysis and Healing Justice practice, she reflected:

> When I was one of the YWEP adult allies, I learned what harm reduction was and how it looked and felt in practice. Later, my understanding of harm reduction would challenge fundamental assumptions about the power relationship between patients and practitioners that I was taught in my four-year master's program in traditional East Asian medicine, and I am so deeply grateful.
>
> Our YWEP practice of harm reduction showed me that when responding to and intervening in generational trauma and violence, attempting to heal and transform the consequences of oppression on our bodies, hearts, and minds, we actually have options. We can take an approach that perpetuates long-standing power imbalances at all levels, or we can try an approach that seeks to challenge these power imbalances.
>
> If we wanted to perpetuate power imbalances, we might use prescriptive models that already exist within the medical-industrial complex and nonpoliticized complementary and alternative medicinal practices. These models are often prescriptive and hold at their center ideal notions of health and wellness based around white, able-bodied, heteronormative people. They therefore allow a variety of -isms to exist unchecked: ableism, fatphobia, heterosexism, white supremacy, misogynoir, and more.
>
> Instead, if we aim to challenge historical, systemic power imbalances, we might choose an approach with harm reduction at its core. Harm reduction offers a nonprescriptive approach that puts the power back in the possession of those most impacted by systemic violence and oppression by acknowledging and centering their self-determination, expertise in their own lives, accountability, and agency to make decisions and take action to heal and thrive on their own terms. Harm reduction approaches meet folks where they are at, introduce and educate folks about their options, and stay present with them as they

> navigate their healing processes at their own pace, on their own terms, and with their own goals in mind.
>
> We took all of this into account when we cofounded Sage, in Chicago. In alignment with our mission, all practitioners were encouraged to work with our community in a nonprescriptive way. Harm reduction (HR) was at the core of every single interaction with our patients/clients, from the time they entered our space to the time they left.
>
> For those who were new to the framework of harm reduction, we offered collective education at our meetings and one-to-one mentorship with those experienced with HR. In the rare case that a practitioner was not able to center HR in their work at Sage, we had to let them go and/or shift their role in the collective.
>
> We offered weekly NADA drop-in hours on Fridays from 5 pm to 7 pm, a harm reduction tool that centers the self-determination of the patient/client, creating space for the people to rest and heal on their own terms for as long as they wish. As practitioners, our role becomes more [that of] a technician. We were there to apply the needles, hold space for the patient/client, and help support them to have a safe and comfortable NADA session. When they indicated that they were ready to have their needles removed, we were there to help remove them. In some cases, patients/clients preferred to remove their needles themselves. In that case, we were there to support and assist as needed.
>
> For me, this kind of harm reduction approach is how we best help to facilitate the healing of generational trauma and the impact of systemic oppression.

I remember Stacy Rubin, a hero of mine, who became the first wellness coordinator at Streetwork Project in New York City in the 1990s, describing how donors and grant funders would react with shock that young people who were using IV drugs cared about salad. *Healthism* is the bias that tells us that people in the sex trade, street economy, or who are street-based cannot care about themselves because they participate in activities that have been categorized as "high-risk." Our complex humanity is dismissed, our identity assigned as either victim to be saved or criminal to be locked up.

The disturbingly quick co-optation of *wellness* shows how efficiently capitalism can take ownership over our ideas of self and community care. Capitalism insists that health is something that must be bought, and only certain people can attain it. The fact is that our wholeness, our power to heal, our ability to care for ourselves and each other cannot be bought or sold. It can only be practiced. And this practice is one of the most painful and joyous experiences I can think of. It is the beautiful mess in communal spaces and alive with laughter through tears. Harm reduction practitioners are using all sorts of language to express the nuance and complexity of a practice that cares for our bodies, minds, hearts, and communities. From a conversation with Elliott Fukui:

> We're supporting each other in the disabled community by fucking surviving right now in this mess of a pandemic. And we're doing that through joyful practice. And that is actually the lineage and legacy of the queer and trans movement. Our movement started on dance floors, and in bars, and in alleyways, and in meat-packing trucks. Joy is also a part of movement and the secret sauce in harm reduction. When we only focus on the trauma, and the crisis—this is where a lot of people make mistakes when they're thinking about safety planning, or even why I think a lot of mainstream approaches don't tend to work longer term—it leaves people to feel like their whole identity is centered around the belief that *You're a crisis* or *You're something that needs to be managed*, and the belief that your relationships all revolve around crisis, that doesn't move somebody towards accountability or healing.
>
> So, we create spaces for joy, practicing joy as a part of harm reduction practice, as a part of liberation practice, because that is what we have to strive for. Even after the Pulse nightclub

> shooting, all of us were afraid and grieving. But then Pride came around, and our asses were all out in the streets again, and half naked, and in our fucking glitter, and living our best lives. And that is what the Black Panthers taught us, that is what Harriet Tubman taught us. . . . It is the joy that calls our people into us, and toward us.
>
> That's why I love it when communities that struggle together also celebrate together and build joyful spaces together, because that is one harm reduction practice of combatting depression and anxiety and trauma. When we only focus on *there's something wrong*, and not *I actually have the control to decide today to do something joyful, and to see how that impacts me, and my community*, then we miss out on an opportunity to deepen healing work. So, yeah, *joy practice* is critical harm reduction strategy for of us.

Liberatory Harm Reduction and Healing Justice allow us to ask what would happen if we intentionally and collectively defined *wellness* and *wholeness* so that we could each come to our own unique understanding of our ideal functioning. What if the medical model and social services accepted our definitions and acknowledged the spectrum we exist in relationship to—and as our status moves one way or the other on the spectrum, we could either seek the support we need or offer support to others? What if, every few months, we checked in with ourselves and each other about our definitions to see if we needed them to shift or change to reflect and embrace our bodies and minds in the given moment?

HEALING JUSTICE

A STRATEGY THAT ASKS US TO INTERVENE, ADDRESS AND TRANSFORM THE ROOT CAUSES OF GENERATIONAL TRAUMA AND RACISM.

A HEALING JUSTICE STRATEGY MUST INCLUDE...

DISABILITY JUSTICE

ENVIRONMENTAL JUSTICE

HARM REDUCTION

TRANSFORMATIVE JUSTICE

REPRODUCTIVE JUSTICE

My Story Is Not on Lifetime Television: Self-Harm/Reduction

Research consistently shows that self-harm is not suicidal behavior*; instead, it's a coping mechanism, a tool, a stress reliever, and, in my case, a way to get back into my body and feel some control.

One of my earliest memories of self-harming is around age four. Almost every night I would use my teeth to gnaw the paint off the headboard to my bed, and then use the paint chips to make cuts in the gums between my teeth until I could taste blood and holes would form between my teeth. As I grew older, my methods became more direct, to inflict the maximum amount of pain in my mouth while leaving the least amount of evidence. By the time I was six, I had a clear ritual. I knew how to heal the wounds, and I knew that I could not stop. Looking back, I don't know how I figured all of that out so young, but I know we are born to heal. Somehow, I knew that self-harm was healing me and that the wound care I was doing was a critical part of my survival. I do believe that in some of us, harm reduction is innate; it forms as adaptive responses to trauma, and it is our resilience and creativity pointing us toward solutions.

When I started leaving home and sleeping outside, I was around other people who picked, cut, burned, banged their heads, or used poison to make themselves sick and bring themselves back. It was a revelation. The setup of my sleeping arrangements at that time was either in bushes in Tompkins Square Park or in squats. This meant that we witnessed each other—there was no privacy—

* Dr. Laura Janine Mintz states, "Research consistently shows that there is a relationship between suicide and self-harm; people that self-harm are about a hundred times more likely than people that don't self-harm to commit suicide. However, the motivations and strategies that people who self-harm use are more complex, and that self-harm is frequently used as a coping mechanism for all kinds of concerns." See Melissa K. Y. Chan, et al., "Predicting suicide following self-harm: systematic review of risk factors and risk scales," *British Journal of Psychiatry* 209 (no. 4, October 2016): 277–83, doi:10.1192/bjp.bp.115.170050.

and that witnessing broke the isolation, even though I don't think we ever discussed what we were actually doing. Not being alone with my rituals was totally new to me, and even though it still took me about ten years to stop lying and hiding my self-harm, feeling safer in the knowledge that there were places in the world where I could be my whole messy self gave me the fortification to keep working on my healing.

At the age I began to self-harm, I had already witnessed and experienced violence. Violence trains us to lie, I think, and teaches us to do whatever we can to avoid being hurt again. Social services and social workers also teach us to lie because we learn to say what is required in order to get a bus pass or help with an application or some other need. Social services need us to fit into criteria and to comply so grants may be fulfilled.

The clean syringe handed to me by the outreach worker in the park when I was in my late teens introduced me to the concepts of how to take care of my cuts and slashes, safety planning, and basic hygiene. By that point, I had encountered social workers enough to know how, and when, to lie. It took me a second to catch up to the fact that I could tell the truth to these grown-ups—the outreach workers—because they were interested in genuinely supporting me to take care of myself on my own terms and to live into whatever version of being well worked for me in that moment. I was not judged for what I thought were my worst behaviors: getting paid for having sex or being sexual, using drugs, self-injuring, and lying to everyone I knew so that I could get as much time as possible away from home. The feeling of being accepted and respected for wherever I was at was so fundamentally different from anything I had experienced that it took me a long time to stop lying to the Streetwork Project case workers. Later, I realized that so much of what the outreach workers were practicing was the art of truly trauma-centered care.

In *Girls Do What They Have to Do to Survive,* YWEP identified self-harm as a form of resilience. We created the term *self-harm resilience* to describe this powerful harm reduction strategy:

> Some young people also find cutting or injuring themselves as a soothing form of self-care. This led us at YWEP to rename what some people call "self-injury" or "self-mutilation." We now call it "self harm resilience." We call it this because so many young people who filled out the Girls Fight Back Journal said that using controlled self-injury was a practice that was an important form of coping. Young people said that they weren't doing this to hurt, they wrote they were doing it to feel better. Many girls wrote stories of body modification, like giving themselves and their friends tattoos and piercings. Respondents talked about reclaiming their body through body modification. "Body modification can mean body autonomy to girls," according to one journal writer. Other girls wrote about more complicated forms of self-harm resilience like breaking bones or making cuts or burns on their skin. Rather than judge this as "bad" or "dangerous," we decided to use harm reduction as a way to understand this. We respect that girls wrote these stories of self-harm resilience in the section of our journal that asked "how do you heal or take care of yourself?" It's important to remember that everyone uses self-harm resilience for different reasons. For example, self-harm resilience was identified as a way for girls to be in control of their own bodies. One girl talked about self-harm resilience as being empowering because she was hurting herself as opposed to someone else hurting her. Self-harm resilience can be a way to prevent or come out of disassociation. Some girls said that it can be a way to deal with being triggered because it draws you back into your body and into the present moment.

Later, after I found a therapist who uses and believes in harm reduction, I learned that so many of us self-harm because we are seeking proprioception. Proprioception is a neuro-physiological process. It is one of our bodies' most critical senses and satisfies the need to feel how our bodies take up space and relate to other parts of our body. Proprioception is the way we unconsciously collect information our surroundings to help us navigate the world. It is an essential function that helps with balance; helps us gauge where we are in relation to other objects and people; and works with our muscles, joints, and tendons to incorporate this information. One possible impact of trauma is that our sense of proprioception can be thrown off, and through the experience of pain, self-harm can help us "land back" into our bodies and reorient us.

Feminists who practice harm reduction taught me that self-harm also interrupts dissociation, which happens when we distance ourselves from our emotions and the world around us. For some of us, dissociation may include detaching from pieces of ourselves and forming new parts with memories and experiences. Dissociation includes so many things, from spacing out in front of the TV to using drugs or alcohol. Among trauma therapists, there is a belief that dissociation is a way that our brains protect us, because it prevents us from fully processing overwhelming danger or emotional or physical pain.

Many people who have labored in childbirth describe "leaving their bodies," as a kind of protection from the physical pain of the moment. Self-harm was one important tool allowing me to regulate my dissociation; I know I would not have survived my trauma experience without drugs, self-harm, and dissociation. I cannot understand why being dissociative is so devalued or characterized as negative. I have come to understand it as a form of "sanism" to value some kinds of mental health functioning over others. Turning off parts of my brain, disconnecting my experiences, and dealing with them in pieces was lifesaving. When we recognize that our body seeks things for healing purposes and release from the shame, we can begin to think about tools for staying safer. Liberatory Harm Reduction gives us the rare opportunity to feel accepted, witnessed, and not judged for what the world sees as morally wrong behaviors, and we can learn to care for ourselves in complex and beautiful ways. When YWEP renamed self-injury as self-harm resilience, we made a trauma-thoughtful, harm reductionist move to shine on our tender spots and reclaim them as strategy. We put Rumi's poem into action—*The wound is the place where the light enters you*—and challenged the world to meet us there.

Healing Justice in Action: Sage Community Health Collective and Casa de Salud

Sage Community Health Collective, based in Chicago, and Casa de Salud, located in Albuquerque, NM, are examples of health care providers that practice community and collective care. Both were formed by longtime harm reductionist practitioners who were also part of building our current ideas of Healing Justice. Sage, founded by Tanuja Jagernauth, Stacy Erenberg, Jennifer Wade, and Liz Apple, provided low-cost, sliding-scale acupuncture, therapy, fat liberation–based food healing, and body work, and offered community space for all those working on healing. Both Stacy and Tanuja had been a part of YWEP for years, and when Sage was formed, I was lucky to be on the founding Community Advisory Council.

I asked Stacy why they decided to form Sage as a Liberatory Harm Reduction, Healing Justice space. She responded:

> When Liz, Jen, Tanuja, and I were visioning together, we knew that any project we created that was going to be working on health care access was going to also be trying to dismantle the medical-industrial complex. It had to be a harm reduction project, because there was no other way to actually create a space where people who experience marginalization could have autonomy over their bodies in the healing process. We learned how to do harm reduction from young people in the sex trade and street economy, from YWEP, and that was precious to us. We said we want to create space to fuck it up, fuck up the MIC, and inter-

> rupt how Eastern medicine has been co-opted by Western laws and values. We wanted to break down this hierarchy of who has knowledge, who has a "special" knowledge, because part of Healing Justice is reclaiming practices that you know have been taken away from us. To take back healing practices that BIPOC folks have used for centuries and were taken away because of colonialism. That's one piece of not relying on the MIC—reclaiming our history and our practices. None of us identify as East Asian, and where we learned acupuncture was in the West, and the Western version of it, too. We had a lot of discussion internally about cultural appropriation: *Who is this medicine for?* But I think it was inspiring to know that the Young Lords and Black Panther Party and Mutulu Shakur and the history of detox acupuncture was a part of our movement history and was actually about self-determined healing that came from Black and Brown people working together to improve our collective well-being.

Sage closed in 2016, after seven years of operation. The loss of Sage in Chicago is still felt every day, and nothing has replaced the care they provided to street-based people seeking harm reduction health care solutions in a nonjudgmental, trauma-centered setting.

Casa De Salud, a similar project based in Albuquerque, is a primary care clinic founded in 2004. They have offered Reiki, acupuncture, syringe exchange, and no-cost services, as well as accepting insurance and Medicaid, from the beginning. They state:

> We were established by health professionals from the medical system, *promotoras* with the Kalpulli Izkalli organization, and community volunteers. We shared the vision of creating a clinic that offered affordable, high-quality, holistic health services to anyone in need. Maintaining the dignity of both the patient and the clinician were essential aspects of our shared vision. We initially named our clinic Topahkal ("house of medicine" in the Aztec language) by the suggestion of a founding member. The medical clinic began in a small, two-bedroom casita on Ann Street, located in the heart of the South Valley of

> Albuquerque. We offered limpias, reiki, massage, herbs, and medical consultation. Our clinic grew by word of mouth, particularly in the Mexican American community.

Casa de Salud is a model of health care that rejects healthism and the medical model while providing life-saving integrative interventions that rely on community relationships, volunteers, and spiritual practitioners. I have never had a health care provider to whom I did not have to lie about my drug use and sex trade experiences. But at Casa De Salud, their mission and the goal of their care is to create the conditions for people seeking help to relax into being whole people. They have flourished and embody astounding solidarity and beauty.

I also want to lift up their revolutionary detox program, which was inspired by the Young Lords' Lincoln Detox Program of the 1970s and combines that approach with local tribal medicine practices. The Strong Roots Program at Casa de Salud is described as

> an intensive outpatient opioid addiction treatment program. Our innovative and holistic approach combines evidence-based life-saving maintenance medication treatment with Suboxone (buprenorphine/naloxone) along with traditional healing, east/west medicine, primary care, bodywork (massage), reiki, case management, and civic engagement to support goals for recovery, purpose, community, and joy, in the lives of individuals and families struggling with addictions.

Whenever mainstream service providers, social workers, and those invested in the medical model tell me that it isn't possible to provide harm-reduction services in a primary care setting, or that they are not able to work with drug users on anything other than abstinence, or that liability laws prevent them from working with people who are actively in the sex trade and street economy, I think of these two projects. I also think about the fear that mainstream providers have of our communities and the desire to see us disappear from their case logs and patient lists. At some point, not offering harm reduction strategies becomes a willful investment in our death.

Healing Justice as a Campaign: Street Youth Rise UP!

YWEP created a political campaign called Street Youth Rise UP! that challenged institutions to change the way Chicago sees and treats homeless, home-free, and street-based youth who do what they need to do to survive. The Street Youth Rise UP! campaign was led by Dominique McKinney, the political director and the executive director of YWEP, who worked alongside adult allies Stacy Erenberg, Cindy Ibarra, and Tanuja Jagernauth to create a political-education, healing-based campaign.

The Street Youth Rise UP! website states the three main research findings:

1. Resilience is a stepping-stone to Resistance—this means that the more we take care of ourselves, the more we have the power to fight back
2. Denied help—young people in the sex trade and street economy are being denied help from social services and nonprofits and even police because they are involved in the sex trade, street economy, or are queer or transgender.
3. Institutional violence makes individual violence worse—this means that when someone goes for help (let's say because someone is hurting them) and then they are turned down for help (because they are in the sex trade or another reason) this makes the situation and the experiences much worse.

YWEP then worked to address these three issues in order to build community resilience and fight back against institutional violence. From YWEP's website:

We started a BAD ENCOUNTER LINE. This form can be completed by a young person or a trusted adult. YWEP is documenting when and where we have been denied help from a social service or someone who was supposed to help you like a doctor or police officer. THIS FORM IS ANONYMOUS and helps us figure out who, where and why our community is being turned away from help. We will release quarterly zines naming these institutions with the data about where and from who we are being turned away the most.

Healing in Action is the part of our campaign that teaches us how to do our own self-exams, about herbs and how we can take care of our bodies in case we can't get to a doctor or we are denied help. We made a universal self-exam guide and a Healing in Action zine with tips and tools for going to the doctor, for how to take care of yourself if you can't get to a doctor and what to do if you are denied help. Tanuja Jagernauth worked with us to learn how to make our own herbal pills from items we can find at the drug store. We have made our own pills for anxiety, headaches, depression and to soothe the bladder. You can come to our office or speak with a youth outreach worker to get information about our herbal medicine. We have also learned how to do NADA—an ear acupressure (no needles just these little beads) that helps with detox from drugs or alcohol. NADA also can help us just relax. Ask a youth outreach worker or come to our office to get ear acupressure.

Chicago Street Youth in Motion is our grassroots organizing city wide task force for street-based youth. This task force is for all genders. For more information or to get involved email. Our task force just wrote a Street Youth Bill of Rights and we will be asking social services to sign on to this Bill and display this poster in their offices to make sure that all young people know our rights and that we can't be denied help!

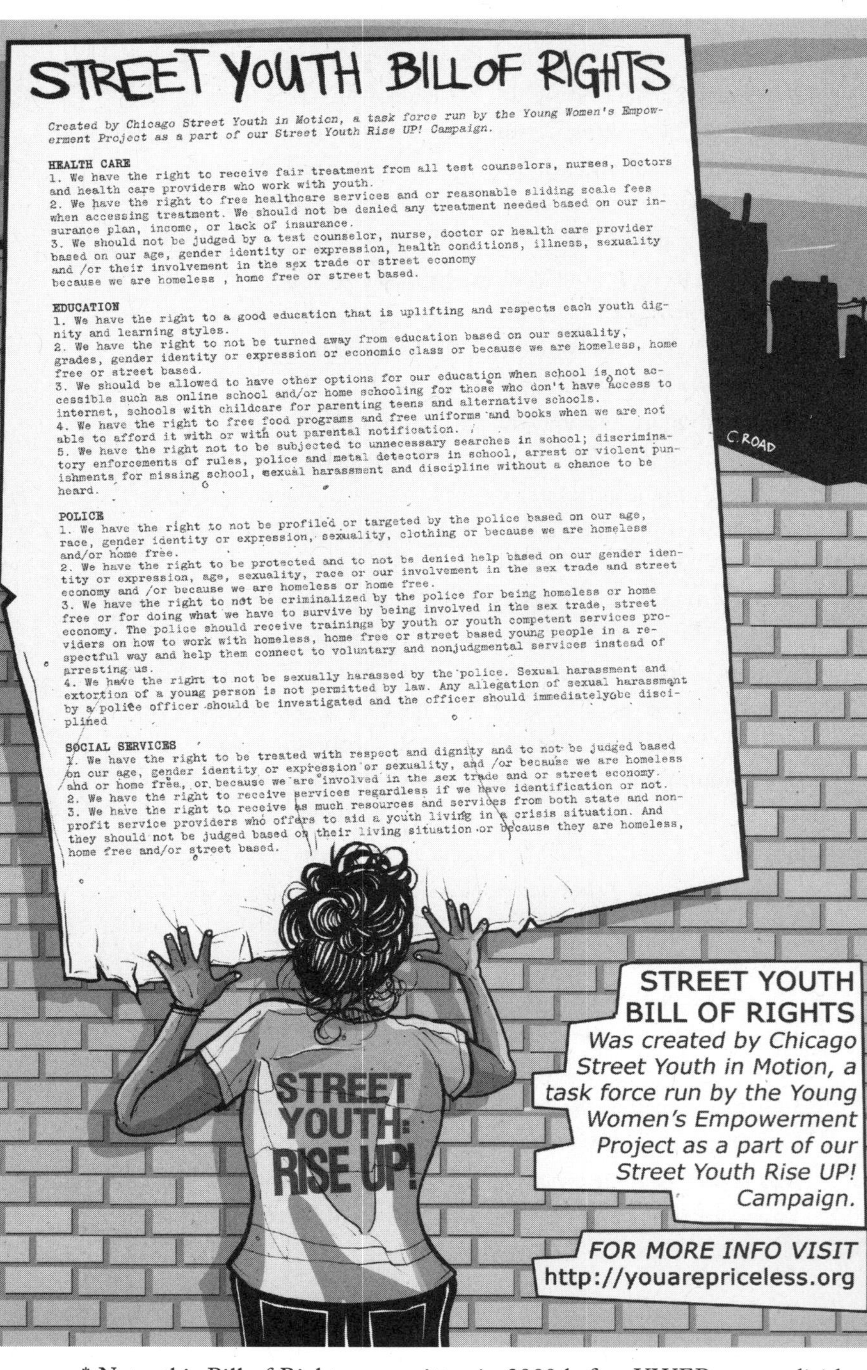

* Note: this Bill of Rights was written in 2009 before YWEP was explicitly abolitionist.

revolutionary love notes

The Intersection of Healing Justice and Harm Reduction in Liberatory Practice

Conversation with Cara Page and Erica Woodland

Cara Page and Erica Woodland are two of my favorite thinkers and activists in my life, and in the current movement for our collective liberation. I met Cara in 2004 through Reproductive Justice organizing, right before she cofounded Kindred Southern Healing Justice Collective, and we became collaborators and chosen family members almost immediately. Cara, Kindred, and Aurora Levins Morales are the founders of the modern incarnation of the Healing Justice framework, naming it in 2005, after Hurricane Katrina devastated Black and Brown communities in the South and local healers created mass mobilization to respond to state and interpersonal violence and urgent healthcare needs. When Cara cofounded Kindred, I was honored to be a part of the first Vision Council that served as an advisory board for the project.

Erica and I met through being raised in the harm reduction community—neither of us can pin down the exact moment we connected. Since 2019, Erica and I have been "thought partners"

—we have a twice-monthly appointment to share thoughts and ideas and solve problems together. His work founding and directing the National Queer and Trans Therapists of Color Network (NQTTCN) beautifully combines his work as a healer, harm reductionist, and activist. I am guided and inspired by the brilliant work of NQTTCN regularly.

Cara Page: I feel like Healing Justice is wrestling with public health. I mean, right now I'm doing a response to that to shut down the Irwin County Detention Center.* And we're calling it a Healing Justice and public health response because . . . we're wrestling with what that means. What we're doing is holding public health accountable for what happened at Irwin County. Because what some of the folks, the physicians that are writing the statement we're working on, who didn't know about Healing Justice, all they're saying is, people hide under the shroud of public health being this progressive land and so they don't have to be accountable anymore for their actions. And so I'm talking to folks inside of public health that are interested in using Healing Justice to push open this political conversation.

And I was like, great. If that's how we could use it, then I'm willing to do the dance. But yes, the fear of co-optation by public health is real—especially in light of what happened to harm reduction and the co-optation of that strategy.

Shira: How do we help them understand how seamless the relationship is between Healing Justice and Liberatory Harm Reduction?

---

* The campaign to shut down the Irwin County Detention Center was catalyzed by Dawn Wooten, a Black woman and nurse who blew the whistle on the systemic abuse of immigrants and hazardous working conditions for staff in Ocilla, Georgia. Abuses include nonconsensual and unnecessary gynecological procedures and massive medical neglect and abuse as documented by multiple Georgia advocacy groups.

Cara: Erica and I have been doing a lot of trainings. Honestly, if I think about it, I don't think most healers are rooted in harm reduction.

I was rooted in harm reduction by way of anti–population control and anti-eugenics work. I wasn't doing a syringe exchange, but I was very aware of it through the Reproductive Justice world. I think the disconnect was to not acknowledge more loudly that harm reduction was a part of the lineage. So, Erica and I have been saying that more in our trainings, but how that lands—we have to unpack it. Because there's just so much mythology on what harm reduction is.

And perhaps that's naive, but I was like, *Oh, snap, people really don't know what harm reduction is!*

Erica Woodland: There's people moving harm reduction into the world, but then there's a lack of coordination, and people aren't rooted in the strategy wholesale, you know what I mean? I think the roots of harm reduction were very much about, *How are we clapping back at the medical-industrial complex so that our people don't die?* You know?

There was much more organization back in the late '80s and '90s, but now with the mainstreaming and professionalization of harm reduction, I mean, people are literally not even getting their hands dirty. Like for real, they're wearing suits and ties at conferences, you know? Not to say that there's anything wrong with that, but when I came into harm reduction there was something so comforting about how close it was to people. You know? It really was led by us and for us before all this professionalization took hold.

When I was in my early twenties looking for a spiritual practice, my spiritual practice was harm reduction. The people who are most disposable, who are experiencing the most suffering, those are my people, and that's who I want to be in community with. Now, I think that the same is true for Healing Justice as was for harm reduction back then. It feels like Healing Justice practitioners who are on the ground, really close to what the needs are and what's happening, articulated an intervention around those needs and have that political framing because of the conditions. Does that make sense?

Cara: What harm reduction did for me is strengthened my analysis on a street economy or survival economy.* It's been called different things, right? When I was talking about Healing Justice at the beginning, way at the beginning, and just having conversations, I was actually very focused on the fact that people could not access different modalities of care that were outside of Western-based medicine, because it would never be covered by insurance.

And then I was also organizing care workers and healers and asking how would they be able to access care. I was working with some elder healers who are like, *I can't even get care, but I'm providing it.* And so, I entered through an economic lens and then that lens got a little bit decentralized.

Let's talk about everyone who's being criminalized. Domestic workers are criminalized. Sex workers are criminalized. Healers are being criminalized for their practice. Healing Justice is a strategy that addresses *all* care-based economies. But right now, the "care-based" economy analysis that's put out there by healers and economic justice organizers is anti–sex work and anti–street-based economy.

People in the sex trade are some of the original caregivers. The frame around worker exploitation prohibits many organizers

---

* YWEP labeled anything that people do to make money untaxed as the street economy. This includes everything from trading sex for money to drug sales to selling socks or batteries on the trains. We even included some kinds of childcare and elder care work as connected to the street economy.

from seeing people in the sex trade as workers and as caregivers. I don't really know what it would take for the US labor movement to include the street economy. Like, it needs to be exploded.

Cara: Boom. Exactly.

Erica, what you were saying about harm reduction as spiritual—I was definitely weeping a little because not only do I feel similarly, but like, if I didn't have harm reduction, I don't know if I would have reconnected with myself spiritually. I feel so indebted to how harm reduction recentered my spirituality through reminding me that I not only had reasons to survive, but that I had a value in helping others survive. I wonder if a lot of Healing Justice practitioners realize the spiritual component of harm reduction.

Cara: No, I don't think so.

Erica: One of the things that I was just going to say is that ride-or-die harm reduction could really fuck up some of the dynamics around Healing Justice right now, because I feel like there's a lot of spiritual performance among healers. And I'm like, *What if you were faced with active drug users who are HIV-positive or engaging in sex work or living outside? What if you were forced to actually interface with the folks who are considered most disposable in our world?* That's not "clean" and pretty. Your whites are going to get dirty. You know what I mean? And it reminds me of when I used to do street outreach—there were people that worked across the street, and they would see us out there at 5:00 a.m., like three times a week. And they'd be like, "What are you guys doing over here?" They nicknamed us the "Little Angels of Jesus." And I was like, I am not a Christian, but I understand what you see, you see people who are dedicated and consistent and [with] radical commitment to people's dignity and humanity. That, to me, is the piece that brought me to harm reduction and brought me to the work that I'm doing now, you know? Because anything that is wholesale against the dignity of the people who are most disposable, I can't get with that. I think there's a lot of healers who need to work at a syringe exchange.

Erica, you just named what would happen inside Healing Justice if harm reduction was more centered. What would happen inside harm reduction, mainstream harm reduction, if practitioners were aware of Healing Justice?

Erica: I think the thing that immediately comes to mind is I don't want to be orienting around just "reducing harm." That can't be the end point. The communities that I worked with in the context of doing strictly harm reduction work, people were engaging in some of the most transformative healing processes in jails, in prison, on the street. It all comes back to how we are navigating and facing into and addressing intense human suffering.

I should not have been doing the work I was doing cause I wasn't trained up, but that's how harm reduction works. I feel like I learned so much by witnessing what people were healing through in conditions that were unimaginable to me. So, I think that the Healing Justice frame in its true form could offer: *What would it mean to consider that healing is always available to us actually, regardless of the situations that we're in?* and *What's the healing that needs to happen inside of the harm reduction community?* I know HJ is getting co-opted by Karens, but I feel like mainstream harm reduction is one of the most racist spaces I've ever worked in. Harm reduction is so important. Why are y'all so inept around navigating race? Like, you all know this shit came from BIPOC communities.

Cara: It's just like, what is the relationship? I think there's human suffering, but I also think there's the land, there's Earth, suffering. And people just have this deep sigh of relief and grief when we ask them to map *What is your relationship to land? What is your relationship to body? What is your relationship to economy? What is your relationship to spirit?*

What would that mean to build power and liberation and heal from some of these things that we've had to go through to be here?

What if harm reduction was asking the question, *What does it mean to build power?*

Erica: Here's the thing. The mainstream harm reduction community is not inside that conversation about building our collective power. And despite issues I have with some of the harm reduction organizations I've been a part of, fundamentally, those projects are centered in *What does it mean to provide care and build power?* I do think there are plenty of examples where people are committed to holding both of those ideas together.

But, on the whole, it's like we almost have parallel play happening in harm reduction. We should all be moving toward the same thing. But we're not. And some of the ways that people are moving are actually counter to building power, because I do think there are actors who don't want, specifically, the most marginalized people to build power. They're not really interested in the redistribution of power and resources. They're interested in replicating the structures of domination—and it might not be wholly conscious, but I think I've seen that, as folks who were OGs on the ground, [who were] super about it.

The difference, I think, between mainstream harm reduction and grassroots BIPOC-led harm reduction is that we're building power, and we're building it while we connect back to care. Taking care of ourselves and each other, while building power—to me, that is Healing Justice. And that is the harm reduction that we're practicing.

Erica: The title of this book, *Saving Our Own Lives*, just intervenes around the whole direct-service model. It gets you all the way together in a couple of words.

Cara: I guess I just want to talk a little bit about the impact of the MIC on people who are currently or formerly incarcerated, who are institutionalized, who are sex workers. To me, that's also a critical connection between harm reduction and Healing Justice, because our people deserve not only to get access to care but to understand how the industries, private corporations, prisons, all the things, Big Pharma, have built their industries literally on our backs.

That, to me, is critical. That's why I think I'm going more through an abolitionist anti-MIC lens, which is part of the Healing Justice analysis, but gets lost.

I am a collaborator of the Healing Histories Project with Anjali Taneja, Susan Raffo, and other partners.* We are co-curating an MIC timeline to map the laws and policies on sex work, immigration, queer, trans, and intersex people, and locate the connections to Big Pharma and state regulations, eugenics, and population control.

It is so wrapped and intertwined as an extension of slavery and colonization from the past to present to our futures. If we do

* About the Healing Histories Project from the website: We are healers, medical practitioners, organizers, media makers, cultural and memory workers who believe that all deserve care and support during times of crisis, vulnerability & resistance. We come together to inform and shape a vision for collective care and safety while integrating models of wellness that seek to transform and intervene on medical violence, harms, and abuses rooted in racism and capitalism. We are engaging individuals, communities and institutions to remember these abuses and harms by catalyzing research, action and movement-building strategies. We do this through the creation of popular education tools, workshop curriculum, cultural and political events and more. The Healing Histories Project works in solidarity with many health and healing practitioners/workers by holding with dignity and respect the lives and communities they care for and by disrupting abuses of the state.

not confront and dismantle the MIC machine it will accelerate in times of war and massive incarceration to dispose of us. I really need people to wrestle with oppression and systemic power inside of harm reduction and Healing Justice to really understand how this plays out.

Reproductive Justice is one of the places where I've met the most hardcore BIPOC Liberatory Harm Reductionists.

Erica: I think the primary definition of harm reduction that has guided my work is around really contextualizing the choices that people have available to them under the conditions of structural violence that we're living in. And this piece around behavior change—not looking at that in a vacuum. Looking at behaviors that are considered "harmful" or behaviors that are criminalized and actually teasing out where is the real harm? Is it in the thing itself? Or is it in the criminalization of that thing? What are the options and resources that people need so that they have more choices? But people get to still do what they do. Right? Harm reduction is the real centering of the inherent dignity of every being, period.

I think it's about having real conversations about what are some collective consequences of substance use, sex work, HIV—not to blame people for their individual choices but to actually be like, *What does it mean to address those collectively instead of holding individual people responsible for choices that they're making?*

I also think, *What if there's a wholesale acceptance of all kinds of behavior that the rest of the world see as taboo*? Right? People use drugs, right? People are fucking, people are paying for sex. Right? People are living with HIV. We don't have to give somebody a scarlet letter because of the circumstances of their life.

Cara: Yeah. I love what you just said. How do we honor our survival strategies—where are we not targeted or criminalized for our behavior or our needs or our desires?

Another important piece on harm reduction is about the street economy and being anticapitalist. When I read what YWEP put out on this, it changed my work and our work in the Reproductive Justice movement—or at least those who were listening to youth and sex workers. Thank you, YWEP, for saying this—the street economy is good shit. These are actually ancestral technologies. These are our survival strategies. This is real work, and we cannot be bought or stolen. We are priceless! It's the name of YWEP's website—youarepriceless.org.

Because everything else says that we are expendable and worth nothing, but everything that we list inside of Liberatory Harm Reduction—if I use drugs, I am not worthless, if I need to do sex work, I am adding to the survival economy—you all just flipped the whole fucking narrative. YWEP said, and a practice rooted in Liberatory Harm Reduction said, *I'm in power and we can be in power together.* If we move in formation with this shared understanding, we're doing what we need to do, because society doesn't give a fuck about whether we live or die.

I was like, that's my definition. You Are Priceless. [laughs]

It's so powerful. I got goosebumps like ten times this during this call, I like almost cried twice. I did cry that one time. 'Cause it is spiritual.

Cara: This makes me think about TJ [Transformative Justice] too, because before I knew what TJ was, I had protocol when I was a kid: do whatever I needed to do to keep my mother out of the hospital and my father out of jail—choosing not to call the police every time my father beat my mom or one of his girlfriends. This also involved my altars in my rooms as a kid. I was like, okay, well, this is my protection. But what will I do to make sure he doesn't come for these women? And I would decide in my mind when it was time to tell them, *You should probably leave and not stay in this relationship.*

Like I would straight up tell them, y'all. *You know, I think it's time for you to go before things get hot and get real.* I eventually told my dad this because he didn't know. And then we went through a huge healing process that lasted for many years until he passed. I told him, *I told your girlfriends to get out of the way before shit got real because your anger and rage was large and I wanted them to know and I wanted you to not be arrested.*

This was my protocol. I don't know where I found out about harm reduction, but it was an affirmation of what I needed to do to survive. Like, yes, you can make your own plan. Children and youth can make our own fucking plan without adults, and it doesn't have to involve the prison-industrial complex. You can do all sorts of things to protect and defend ourselves and each other. I could map different ways I've done that to avoid, for me *not* to choose, to go into the sex trade, which has happened multiple times, but to decide [about] making the choice. Feeling like I had fucking agency to decide what was powerful. And people just don't talk about that. Knowing that I have survival protocol, and this will get me to the next place. I'm talking as like a nine-year-old Black girl saying, *I'm going to fucking change this reality. This is not the end of my game.* That is Liberatory Harm Reduction.

Harm reduction gave me affirmation. And it saved me.

Yeah, we both have survivor moms.

Erica: Makes me think—that we have a right to survive, and we have a right to have access to the things that we need to survive, period, point blank. That, I think, is the piece that ties Healing Justice, Reproductive Justice, harm reduction, Transformative Justice, and Disability Justice together. As you know, this is non-negotiable.

Cara: That's beautiful. That's right. But this worth piece is very powerful. The Shame. To move through shame. I never called it that. I didn't say, *We're moving through shame now*, but the people that I chose to surround myself with, we were like, *Fuck you, shame*, like, we were willing to say, *You are better than your shame.*

That was Claudine O'Leary who named our website youarepriceless.org.

Cara: I was like, *Fuck yes, we are priceless.* How many times do you hear that? I was like, *Stop it. Stop everything.* It was beautiful, so simple. The worth, the worth piece, and the shame. That would have killed me if I didn't have other ways to live beyond the shame. Healing Justice wants to reckon with the institutions that shame us and imagine something new, affirming, rooted in power and transformation and Liberatory Harm Reduction that you are naming, Shira, in this book.

Erica: Right. And to actually put the shame where it belongs, which is on the state.

I just had a realization, because one of National Queer and Trans Therapists of Color Network's values is exquisite care, and I'm like, *Oh, right, that comes from harm reduction, actually*, because that was how I was trained up.

I didn't even need to be trained up cause that's my natural way of being, but that was one of the things that I received really explicitly: you go out of your way to treat those who get mistreated the most with all the dignity and respect. Not in some performative way or condescending or paternalistic way, but in some way [that honors] what people are able to survive and heal through.

And, ultimately, it's why I chose to get more skills. I shouldn't have been doing case management with people much older than me who had lived experiences that I didn't have. I did the best that I could, but ultimately I was like, *Oh, this is irresponsible. These folks need a certain level of expertise that I don't have.* And no one's going to give it to me, you know?

Cara: We need to hear more from practitioners who understand their role of [providing] safety and reducing harm and bringing dignity and respect to care and healing practices.

Yeah, I'm going to be sitting with this for a long, long time. I'm so grateful. This conversation is what happens when we also weave our whole selves together. This was a real gift. Thank you.

We Are Not the Problem—We Are the Solution

Dominique McKinney is a fierce mother and activist and harm reductionist born and raised in Chicago, IL. She grew up as a ward of the state and faced many challenges with institutional violence. Her life experience has led her on a journey to continue to fight back for change and accountability within those very same institutions that are causing violence in homeless, street-based youths' lives today. Dominique has been organizing since the age of fourteen. Her experience led her to become the very first youth executive director of the Young Women's Empowerment Project at age twenty-two. She has engaged in activism against many injustices including Reproductive Justice, sex workers' rights, gender justice, juvenile justice reform, and her very own passion, holding those institutions that cause violence in our lives accountable. In 2009, Dominique founded the Street Youth Rise UP! campaign—a youth-led campaign that focuses on the youth leadership and voices of street-based youth impacted by these systems and on creating safe spaces for youth to heal while providing peer-to-peer outreach and conducting youth participatory action research. In 2018, Dominique was granted the Soros Justice Fellowship and is now using this fellowship to revamp the youth work that needs to happen while challenging state practices that funnel vulnerable youth into juvenile and adult justice systems.

Shira: What do you see as the difference between the harm reduction that we practiced at YWEP, that I'm calling Liberatory Harm Reduction in this book, and the harm reduction that you see in public health settings?

Dominique: In a way, the harm reduction we practiced at YWEP is kind of indescribable because it changes so much from person to situation. It's a feeling and a set of strategies. But those can change and grow over time. Liberatory Harm Reduction teaches you how to be aware of yourself and how to name your needs. I felt like the tools and the support offered to me were helpful because it gave me space to grow. YWEP didn't shut me down and it didn't shut me out because I didn't get it right or I didn't do it perfectly.

Liberatory Harm Reduction is a way of life for me, and I'm pretty sure that's true for a lot of young people who grew up at YWEP. It's just who we are now. It became a part of our everyday life. What we chose to eat, how we chose to stay safe. It wasn't like, *Okay, don't go out there with a knife.* It was like, *I know you have to protect yourself, so let's think through the risk of having a knife on you versus the risk of not having one. Like if you're stopped by a cop and you're carrying a knife, that's a weapons charge, sure, but the reality of making it back to your spot if you don't have a weapon—that has its own risk.* So yeah, Liberatory Harm Reduction is a way we can hold all of those parts of someone's life and not judge or give an easy answer.

I feel like harm reduction done in public health settings is an injustice to what harm reduction really is, especially because they so rarely use Transformative Justice and healing. I'll give an example. There was a young person who was having suicidal ideation, and to cope with those feelings they used self-injury. They cut in the bathroom of the public health social service I worked at. Workers there got so alarmed and were like, *We've got to call an ambulance.* I'm like, *No, no, no! Let me check in with this person and talk with them.* In the back office, I put together a kit that we used to have at YWEP with alcohol, cleaning pads, and triple-antibiotic gel. Then I talked to the young person about what was going on and gave them the kit. I was able to meet them where they were at so they didn't feel judged, and they could actually talk about what was happening. The other workers there were so in shock by how I handled it and kept wanting to call 911. But I said, *No, don't fucking call the police because that's going to put them into a hospital, or it will somehow add another trauma to their life.* This person needs to just be heard and supported and given safety information about what they're doing. From that talk and that kit, we were able to form a solid bond, and I was able to ride their highs and lows with them without adding any trauma to their experience by calling cops or forcing them to be hospitalized.

It really means truly respecting self-determination, and social services can't get down with that.

Why is harm reduction so important for young people, especially young people in the sex trade, street economy, and sex work?

Because it's all about having ownership and autonomy over ourselves. It gives young people in the sex trade, street economy, and sex work the power to make the decisions that they need to make for themselves in those moments. Because Liberatory Harm Reduction is peer based, it also helps give space for a person to grow and to teach other people. It becomes a way of educating each other on what works and what doesn't work, and ways on how to take better care and just how to survive.

Harm reduction isn't forcing someone to stop doing what they're doing. It looks like helping them know they are in control to make the decisions on their own: that's empowerment. YWEP didn't leave us powerless. I felt powerful even when shit was fucked up. I want young people to know that how they survive does not define who they are. There are always aspects of your survival that are totally within your control. Sometimes the world is so messed up that we get pushed into these situations, and we figure it out. That's the resilience part of it. I want young people to know that they're resilient, that they're smart, that they are capable of doing whatever they put their fucking minds to.

I want adults to understand that young people in the sex trade and street economy are the shit. We survive. We're in the middle of the pandemic and folks are able to just do what they need to do to make it happen for themselves. I want young people to know that they are in control of their own lives, that they are powerful.

What was it like to be director of YWEP?

That was one of the best moments of my life. When I was a kid, I used to dream about this stuff. When I was in foster care growing up, I used to kind of fantasize about there being this cool space that was for young people. Becoming the director of YWEP was the most empowering thing that has happened to me in my life besides being a mother. It just felt surreal. Here I was, a young Black woman as executive director of a nonprofit organization that worked with other young women and trans girls in the sex trade.

I carry it with me even though YWEP is closed now, because I know what works. I've seen how harm reduction really works. Watching other organizations, public health or social services, makes me cry because I am thinking that these organizations get it because they say, *We do harm reduction work. We have youth leadership development. We do Transformative Justice*, but then they're calling the police on young people who are coming for help. They're calling children's services on them. They're requiring

ID and for young people to stick to certain stipulations in order to move around in your space. They have these punitive policies that exclude young people from getting services when they need it.

I'll give you a good example. I was working at another organization that claims to do harm reduction. Whenever they had an issue with a young person in the space, that person would be asked to leave the space or be banned from the space. If a young person and the setting are not a fit, it's not going to work; I get that. But, if we are really using harm reduction, how can we create something with this young person so that they're still able to get their needs met? Because even though they can't be in the space, service providers still have to do due diligence and make sure the young person's needs are getting met. If this is really practicing harm reduction, then meet the young person down the street or somewhere away from the space so they can get the things that they need and not be cut off from access to resources and help.

But harm reduction isn't coddling people, either. For instance, I had a big mouth when I was a young person; I was a debater and used to be combative, questioning everything. YWEP saw it as a positive quality, even though everywhere else in my life—school, group home, everywhere—it was seen as a problem. I had started to feel like that quality was negative about me. But YWEP saw something in me that was like, *Okay, so this person is a debater, that's a good thing. You would be a good organizer and advocate. Here is an opportunity to do an internship to do social justice organizing so you can learn how to take that and fight back against these systems of oppression.*

That's the other thing about harm reduction: there are no experts. We are all just teaching and learning all the time. YWEP was a learning exchange in a way; there were things I learned from YWEP, and there were things YWEP learned from me. And that's what empowerment and Liberatory Harm Reduction looks like too.

You talked about how harm reduction, Transformative Justice, and Healing Justice are connected. Can you talk about how this looked at YWEP?

I think the best example is if you look at Street Youth Rise UP! (SYRU), because it was a Transformative Justice campaign; it wasn't focused on policy. It was focused on transforming the root causes of harm by building up our community's resilience and by holding institutions accountable. Our campaign used the strategy of Healing Justice and was soaked in harm reduction because of who we were.

A portion of the campaign was called "Healing in Action." This was a Healing Justice approach that was intervening in people's experiences with medical neglect and violence and also was holding institutions accountable for how young people in the sex trade and street economy were being treated. On an individual level, we used holistic alternative methods to heal ourselves. YWEP activists learned how to make our own herbal pills using kava kava and astragalus root. Then, we distributed them along with information about how to use them and what to do when you're experiencing discrimination from a doctor, hospital, or clinic.

We created self-exam guides for all bodies and used our outreach to provide one-on-one support and resources. YWEP knew from our research that young people in the sex trade and street economy were being denied help from social services, health care settings, the police. We decided to track this information by starting a second participatory action research project called the "Bad Encounter Line," so that we could report when we were being turned away or harmed by places that were supposed to help us. We used participatory action research as a Healing Justice tool, because it was action that worked to heal our community through the power of story and naming our experiences. We also published it in a zine and distributed it as a callout, so organizations knew we were watching them. We would call those organizations that were being reported by young people as either harmful or neglectful, and we would offer them training and resources to improve their relationships with us and learn how to treat us better.

Tell me more about Street Youth Rise UP! SYRU takes the YWEP campaign to the next level. You founded this new organization with Alex A., Skylar, Desi, and Daph, who were part of the Youth Activist Krew at YWEP.

Street Youth Rise UP! is a youth-led project that focuses on changing the ways Chicago institutions and service providers see and treat LGBTQAGNC and cisgender homeless, home-free,* and street-based youth of color who do what they have to do to survive and are involved in the sex trade and street economy throughout Chicagoland. We use harm reduction, Transformative Justice, peer-to-peer outreach, crisis intervention, participatory action research, and grassroots policy-change approaches to hold institutions accountable to our constituency.

SYRU practices Healing Justice in the ways we were taught by YWEP. We believe we are the solution and have the right to take care of our own bodies in ways that feel good to us. For example, when the pandemic began, SYRU used its knowledge of holistic and herbal medicines from YWEP to create self-care packages for street-based homeless, home-free young people. We also teamed up with a Healing Justice group in New Orleans to provide more packages for folks in the sex trade. Healing Justice for us is practiced in so many ways in our work because we believe in autonomy and self-determination. We use it when handling a crisis, during de-escalations, and during our outreach services.

---

* *Home-free* is a term created by the organizers at YWEP to describe a young person who left home by choice, as a positive step toward self-preservation and self-care, and generally feels like leaving home was the best decision they could make at the time to ensure their survival.

How did YWEP and SYRU change Chicago?

Both YWEP and SYRU changed Chicago by helping to bring the voices and resiliency of youth in the sex trade to the forefront of conversations that are about us. We do this by showing that youth leadership development is real, and young people are leaders and experts in their own lives. With the right support, *all* young people can thrive—not just the ones in schools. We can all be leaders. Our research helped to shine a light on Chicago police violence and abuse. Our work has impacted organizations and intersecting movements working on prison abolition. We have forced social services, institutions, and even movement organizers to look at the ways they engage, address, or especially benefit from institutional violence. I believe we made Transformative Justice, Healing Justice, and harm reduction something that people in Chicago have heard of, partly because of our work, and want to know more about. I believe we made sex workers, people in the sex trade and street economy a homeless or home-free youths and know they could be leaders. It made other people know that they couldn't push us around because we are a force. We made street-based survival a flex!

Applying Liberatory Harm Reduction to Mental Health and Psychiatric Medication

This chapter has been excerpted from the Harm Reduction Guide for Coming off Psychiatric Drugs *by the Icarus Project and Freedom Center.*

Absolutist approaches to drug and sex education teach abstinence, "just say no," and one way for everyone. These work for some people, but not most, and if you don't follow the model you can end up being judged, not helped.

"Harm reduction" is different: pragmatic, not dogmatic. Harm reduction is an international movement in community health education that recognizes there is no single solution for each person, no universal standard of "success" or "failure." Getting rid of the problem is not necessarily the only way. Instead, harm reduction accepts where people are at and educates them to make informed choices and calculated trade-offs that reduce risk and increase wellness. People need information, options, resources, and support so they can move towards healthier living—at their own pace and on their own terms.

Applying harm reduction philosophy to mental health is a new but growing approach. It means not always trying to eliminate "symptoms" or discontinue all medications. It recognizes that people are already taking psychiatric drugs, already trying to come off them, and already living with symptoms—and that in this complicated reality people need true help, not judgment. Harm reduction encourages balancing the different risks involved: the harm from extreme states, as well as the harm from treatments such as adverse drug effects, disempowering labels, and traumatic hospitalization.

Making harm reduction decisions means looking honestly at all sides of the equation: how drugs might help a life that feels out of control, how risky those same drugs might be, and the role of options and alternatives. Any decisions become a process of experimentation and learning, including learning from your own mistakes and changing your goals along the way. Harm reduction accepts all this, believing that the essence of any healthy life is the capacity to be empowered.

Everyone's
experience is
different.

There is no formula for coming off psychiatric drugs. What there is, and what this guide presents, is some common experience, basic research, and important information that can potentially make the process less difficult. Many people successfully come off psychiatric drugs, with or without guidance, while others find it very hard. Many continue on psychiatric drugs because the benefits are greater than the drawbacks. But many people end up staying on psychiatric drugs without ever exploring options, just because they don't know any other way.

When we've relied only on doctors, television, and mainstream sources, it might seem impossible to imagine dealing with our emotional extremes without psychiatric drugs. Maybe we've never heard of anyone going through what we go through without medications. Maybe a prescription was the beginning of people taking our need for help seriously, and medications feel like the only way to recognize that our problems are severe and out of control. And when everyone around us has come to view medication as essential to our survival, considering a new path can feel too risky to even try.

Many of us get help from psychiatric drugs but might not understand how they really work or what the other options are. Some of us never found medications useful, or medications even made our problems worse, and we are ready to try living without them. Sometimes people are torn between the risks of staying on and the risks of going off, or we take multiple drugs and suspect we don't need all of them. Others may want to go off but it's not the right time, or may have tried in the past, experienced a return of frightening symptoms, and decided to go back on for now.

Our paths to healing are unique. Some of us don't need to make any life changes, letting time and patience make change for us. Others may need to make big shifts in nutrition, work, family life, or relationships; we may need to focus more on self-care, expression, art, and creativity; adopt other approaches like peer support, therapy, herbalism, acupuncture, or homeopathy; or find new life interests like going to school or connecting with nature. We may discover that the first step is getting restful sleep; we may need structure to help get us motivated; or to stop taking any recreational drugs or alcohol. Our priorities might be to find a home or a new job; we may need to establish stronger support networks of trusted friends; or it may be important to speak up with greater honesty and vulnerability about what we are going through.

The process might feel mysterious and arbitrary, and an attitude of acceptance and patience is vital. Learning means trial and error.

Because each of us is unique,
it's as if we are navigating
through a labyrinth, getting lost
and finding our way again,
making our own map as we go.

Looking Critically at "Mental Disorders" and Psychiatry

Doctors put people on psychiatric medications for experiences labeled "mental disorders:" extreme emotional distress, overwhelming suffering, ARWR mood swings, unusual beliefs, disruptive behaviors, and mysterious states of madness. Currently millions of people worldwide, including infants and elders, take psychiatric drugs when they are diagnosed with bipolar disorder, schizophrenia, psychosis, depression, anxiety, attention deficit, obsessive-compulsive, or post-traumatic stress [disorders]. The numbers are climbing every day.

For many people, psychiatric drugs are very useful. Putting the brakes on a life out of control, being able to function at work, school, and in relationships, getting to sleep, and keeping a lid on emotional extremes can all feel lifesaving. The sense of relief is sometimes dramatic, and the medications can stir very powerful emotions, and even feelings of salvation. At the same time, the help psychiatric drugs offer many people can leave little room to see more to the picture: others experience these drugs as negative, harmful, and even life-threatening. As a result, it is rare in society to find a clear understanding of how and why these drugs work, or an honest discussion of risks, alternatives, and how to come off them if people want to.

Many doctors and TV ads tell people that psychiatric medication is necessary for a biological illness, just like insulin for diabetes. They promote the idea that the drugs correct chemical imbalances and treat brain abnormalities. The truth is different, however. "Biology" and "chemical imbalances" have become simplistic sound bites to persuade people to put their faith in doctors and quick fixes. These words are in fact much more complicated and unclear. Biological factors (such as nutrition, rest, and food allergies) affect everything we experience: biological "cause" or "basis" plants the belief that medication is the key to solving our problems. To say something has a biological cause, basis, or underpinning can give a message that the solution must always be a medical one and that "treatment" has to include psychiatric drugs. Once people have a diagnosis and start taking medication, it is easy to think of the medications as physically necessary for survival.

Not only is there no solid science behind viewing mental disorders as simple malfunctions of biology "corrected" by drugs, but many people with even the most severe diagnosis of schizophrenia or bipolar go on to recover completely without medication. The experiences that get labeled mental disorders are not "incurable" or always "lifelong": they are more mysterious and unpredictable. For some people, psychiatric drugs are helpful tools that change consciousness in useful ways, but they are not medically necessary treatments for illness. Once you acknowledge this, more options become thinkable. And the potential risks of psychiatric drugs come under greater scrutiny, because they are very serious—including chronic illness, mental impairment, dependency, worse psychiatric symptoms, and even risk of early death.

Universal Declaration of Mental Rights and Freedoms

1. That all human beings are created different. That every human being has the right to be mentally free and independent.
2. That every human being has the right to feel, see, hear, sense, imagine, believe, or experience anything at all, in any way, at any time.
3. That every human being has the right to behave in any way that does not harm others or break fair and just laws.
4. That no human being shall be subjected without consent to incarceration, restraint, punishment, or psychological or medical intervention in an attempt to control, repress, or alter the individual's thoughts, feelings or experiences.

Psychiatric medications have become a multibillion-dollar industry like Big Oil and military spending, and companies have incentive and means to cover up facts about their products. If you look more carefully into the research and examine closely the claims of the mental health system, you will discover a very different picture than what pill companies and many doctors lead us to believe. Companies actively suppress accurate assessments of drug risks, mislead patients about how controversial mental disorder theories are, promote a false understanding of how psychiatric drugs really work, keep research into alternative approaches unfunded and unpublicized, and obscure the role of trauma and oppression in mental suffering. For much of the mental health system, it's one-size-fits-all, regardless of the human cost: scandals are growing, and the fraud and corruption surrounding some psychiatric drugs are reaching tobacco-industry proportions.

In this complicated cultural environment, people are looking for accurate information about possible risks and benefits so they can make their own decisions. Too often, people who need help reducing and getting off these drugs are left without support or guidance. Sometimes they are even treated as if the desire to go off the drugs is itself a sign of mental illness—and a need for more drugs.

In discussing "risks" and "dangers," it is important to understand that all life involves risk: each of us makes decisions every day to take acceptable risks, such as driving a car, working in a stressful job, or drinking alcohol. It may not be possible to predict exactly how the risks will affect us, or to avoid the risks entirely, but it is important to know as much as we can about what the risks are. Looking at the risks of drug treatment also means looking at the risks of emotional distress/"psychosis" itself, and making the best decision for you. Maybe psychiatric drugs are the best option given your circumstances and situation, or maybe you want to try to reduce or come off. This guide is not intended to persuade you one way or the other, but to help educate you about your options if you decide to explore going off psychiatric drugs.

Because of pro-drug bias, there has been very little research on psychiatric drug withdrawal. We based this guide on the best available information, including excellent sources from the UK, and worked with a group of health professional advisors including psychiatric doctors, nurses, and alternative practitioners, all of whom have clinical experience helping people come off drugs. We also draw on the collective wisdom of an international network of survivors, allies, colleagues, activists, and healers who are connected with the Freedom Center and the Icarus Project, as well as websites such as Beyond Meds. *We encourage you to use this guide not as the definitive resource but as a reference point to start your own research and learning.* And we hope that you will share what you have learned with others and contribute to future editions.

Eating Disorders and Liberatory Harm Reduction

Let me start by saying it is scary to talk about eating disorders in the context of fat liberation.* Deep Breaths. I'm going to do it, probably imperfectly, because we deserve it. We deserve complexity in conversations about food, harm reduction, and bodies. I write this as a fat person who loves fat bodies and also has an eating disorder. I write this as someone who loves many people with eating disorders, who represent a multitude of body shapes. My own shape has changed dozens of times over the last several decades—my size serving as a fictitious indicator of my "health" or status of my "disorder."

To write this section, I had so many conversations with my radical fat activist community and I want to point you to some essential reading for fat liberation that can support your politicization process, such as *Fearing the Black Body: The Racial Origins of Fat Phobia* by Sabrina Strings, *Belly of the Beast: The Politics of Anti-Fatness as Anti-Blackness* by De'Shaun L. Harrison, *The Body Is Not an Apology* by Sonya Renee Taylor, and *What We*

* Sociologist Charlotte Cooper dates the fat liberation movement to the late 1960s, when feminist therapists known as the Fat Underground began fighting to remove "obesity" from the Diagnostic and Statistical Manual of Mental Disorders (DSM) published by the American Psychiatric Association.

Don't Talk About When We Talk About Fat by Aubrey Gordon.

The eating disorder world is shockingly binary. The widely held belief that all people who struggle with anorexia are thin costs fat people their lives every day. The myth that only cisgender women have eating disorders costs transgender people their lives every day. The belief that one has to stop their eating disorder means that we lose the opportunity to be in meaningful connection about our struggles and strategies to eat and survive. In 1983, I was the youngest kid in Weight Watchers in my area, and they had to get special permission for me to attend the adult groups. I was eight years old. I grew up being told that because I was fat, I was an overeater, but in reality, my habits were of extreme food restriction.

Mayadet Patitucci Cruz, a queer Puerto Rican Liberatory Harm Reduction practioner shared this with me:

> Is it still called restrictive eating when there is no food to eat? Capitalism and white supremacy can force poor folks to develop an eating disorder, and that was true for me and my family. We had so many harm reduction practices. If there was a whole week until the food stamps came in, you made random meals out of whatever was left in the pantry, and you stayed in bed and didn't go out to conserve your energy because you were fucking starving. I remember our local food banks gave us bags of expired Hostess cakes. Days of that will definitely make you purge. When the first of the month hits, there was a grocery splurge and we binge ate—yes, because there wasn't any "long-term thinking" when in crisis, or whatever it's called to blame poor folks for being poor—but also there is crushing shame and powerlessness when you are not able to feed your four children. When the stamps come in, splurging on groceries is taking control back in an otherwise violent and powerless situation. What we do to navigate and survive that harm are all Liberatory Harm Reduction practices.

The first place I felt safe as a fat person was in harm reduction, where my coping strategies were honored and we all had value exactly as we are. Most conversations about food were about how to get it, how best to prepare it, and the exact right way to spice and flavor. When I attended a NOLOSE conference in 2003, it was the first time I was in a fat liberation space, a place where we all agreed on the baseline: all bodies are good bodies; we all deserve competent health care, to fly on a plane, to have access to basic safety. These truths are critical to BIPOC survival.

I met Naima Lowe through the Sex Workers Art Show. We connected immediately, and our decades-long friendship holds so much. She is one of the few people with whom I have been able to discuss being a fat liberation activist who also struggles with an eating disorder.

Wait, There Are People Who Can Just . . . Eat?

NAIMA LOWE

Between chronic illness, forced childhood dieting, fatphobic medical neglect, and intergenerational traumas including food scarcity, sexual assault, and chaotic substance use, I feel set up to fail at eating. You try having Black parents in their seventies without feeling anxiety about salty, sugary, or fatty foods. You try getting fatter in your forties for reasons that are not NOT related to the eating disorders that you're finally treating, now that the field understands that you exist.

When I first learned about orthorexia (obsession with eating healthy), I thought, *Shit, someone invented an eating disorder especially for Black people!* We love a clean diet. We love the promise of outfoxing the medical-industrial complex that's out here neglecting, experimenting on, or murdering us for five hundred years. We can fix our diabetes with prayer, eat like our ancestors, get off that white man's white sugar. We can master-cleanse.

But I've failed this test of will; this endurance trial designed to (not)eat our way out of the impacts of colonialism. My unapologetically fat body must seem like evidence of every structural, cultural, and personal failure imaginable. Fatness is the symptom and illness, and the prescribed cure (constant dieting) has equally fucked up my metabolism, interoceptive hunger/fullness cues, and my emotional reaction to food. Or maybe I'm just a stubborn fat bitch who hates being told what to do.

I'm committed to fat liberation and body sovereignty, so it's terrifying to describe any fat body, including my own, as pathological. My orthorexia, anorexia, and binge-eating disorder have been dangerously out of control at times, but they've also saved me. Liberatory Harm Reduction helps me release shame and understand how pushing myself into extreme states of hunger or fullness has grounded me through trauma. Hyperfixation on the science and art of food gives me deeply healing social and cultural connections. Bingeing gives me a thrilling sense of release through uninhibited indulgence, pleasure, and the power to reject prescriptive notions of my body.

Trusting my intrinsic food desires means healing the inner kid who fought for control of her own body. There's deep relearning that I've experienced in both intentional fat liberation spaces like NOLOSE as well as sharing intimate dinners and anti-inflammation recipe hacks with chronically ill friends. These respites from isolation can be challenging to navigate due to conflicting needs around witnessing and naming stigmatized food behaviors. But these sacred spaces are worth the energy it takes to preserve and hold multiple truths about how fat bodies survive eating in a fatphobic world.

Spaces to talk about how we feel in our bodies without weight-loss pressure, fat shaming, or transphobia are scarce. Five years ago, I began searching for harm reduction projects focused on eating disorders. I found two: Fighting Eating Disorders in Underrepresented Populations (FEDUP): A Trans+ & Intersex Collective and Nalgona Positivity Pride (NPP). The vision and values of FEDUP represent Liberatory Harm Reduction in action. When I discovered Gloria Lucas's Tumblr account, I scrolled and cried for hours. I cried for the years of my life lost to distraction about how and what to feed myself. I cried for the lack of accurate information about how to reduce the harm from my own struggles with eating disorders. Finally, I cried for all the people I know who are unable to be seen and witnessed in their attempts to make sense of how to eat.

I dove into NPP's Instagram and learned that the mission is

> an in-community eating disorders and body-positive organization dedicated in creating visibility and resources for Black, Indigenous, communities of color (BICC). Since 2016, NPP has been raising awareness around the specific needs of BICC through digital media, education, grassroots eating disorders treatment models, and art. Rooted in Xicana indigenous feminism and DIY punx praxis, NPP emerged out of a great need not only to shed light on the experiences and barriers that exist in BICC affected by body-image and troubled eating but to create opportunities of healing by and for BICC.*

* For more information about NPP, go to www.nalgonapositivitypride.com.

Nalgona Positivity Pride: *Conversation with Gloria Lucas*[*]

Content Warning: mention of specific eating disorder behavior.

Gloria: I've dedicated most of my youth to eating-disorder awareness. I've had the opportunity to speak in front of dieticians, doctors, nurses, and others, expanding the narrative of who is affected by eating disorders and why they happen in groups affected by systemic racism. Yet eating disorder treatment is not only not accessible to me, but it is not a safe place for me. Like the majority of the MIC, the eating disorder treatment industry is broken. The reason I say eating disorder treatment is not a safe place for BIPOC is because the eating disorder field has not principally and historically been invested in the well-being of BIPOC. BIPOC have been an afterthought. The whole foundation of eating disorder treatment

* All information presented does not provide a substitute for medical advice, an examination, diagnosis, or treatment. it is important to consult with a doctor before making any changes to your health. The information shared in this interview may or may not be evidence-based and can only be used for informational purposes. Nalgona Positivity Pride further disclaims any and all liability whatsoever relating to any information, material, or content that may be accessed through this information. If you or a loved one is struggling with an eating disorder; you can call the toll-free, confidential National Eating Disorder Associations (NEDA) Helpline at 1-800-931-2237.

is submerged in whiteness—everything from diagnosis to who makes up the field to where treatment centers are located. I have yet to see a treatment center in a BIPOC community.

Treatment is not made equally, from who can access it to its effectiveness. If eating disorders affect at least 9 percent of the population worldwide, and 1 in 10 people struggling with eating disorders receive treatment, that informs us that the majority of people, regardless of socioeconomic background, are not receiving help. BIPOC with eating disorders are half as likely to be diagnosed or to receive treatment.

I first became aware of harm reduction when I was introduced to punx politics and feminism by other amazing folks in Riverside, CA. Once I started Nalgona Positivity Pride, I thought, *Why isn't more information bridging eating disorders and harm reduction?* Harm reduction started in the streets by the people themselves: people outside of medical institutions. Harm reduction is sacred work; it is ancestral work. Harm reduction is a compassionate model for those who are left to grapple with coloniality-induced grief and the multigenerational maladaptive skills that were developed to survive unutterable compounded destruction and dysfunctionality.

Throughout my ten-plus-year course of struggling with eating disorders, there have been moments when I wanted recovery but didn't have the support. There have been other times when I did not want to stop the behaviors. Regardless of where I've been on the "recovery" spectrum, I deserved information that made my life more bearable in moments of extreme depression and depletion. I deserved information that provided accessible symptom management and information on reducing mental and bodily harm.

I first found eating disorder harm reduction information in blogs and on Tumblr. I also found information that I would categorize as harm reduction in pro-mia and pro-ana sites.* Eating

* *Pro-ana* and *pro-mia* are terms that support the eating disorder practices asso-

disorder harm reduction was minimal five years ago. Recently, I did a Google search and was surprised to see a handful of academic articles on the subject. It is nice to see more harm reduction conversations taking place in the eating disorder field, and I hope more is done outside of anorexia.

The first time I sought help and wanted recovery I went all in, but there was nobody waiting for me on the other side. The world did not care. It was left up to me to do it all on my own, and it was one of the toughest things to go through. Everyone around me did not understand and didn't know how to help.

What I want the eating disorder awareness community to know is that my eating disorder does not care if a community (professional or not) disagrees with harm reduction, but my life is immediately impacted when I am not met halfway or if my struggle is further stigmatized. Harm reduction is not up for intellectual debate; it is an urgent, realistic approach. It is about helping people on their own terms. Enough time has been wasted on rigid "recovery-only" models that do not fit neatly with the reality of eating disorders and its comorbidities. It is unethical to withhold essential information that breaks isolation and improves quality of life from a group affected by a mental health disorder with a high rate of suicidality and early death. Harm reduction can help reduce anxiety and depression. It might be the first introduction to self-care for people with eating disorders. It's a way to gain self-awareness. It provides dignity, compassion, and autonomy for those struggling with eating disorders.

The only reason why I am staying afloat, and why my eating disorder and other self-harm practices are not worse, is because of harm reduction. I call that winning. The eating disorder treatment industry might have the best of intentions in promoting recovery, but they fail to recognize that recovery is often achieved with a lot of privilege. The "recovery-only" approach is profit-driven. This

---

ciated with anorexia nervosa and bulimia nervosa.

society is obsessed with food while simultaneously hateful toward fatness—"recovery" becomes an MIC attempt to immediately appease fatphobic anxiety and jump over the discomfort of navigating active eating disorders. These same factors are the reasons why saviorism exists within the eating disorder recovery community. Pushing a "recovery-only" approach is a self-gratifying practice to opt out of analyzing the factors that contribute to and exacerbate eating disorders in the first place—childhood adversity, food insecurity, historical/intergenerational trauma, racism, poverty, fatphobia, sexism, and more.

The "recovery binary" is the same philosophy found throughout white settler systems (gay/straight, fat/skinny, man/woman). This rigidity and lack of flexibility is a reflection of an eating disorder itself. These all-or-nothing spaces leave people like myself out: people who, for valid reasons, are not ready to commit to eating disorder abstinence.

People with eating disorders deserve a bearable life and should not receive proper support only when they are in "recovery." I don't always want to hear "recovery" messages. Personally, it makes me feel more isolated. It makes me feel that I am in the wrong for not wanting what everyone else wants for me. It reminds me of how I failed in treatment, and it reminds me of how eating disorder treatment failed me. It gives me no space to speak truthfully, to speak from my heart. Sometimes I just want someone to see me and validate that this shit is hard. Accept me where I am.

In my vision, harm reduction should apply to every medical encounter for eating disorders. Since eating disorders are often accompanied by substance use, there should be multiple harm reduction strategies offered. Having said that, harm reduction should not only exist in white therapy rooms but also in our communities and should be spread and made easily accessible through social media and printed materials.

Shira: What are some harm reduction strategies?

Gloria: There is a lot of basic information that can positively impact people struggling with eating disorders. For instance, not brushing teeth after self-induced vomiting; brushing acid directly onto teeth surfaces can cause more damage. It is safer to induce purging when vomit has less acidic contents. After vomiting, using a baking soda mouthwash and a tongue cleaner can reduce dental erosion. Also, drinking lots of water along with consuming food helps with rehydration.

Many people with eating disorders have found it helpful to take probiotics and drink cuachalalate tea to improve gastrointestinal issues. For indigestion discomfort, applying a heating pad on the stomach area is helpful. Last, Epsom salt baths can be helpful for constipation.

Food is such a sensitive and multifaceted topic. Then add racism, history, media, and gender—the plot thickens! A lot of white folks aren't ready for that. A lot of BIPOC aren't ready for it either. It's too messy! But we—BIPOC—truly do not live single-issue lives.

When I think about my own story, it is hard to put the pieces together. For most of my life I have had an eating disorder, and it is hard to contextualize. I can combine living in an immigrant home where there was toxic masculinity, violence, organized religion, mental health disturbances, disordered eating, fatphobia, and limited resources as factors that deeply impacted me. I can't help but also consider my mother's childhood experiences with child abuse and extreme food insecurity and my dad's Indigeneity and his rage. What were my ancestors' stories? I am sure these traumas played a role. Add on cortisol levels from day-to-day stress and environmental racism; now that's another story. There's unaddressed trauma because debilitation is normal. There's no language to talk about it because the demands of capitalism do not allow time to process and grieve. A lot of us grew up in environments where we were taught that we weren't smart enough or capable enough. We constantly measured our self-worth to the standard of whiteness.

Eating disorders are not just an *Oh, I want to feel sexy in my jeans* matter. It's more, *I come from a DNA trajectory that endured a lot of violence and through the course of generations maladaptive coping skills were developed to survive. These memories are trapped and they want to be released.*

Do you think about eating disorders serving a healing purpose?

In many ways, eating disorders serve as a sedative, a way to numb ourselves from the disorderly world. Many of us feel that the world has become unbearable, and eating disorders make it more tolerable. Sometimes eating disorders serve as slow suicides. Sometimes eating disorders develop as an attempt to find love in a world inundated with toxic masculinity. Being a woman of color or being an Indigenous woman with no real place to call home, eating disorders allow us to have some regularity or control. The land has been teaching us since time immemorial even when we are not cognizant of it. We can't help internalize this and treat ourselves the way the land/earth is treated under settler colonialism.

Does harm reduction affect how you see your eating disorder?

Oh, for sure. Small acts of harm reduction do add up and make a difference in your mood and health. There's so much shame when you "relapse," and harm reduction has allowed my life to be more manageable; I'm not always in this dark place. Having an eating disorders awareness social media platform comes with a lot of pressure, but harm reduction has made it more possible for me to talk about my eating disorder status. Harm reduction reduces the stigma around having an eating disorder. It teaches me to be transparent with all of my providers and say things such as, *I have bulimia and I'm not planning to stop. I am looking for ways to still take care of myself and reduce the harm. Can you meet me where I'm at?*

For thousands of years, Indigenous societies worldwide healed inside community. When we look at the most common eating disorder treatment model, you have to leave your home to do in-patient, which might not always be the best thing for some folks. Alternatively, harm reduction creates community—this is important, because eating disorders thrive in isolation. Each time I speak on harm reduction, I love to see who gathers and how community is built. Harm reduction has allowed me to define what eating disorder symptom management and eating disorder healing look like for me. I get to decide who is part of my support team, and this has proven how important it is to have both the community and professionals on your side.

As I am preparing the content for my eating disorder harm reduction e-course, I am learning so much about my body and what stress it is experiencing. I believe that knowledge helps you make better choices. Knowledge is power! I keep asking myself, *Why didn't anyone tell me this before?* This information has to be made available to sufferers.

You could be engaging with harm reduction at any stage—from dieting to enduring eating disorders—harm reduction leaves nobody out. It is unconditional support, and I don't think there are many things out there that are unconditional anymore.

Harm reduction has allowed me to exist within my own brilliance, my own power, my own relapse—and be all of that, be completely vulnerable and completely human.

HARM REDUCTION STRATEGIES FOR EATING DISORDERS

w/GLORIA LUCAS OF THE NALGONA POSITIVITY PRIDE PROJECT

ORAL CARE

OVER-THE-COUNTER SUPPLEMENTS

GASTROINTESTINAL CARE

POTASSIUM PILLS

DIARRHEA MEDICATION

THIS DOES NOT CONSTITUTE MEDICAL ADVICE.
PLEASE ASK YOUR DOCTOR
FOR THE MOST ACCURATE SUPPORT.

Transformative Justice and Liberatory Harm Reduction

What we believe:
We can and must end violence.
Healing is possible.
We need a model that isn't prisons and isn't police to keep our communities safe.
This is hard work and it's a work in progress...it's on us to keep building the work.

—API Chaya*

How do we end violence? How do we reclaim our imaginations from police, prisons, funding limitations, liability insurance, laws, and state systems?† I think that these questions are so large and so open-ended that our answers will come through conversation with each other, through mistakes, and through reflection. All we can do is seek answers together and begin the process of experimentation, practice, and healing. In many ways, the everyday practice of harm reduction is how we make a world

* Shared in the Transformative Justice track at the Allied Media Conference, June 2014. Learn more at www.apichaya.org.

† Liability laws greatly impact nonprofits' abilities to respond to violence and harm without calling the police or filing paperwork with the state.

without violence because it gives us steps, tools, and rituals to strengthen our community interdependence, build our collective power, and reduce our need for state systems and social services.

Although many harm reduction projects have build up community resilience, strengthened capacity to interrupt and transform violence, and reduced dependence on state systems and social services, many public health harm reduction programs would not include these outcomes as explicit goals of the work. These goals are a by-product of public health harm reduction because, often, people seeking services from community groups that operate from a harm reduction approach are locked out of traditional social services, as their survival is criminalized. The intersections of the law with health care and other service organizations make accessing help dangerous. Consider the first person you encounter when going to an emergency room—do you first meet a nurse? No. In most cities you are greeted by a security guard, pat downs, and metal detectors.

People who create and attend harm reduction programs are often unable to access social services because of gatekeeping restrictions barring participation in the sex trade and limitations such as mandatory abstinence from all substances or required identification or other paperwork that many street-based community members and immigrants cannot easily access. Mandatory reporting creates another barrier. These laws require people to report child abuse, elder abuse, abuse of people with disabilities, and, in some cases, can force hospitalization on those who are suicidal or experiencing signs of mental health crisis. This keeps many drug users and sex workers away from social services and health care settings out of fear of losing their children or being incarcerated or locked up in psychiatric facilities.

In harm reduction communities and organizing projects, we have to figure out how to solve problems without using the police or the state. Harm reduction not only demands the centering of survivors, but also that we lead the work and that our thoughts and expertise as the people most impacted by the criminal injustice system are valued, paid, and recognized. We possess the relevant skills and creativity to end the violence of police and prisons.

In cities such as Chicago, the police are notorious for demanding sexual favors in exchange for dropping charges against people in the sex trade.* They target transgender women and girls and profile people for "looking like they are involved in the street economy." Yet many social service organizations still insist on positioning security guards or plainclothes police officers as the first points of contact at building entrances because the liability laws that protect the nonprofit or health care setting are embedded in a law-and-order politic that disregards the safety and security of the most vulnerable and instead protects itself.

As a response to systemic injustices and barriers, harm reduction projects are less likely to have security guards in their settings. We start our own food banks that don't require IDs, support squatters and squatters' rights work, and create childcare collectives to support young parents. Harm reduction puts into everyday practice the idea that *we are not our worst behaviors.* It gives us permission to be accountable, grow, and change, and acknowledges that all survivors and all human beings are complex. There is no such thing as a good or bad person; there are only good or harmful actions. As a survivor- and trauma-centered philosophy, Liberatory Harm Reduction runs counter to the popular expression, *You can't love anyone until you love yourself.* As a feminist, survivor, and someone socialized to be a caregiver first, I have always struggled with this concept because learning I had a *self* to love has been a long-term process through years of therapy and living a life focused on healing. If I believed I had to love

* The report by YWEP, *Girls Do What They Have to Do to Survive: Illuminating Methods Used by Young People in the Sex Trade and Street Economy to Fight Back and Heal,* first identified the trend of police bribing young people for sex in exchange for not arresting them and then arresting them anyway. This is within the law in most cities.

myself before being able to be in loving relationships with others, then in effect I would be telling myself that I don't deserve love right now—only in an imaginary "healed" future with a constantly moving end date. At YWEP, self-care was emphasized as a part of community care; we learned how to love ourselves through how we cared for others in our community. We learned that we were worthy of love through receiving love from the other people in the sex trade around us who gave us the gift of radical acceptance by allowing us to show up as our best selves every day.

In Transformative Justice, the harm reduction practice of risk reduction can happen on the quick and can also be a long-term investment. We can all come up with immediate ideas that will change the outcome of a scary or higher-risk situation using strategies such as needle exchange, safety planning, care plans for surgeries, and medication detox planning. These strategies must be directed by the individuals and the survivors and be negotiated with the larger community when needed. For example, as we allowed our office space to be used as a "safe house"* for young people in the sex trade and street economy who were in danger, we had to learn to balance the individual and collective needs so that our whole community was engaged in keeping each other safe. To do this, we listened to the needs of each young person in danger and shared those needs with the staff collective, who decided if we had the resources to be helpful and make a positive difference. Most of the times we agreed to temporarily host someone in our office until we could figure out a longer-term solution. However, there were also moments we knew we couldn't make enough of a difference or that the larger YWEP community would be in danger if we used our space. In those times, we paid for a few nights of a motel room, provided meals, and made a round-the-clock plan of check-ins and companionship.

---

* A safe house is a secret location where people who are seeking refuge from interpersonal and/or state violence can be protected by activists who work to create and maintain networks, that at times, can even help people move safely throughout the country.

We invested in long-term relationships with each other instead of following the landlord's rules of "no overnight guests" and made clear boundaries with everyone who came to and from YWEP's offices so that we could work together to maintain our safety. In this way, we carefully knit ourselves into each other, creating a system of interdependence. At staff retreats, we would spend time on a visualization activity where we imagined our entire office as an aquarium filled with water. We pictured the waves and ripples moving out from each of our subtle arm motions to help us make sense of the ways in which our individual decisions impacted the whole.

But What Is Transformative Justice?

There are any number of books, articles, and zines that should be read about Transformative Justice and prison abolition before you begin your work to end violence without police, prisons, and the state. From *Beyond Survival: Strategies and Stories from the Transformative Justice Movement* by Ejeris Dixon and Leah Lakshmi Piepzna-Samarasinha to *We Do This 'Til We Free Us* by Mariame Kaba to the books that started it all—Angela Y. Davis's *Are Prisons Obsolete?* and *Color of Violence* and *The Revolution Will Not Be Funded* by INCITE! Women of Color, Gender Non-Conforming, and Trans People of Color Against Violence, and the Creative Interventions Toolkit, stewarded by Mimi Kim and an entire collective of people practicing community accountability. Each of these books gives us a foundational framework and real-life examples of how we can respond to violence without relying on the state.

As defined by YWEP in 2009, Transformative Justice means

> acknowledging that the state can and will cause harm in our lives, so we work to solve problems together that don't rely on police or social services. We believe that we will reduce violence in our lives and community the more we build together. We believe that we have to confront systems when they stop us from getting

> the help we need—this is called attacking the "root cause" of violence. We believe that state systems are the ones most responsible for what causes violence in our lives. We believe that survivors use harm reduction every day to survive violence.

Just as harm reduction was created by the people, so was Transformative Justice and community accountability created by women of color and trans People of Color who were antiviolence activists working in domestic violence shelters, rape crisis hotlines, and peer-based counseling projects for survivors. In recent years, we have begun to think of Transformative Justice as a broad philosophy that can encompass everything from having our own safety teams at conferences and marches to safer workplace culture to safety planning for sex workers. Put simply, Transformative Justice names the role of state harm in the lives of BIPOC and requires us to find solutions outside of state systems to solve problems. Miss Major Griffin-Gracy, an early harm reductionist, prison abolitionist, transgender activist, and sex worker organizer said,

> The interesting thing is, by the time I got to prison, and I was talking to Frank Smith [the leader of the Attica prison uprising], I realized the stuff we were doing to try to keep the girls safe was good, but it wasn't enough. We didn't have enough information about what harm was being done to us, and until you understand how oppression works, where it's coming from, and what it means, it's really hard to fight it because you didn't understand what the fight is all about.

It is this naming of structural violence that is essential to our liberatory practice of harm reduction and it is the everyday, sometimes small things that we do to keep ourselves and communities safe that makes harm reduction inextricable from and necessary to our understanding of Transformative Justice.

If Liberatory Harm Reduction is what we do on an individual level to increase our daily safety and personal accountability and to build deep relationships, Transformative Justice is what we do on a community level to address the root causes of violence and create alternative solutions to calling the police and depending on social services. What many people who are newly attracted to the work to end prisons and policing do not realize is that most activists who have been working on Transformative Justice and community accountability for the last two decade have also been grounded in harm reduction philosophy, and they use it to weave their politics and practice together into tangible action. This is in part because Liberatory Harm Reduction is nonbinary and helps guide us in the release of things like "innocence" versus "guilt" and "good people" versus "bad people," "clean" versus "sober," and so on. Releasing these concepts and the trappings of the success/failure dichotomy is essential to our work in Transformative Justice.

When Mariame Kaba and I wrote *Fumbling Towards Repair: A Workbook for Community Accountability Facilitators* in 2018, our purpose was to offer tools, skills, and a way of thinking about how devastating harm like sexual violence can be responded to without relying on the state. This section of *Saving Our Own Lives* digs into how harm reduction is the critical axis on which so much of repair, transformation, accountability and healing is held.

In my community of drug users, people in the sex trade, trans and queer, young, and BIPOC, harm reduction is part of our breath. Sexual violence and harassment from law enforcement are common experiences, and calling the police for help is almost impossible without risking rape, arrest, or death. As a survivor of multiple forms of violence that started when I was very young and spanned to the last time I experienced sexual violence, a few years ago during a date with someone I was attempting to partner with, I am writing from a perspective of complexity.

HOW HARM REDUCTION INFORMS Tranformative Justice

The Dangers of Reformist Reforms

Transformative Justice is a belief and practice that invites us to transform the root causes of violence, and to respond and repair interpersonal harm without the involvement of the state. The last element is critical: Transformative Justice does not engage the state *at all*. For example, the critical push in 2020 to defund the police and reinvest in communities is an essential campaign to abolish police and prisons. We consider it to be necessary *nonreformist* reform work. *Nonreformist* reform simply means working on policy or legislation that reforms the prison system *without expanding it*. This is important to distinguish because most reform work winds up expanding the footprint of the carceral state.

An important early example of this was the creation of the juvenile justice system. When Jane Addams, a Chicago activist working at the turn of the twentieth century, advocated to remove children from the adult prison system, it was because they were being brutalized through incarceration in jails and poor houses. Many reformers view the creation of separate courts—family court, drug court, domestic violence court, prostitution court—as significant advances in social change work. However, all these courts have succeeded in one thing only: expanding the carceral system's reach in the lives of children and their families.

Some mainstream harm reduction policy advocates point to Addams's work as an example of progress and positive reforms. But her work actually sparked an expansion of the carceral system and the reach of the state in lives of poor people and young people. Mischaracterizing her work as harm reduction has led to confusion and contributed to harm reduction becoming part of a liberal framework, especially on the West Coast, where harm reduction was adopted by public health systems and social services through the state's public health policies early in the AIDS crisis. A true Liberatory Harm Reduction policy would be focused on reducing carceral reach, removing laws against prostitution and drugs, and would focus on the root causes of harm. This kind of policy work is often referred to as nonreformist reform.

Liberatory Harm Reductionists must use both nonreformist reform and Transformative Justice strategies in order to abolish prisons and policing. To do this, it is essential to understand the difference between these two concepts. Nonreformist reforms seek to bring an end to prisons using abolition and harm reduction values by removing laws and shifting funds away from policing and toward addressing the root causes of violence. Nonreformist reform *is not* a Transformative Justice strategy because the latter's reforms must engage the state to be effective.

Without replicating policing and surveillance, some Transformative Justice strategies are part of the daily harm reduction we use in our lives, like using public transit instead of driving while intoxicated, and some are more complex, such as creating safety at parties, offices, movement spaces, and online.* Other strategies are more about avoiding actions, such as not calling 911 on your loud neighbors. Still others are about slowly changing how we think about the critical difference between punishment versus consequences, accountability versus justice, healing versus revenge.

These separate, critical strategies that Liberatory Harm Reductionists use to dismantle oppressive systems have a crucial difference. For example, campaigns seeking to defund the police and reinvest in communities are excellent examples of harm reduction/nonreformist reform strategies, informed by abolitionist goals and dreams, to tackle and untangle the reach of the carceral state. Liberatory Harm Reductionists should support Defund the Police campaigns until we win and we have ended policing and abolished prisons.

---

* *Beyond Survival: Stories and Strategies from the Transformative Justice Movement* by Ejeris Dixon and Leah Lakshmi Piepzna-Samarasinha is an essential read for anyone working on dismantling the prison system and building a world without police.

Transformative Justice and People in the Sex Trade, or Don't Forget to Thank a Young Person in the Sex Trade for Making Your Life Safer

People inside and outside of movement spaces tend to think of people in the sex trade as living and existing outside of Transformative Justice. The truth is that people in the sex trade are integral parts of movement spaces and largely ignored. Sex work is treated as something to be ashamed of and othered. One of the main missions of my life is to remind the harm reduction and prison abolition movements that people in the sex trade not only exist but are also the architects of so many of these practices.

Let's be clear: people in the sex trade coexist with you in every facet of your life. You passed by someone in the sex trade many times this week alone, I am sure of it. It has to be said in a section on Transformative Justice that we are here and everywhere doing care work and community work to make life less violent and worth living.

Something that is often left out of mainstream conversations about harm reduction and prison abolition is that *people who sell drugs are included in our communities, and their rights are a part of our fight for safety and freedom.* People who sell drugs are vilified and often not welcome in social services, schools, or even organizing spaces. As discussed in this book, there is no Liberatory Harm Reduction without prison abolition and ending policing. To do that we must end the War on Drugs and end the criminalization of people in the sex trade and sex workers. This is to ensure that people who use drugs do not face prosecution, and it is also to ensure that people who sell drugs are not criminalized.

The dilemma with most campaigns to decriminalize sex work is that additional laws don't necessarily make things better for our community, and the removal of laws doesn't necessarily decrease violence or policing in our neighborhoods because criminalization does not originate in the law. Rather, criminalization is based on racism, transphobia, poverty, and other forms of structural violence. In fact, a lot of the laws that are supposedly designed to protect us end up hurting us, our families, and our communities. I write about decriminalization as a necessary step to making people in the sex trade and street economy safer. But decriminalization, while critical, should not be the end of goal for Liberatory Harm Reductionists and sex worker activists because it does not go far enough. In organizing work led by and for girls, women, and trans People of Color who have experience in the sex trade, sex work, and street economy, we have been trying to make clear that anti-criminalization should be our focus.

During the mid-2000s, YWEP, Different Avenues, Native Youth Sexual Health Network, Streetwise & Safe, and Emi Koyama joined to form an organizing body called Fuse. Our intent was to light a fuse in the mostly white sex worker movement that lacked analysis about the impact of the criminal legal system in the lives of transgender people, girls, and women of color and to make clear the distinction between doing anti-criminalization work—which seeks to end this racist police state we are living in—and the work of the more visible decriminalization movement, which is working to abolish laws that regulate sex work. The activism of people such as Kelli Dorsey, Emi Koyama, Andrea Ritchie, Deon Haywood, and Dominique McKinney has changed the sex worker organizing world forever. Their work has also impacted mainstream public health harm reduction and created the analysis for Liberatory Harm Reduction.

To help you understand just how important people in the sex trade are to prison abolition work, I want to tell you about Danzine, the Bad Date Line, and Bad Date sheets. Danzine was created by and for sex workers in Portland, Oregon, during the mid-1990s. They created a gorgeous zine series that was as colorful as it was brilliant and ran a needle exchange from 1995 to 2005 before they taught the county to take over. (This syringe services program is still in operation, on the same street corner.) These folks created the first Bad Date sheet as a tool for sex workers to use to help keep them safe. Later, Danzine created the project called the Bad Date Line whose mission was the following:

> The Portland Bad Date Line (PBDL) is meant for us to share and circulate descriptions of harmful people. A bad date is a violent and/or abusive customer in the sex industry. Our hope is that someone would refer to the PBDL as an option to reduce risk for violence, abuse, rape, unwanted pregnancy, hepatitis/STD and HIV transmission.

Joanna Berton Martinez, formerly known as Teresa Dulce, is the cofounder of Danzine and the person responsible for elevating the Bad Date sheet to become an almost commonplace tool among sex worker organizers. I learned that it started as a response to a particular violent incident that happened to someone known to the peer workers at Danzine. Danzine peer outreach workers were involved in the sex trade in ways ranging from stripping to fantasy work to phone sex to trading sex for money. They would go out onto the track* in the evening and make sure people had condoms, new syringes, and sharps containers in which to safely put their used syringes. As they talked with folks, they collected identifying information about bad dates on a piece of paper, photocopied the descriptions, and handed out these half-page tools to other people in Portland to warn them of potential harm. The goal of this work was straightforward: "It is our goal to collect and share descriptions of violent and/or abusive customers in the sex industry." Since then, examples of these bad date sheets have been distributed around the world so that other sex workers would know how to start their own Bad Date Line.

Joanna describes this work here:

---

* A track, cometimes called a stroll, is a known place where sex workers and people in the sex trade are available to be picked up outdoors. In most cities, there are recognized blocks or neighborhoods that are a track or a stroll.

> The Portland Bad Date Line started in 1998 when a working girl told us (at outreach) about a bad date she had in a truck. We faxed his description to other agencies that served survival-based prostitutes. Later that year, one of our friends got hurt in-call during a private show. A group of us made a phone tree and called escorts who had ads in local adult magazines. Then the PBDL became a monthly sheet, primarily distributed through direct-service agencies and in the jails. The PBDL has changed many hands and still keeps ticking—a project with heart. Thank you Invisible Fringe, Sex Workers Action Group (SWAG), Danzine, and Outside In's syringe exchange Program, and the Trans Identity Arts Resource Center (TIRC). The PBDL is currently being facilitated by Outside In and volunteers from the community. By 2001, we were sending the sheet to over fifty agencies in the USA, mostly in the Portland Metro Area and up and down the I-5 corridor.

When I was working at NYPAEC in the 1990s, I started to get fax transmissions from the Bad Date Line. I was already a devoted reader of the Danzine zine—which was the only publication I knew of that was written by and for sex workers. It was a beautifully illustrated comic book–like printout that we would covet and take turns reading to each other. So when the first fax came through, I remember not being able to hold the paper still as my hands trembled with what felt like grief and power surging through me simultaneously.

I asked Joanna if they thought of the Bad Date Line as a participatory action research project, and she said they did not—they just thought about the best way to get the word out so people in the sex trade could make the most money with the least violence. I also asked her if they thought about it as a Transformative Justice action or as a pushback on the police or the system. She said that at the time, all they wanted was for the violence to stop.

Bad Date Report Form *4/06*

A bad date is a violent and/or abusive customer in the sex industry. It is our goal to take anonymous reports and share their descriptions in the hopes of decreasing harm. **Please check ALL the boxes that best describe the situation and feel free to fill in the blanks. (If there is more than one perp, check to the left of the boxes for second perp.)**

THERE ARE TWO SIDES TO THIS SHEET.

LOCATION + TIME

What day did this bad date occur?

- ☐ Monday
- ☐ Tuesday
- ☐ Wednesday
- ☐ Thursday
- ☐ Friday
- ☐ Saturday
- ☐ Sunday
- ☐ Don't know

Time:

- ☐ Morning
- ☐ Day
- ☐ Night
- ☐ Wee hours
- ☐ ____________________

Where:

- ☐ Street____________
- ☐ Strip club____________
- ☐ Modeling studio____________
- ☐ Out call____________
- ☐ Other____________

VEHICLE

Were you picked up in a vehicle?

- ☐ Y
- ☐ N

License plate #____________________

What type?

- ☐ Car
- ☐ Truck
- ☐ Van
- ☐ SUV
- ☐ Other____________
- ☐ New
- ☐ 2-door
- ☐ 4-door
- ☐ Other____________
- ☐ New
- ☐ Old
- ☐ Clean
- ☐ Wreck
- ☐ Other____________

____

____

____

VEHICLE *continued*

Color:

- ☐ Red
- ☐ Yellow
- ☐ White
- ☐ Black
- ☐ Blue
- ☐ Green
- ☐ Brown
- ☐ Other____________

BAD DATE DESCRIPTION

Was there more than one person?

- ☐ Y
- ☐ N

(If yes, please describe on flip side)

Gender:

- ☐ Male
- ☐ Female
- ☐ Trans
- ☐ Don't know

Approx age:____________________

Appearances:

- ☐ White
- ☐ Black
- ☐ Hispanic/Latino
- ☐ Asian
- ☐ Native American
- ☐ ____________________

Speak with an accent?

- ☐ Y (what type?)____________
- ☐ N

Body Type:

- ☐ Short
- ☐ Tall
- ☐ Thin
- ☐ Medium
- ☐ Fat
- ☐ Muscular/Beefy
- ☐ In-shape/Fit
- ☐ ____________________

BAD DATE *continued*

Hair:

- ☐ Short
- ☐ Long
- ☐ Bald
- ☐ Shaved
- ☐ Crew cut
- ☐ Curly
- ☐ Dreads
- ☐ Straight
- ☐ Blonde
- ☐ Brunette
- ☐ Grey
- ☐ Black
- ☐ ____________________

Eyes:

- ☐ Blue
- ☐ Brown
- ☐ Green
- ☐ Hazel
- ☐ Eye Glasses
- ☐ Don't Know

Facial Hair:

- ☐ Beard
- ☐ Mustache
- ☐ Sideburns
- ☐ Clean Shaven
- ☐ Stubble
- ☐ ____________________

Marks on the body:

- ☐ Tattoos
- ☐ Scars
- ☐ Warts
- ☐ Birth Mark
- ☐ ____________________

Where on the body?____________________

____

Describe:____________________

____

____

____

____

YWEP's Participatory Action Research

In 2006, Catlin Fullwood spent sixteen months teaching YWEP folks the methodology and application of participatory action research. We learned how to develop research questions, different ways to collect data, how to analyze data, and how to present our findings so that everyone could understand them. At some point, we realized that the Bad Date Line was, as Joanna described it, "the first participatory evaluation research project done by and for sex workers with lead players who were women of color and mixed heritage in the country."

As YWEP began to do our own participatory research, we knew that we wanted to examine the impact of institutional violence on the lives of girls and transgender young people in the sex trade and street economy. Previously, every researcher who had asked us to participate in their focus groups or surveys always ignored our resilience and resistance to interpersonal violence, ignored our stories of police sexual assault, and positioned us as flat victims whose only daily experiences were multiple crimes including abandonment, neglect, and violence from pimps and johns. We read the studies after they were published and said to each other, *But that isn't right—that isn't what we said—that just erased every part of our story.*

We knew we had to start doing our own research, when, in 2007, a staffer from Illinois Criminal Justice Research Information Authority, whom we agreed to help understand the prevalence of the sex trade among people under eighteen in Chicago, led the police to the door of a YWEP outreach worker. The cops ran into her house while she was in the shower, pulled her out, and confronted her with the flyer she had been distributing on behalf of the researcher to recruit participants for the study. The cops accused her of being a trafficker recruiting girls into the sex trade, and brought her in to face charges. As it was Friday afternoon, the researcher had left work for the day, and no one from her office would contact her at home on our behalf. It took us hours to make the police believe us, and, in the end, I had to produce signed contracts and printed emails to get them to drop the charges.

The next morning, YWEP folks met at the office and agreed that we would never work with another professional researcher again. We decided we would study the impact and intersections of institutional violence in our own lives. We adapted the bad date sheet to track institutional harm, including when institutions deny help based on the assumption of an individual's being involved in the street economy, and to track how we fight back and heal. In 2009, we self-published our research and conducted two national tours, where we presented our data to movement activists, funders, and other sex workers. The opening page of our study stated:

> This research is for US. It's for YOU and for all girls, including transgender girls, young women and trans people involved in the sex trade and street economy. This research study was created by us, collected by us, and analyzed by us. We did this because this is OUR LIVES. Who knows us better than us? We did this to prove that we care—that we are capable of resisting violence in a multitude of ways. We take care of ourselves and heal in whatever way feels best for us—whether society approves of it or not. This research study honors all of the ways we fight back (resistance) and our healing (resilience) methods. We proved that we do face violence, but we are not purely victims. We are survivors. We can take care of ourselves, and we know what we need. This research is a response to all of those researchers, doctors, government officials, social workers, therapists, journalists, foster care workers and every other adult who said we were too messed up or that we needed to be saved from ourselves. The next time someone tells you that you don't know what's best for you, look towards our tool kit for inspiration. We wrote the tool kit with the intent of giving you ideas about how us have survived this life—not to tell you what to do.

> We did this. We did the research. And now we are sharing it with you so that you know that girls do what they have to do to survive.

Once we began our speaking tour, our research had wide-ranging impact. We were quoted in the *New York Times* and interviewed on National Public Radio, and our research went to the United Nations twice. The first time our research was used was during the Ninth Periodic Universal Review of 193 UN member states' human rights. Our research was embedded in a report written by the Best Practices Policy Project about the treatment of people in the sex trade in the United States. Based on this report, the United Nations found in our favor and demanded that the United States be held accountable for the police violence, systemic neglect, and health care discrimination that people in the sex trade face in this country.

The second time YWEP's reporting tool went to the UN was with We Charge Genocide, a group of activists in Chicago who were tracking police violence against young BIPOC people. We Charge Genocide was a grassroots, intergenerational effort to center the voices and experiences of young BIPOC people in communities most targeted by police violence in Chicago. From the group, six Black and Brown youth organizers went to Geneva, Switzerland, for the Fifty-Third session of the United Nations Committee against Torture, during which the United States was under review.

The shadow report written by We Charge Genocide to present at the UN used a data-collection method adapted from YWEP's "Girls Fight Back" zine (a version of the Bad Date Line). The tool was recalibrated so that it could be used to collect data when young people had any kind of police encounter. We Charge Genocide staged a powerful protest in the UN session—one of the first of its kind.*

* WeChargeGenocide.org, "We Charge Genocide Holds Historic Protest Inside the United Nations During UNCAT Review of US Torture," Geneva, Switzerland, November 14, 2014—Chicago youth organizers presented a report this week to the United Nations Committee Against Torture (UNCAT) in

The Intersection of Reproductive Justice, Disability Justice, Transformative Justice, and Liberatory Harm Reduction

The reality of the sex trade, sex work, and the street economy in our lives means that Reproductive Justice *and* Transformative Justice must be a critical part of Liberatory Harm Reduction. I have too often been in conversations with people who root their understanding in public health harm reduction and therefore miss the critical intersections of how criminalization and Reproductive Justice come together.

Andrea Ritchie is a Black, lesbian, immigrant survivor who has been documenting, organizing, advocating, litigating, and agitating around policing and criminalization of Black women, girls, trans, and gender-nonconforming people for the past three decades. Andrea cofounded Interrupting Criminalization with Mariame Kaba and is the author of *Invisible No More: Police Violence Against Black Women and Women of Color* and coauthor of *No More Police: A Case for Abolition* and *Queer (In)Justice: Criminalization of LGBT People in the United States*. She is also a former member of INCITE! Women of Color, Gender Non-Conforming, and Trans People of Color Against Violence and a former board member of YWEP. We have known each other as collaborators, co-organizers, and friends for nearly twenty years. Andrea shared this with me:

> I can tell folks to read Sarah Haley and Talitha L. LeFlouria and Cynthia Blair's work, about how immediately after the proclamation of emancipation, Black women just left white homes in droves, where they had been forced to care for white people's children, engage in reproductive labor for other people, and were severely limited in their ability to use their reproduc-

---

Geneva, Switzerland. Questions they wrote on police violence in Chicago were asked by the committee to U.S. representatives. During the U.S. response, We Charge Genocide delegates staged a historic protest, standing with their fists in the air for over a half hour."

tive labor in the way that they wanted to, for their own families, or their own lives. They were also subject to systemic structural sexual violence that sought complete control of their sexual and reproductive autonomy, including through forced parenting and forced abortions, which is the forced control of Black women's reproductive capacity and autonomy. Following the legal end of slavery, criminalization facilitated continued control over Black women's labor and bodily autonomy. Cops would arrest Black women under prostitution laws, vagrancy laws, or disorderly conduct laws that were being put into place or increasingly enforced across the country at that time to then convict them of a crime. Then, re-enslave women into domestic servitude through convict leasing and put their reproductive labor back in the houses of white women because there was an exception to the abolition of slavery for people convicted of a crime. Criminalization of prostitution was directly about reasserting reproductive control over Black women's reproductive capacity, economic capacity, labor, and sexual agency. Criminalization of the sex trade is at the core a Reproductive Justice issue on all those levels, and the ways that it is criminalized interfere with people's relationships and use of harm reduction tools, like condoms.

Harm reduction and Reproductive Justice intersect in a number of places, for example: drug use and pregnancy, which is definitely a prime site of profiling, policing, and criminalization. Another is police and prosecutors using possession and presence of condoms as evidence of intent to engage in prostitution, which is definitely a Reproductive Justice issue, in the sense that the state is literally reaching its hands into your purse or pocket, to take out the one form of birth control/STD protection that you could get without a doctor and taking it away from you, and then trying to use it against you as evidence of a crime. Condoms are a primary tool of harm reduction. Outreach workers in harm reduction programs give out condoms all the time. But the outreach workers were being criminalized, and so were the sex workers, which affected their ability to exercise reproductive autonomy and sexual autonomy.

Harm reduction groups led in organizing to resist those policies and practices because their outreach workers were being criminalized. The state was literally interfering with people's ability to engage and use birth control and engage in STD prevention. It was also about the Reproductive Justice issue of being allowed to do with your body what you want to do with your body, whether it's by choice or a circumstance that you're engaged in the sex trade, that you should be able to use these tools.

Just like Reproductive Justice isn't about *only* your ability to access an abortion, and Disability Justice isn't *only* about elevators, Liberatory Harm Reduction isn't *only* about your ability to access a clean needle. Liberatory Harm Reduction is not only about your individual choice to smoke if you're pregnant but also about transforming conditions that make all the demands and visions of Reproductive Justice possible, and giving people structural and individual tools to live their best lives. Disability Justice, Reproductive Justice, and Liberatory Harm Reduction together give us the tools to reclaim body autonomy from the state and demand that we leave no one behind as we organize to fight the MIC and PIC simultaneously.

From *Reproductive Justice Is Disability Justice* statement, Sins Invalid 2019:

> Recent attempts to ban abortions have led to many nonconsensual conversations about women, trans, and nonbinary people's bodies. In these discussions, we must remember how disability justice values an intersectional analysis which requires us to consider the complexities of reproductive justice in the context of ableism. Choosing when to become a parent is a basic principle of reproductive justice. On one hand, the fear of disability has been used as a tool to manipulate individuals' reproductive choices, sometimes causing people to opt for selective abortions to avoid disability, which is in line with eugenics. Simultaneously, dis-

> abled people have often been forced to terminate pregnancies under the pretense that we cannot be good parents because we are disabled. Additionally, because of the isolation of ableism, people with disabilities will be less likely to find safe options to terminate pregnancies when they choose. This context, along with the struggle of disabled people to obtain comprehensive sex education and healthcare, means these abortion bans will be catastrophic for disabled folks.

The critical intersections that mean that Disability Justice is Reproductive Justice have guided Liberatory Harm Reductionists in their work to challenge the state. Earlier, this book presented the story of the Lincoln Hospital takeover that was sparked by a botched abortion. The Jane Collective in Chicago was a radical underground network of feminists who, after finding out that one of the doctors they had been referring to had no medical training, worked from 1969 to 1973 to provide abortions by teaching lay people how to safely perform a dilation and curettage procedure (D&C). This was a coordinated pushback on the MIC. Even though the language for harm reduction did not fully exist yet, the Jane Collective's work is an example of how radical activists connected critical dots between the ideas of collective liberation and people's everyday struggle to survive.

Viva Ruiz is working to connect these dots. Viva, a queer sex worker of color and artist-activist, founded Thank God for Abortion (TGFA) to push back on not only the Christian right but also on leftists who disregard the full personhood of sex workers, people in the sex trade, and people in the street economy as a whole. In my conversations with her, we talked about how nightclub life and harm reduction tools helped her establish this current radical project:

> One of the first groups I started going to was started by Annie Sprinkle when she was doing PONY, Prostitutes of New York. In her living room, it was hustlers, it was people on the stroll, it was dancers—it was really beautiful, because it was really

real—that we all needed each other.

Thank God for Abortion (TGFA) is really the same as PONY because things haven't changed, things that are life-threatening—I still don't have possession of my own body, and people still don't let women, gender-nonconforming people, trans people, Black, Brown, and immigrant people have possession of our own bodies. Personhood is a basic building block of liberation movements. I had a decade of stripping at night clubs and go-go dancing, just using my body for work and declaration that helped me form this practice of making my body the proof my liberation. And punk music, and being outside of/never outside of capitalism, but outside of that striving, outside of a corporate ladder, outside of institutions, outside of schools and pipelines, or whatever.

The nightlife was a big part of what led TGFA. The amniotic fluid of the nightlife that includes sex work and drug use, that world is where I learned how to organize from being in bands and working in clubs and having the skills that I have. My life goal, my vision, my ambition is shamelessness.

TGFA was born from anger because of being invisibilized; the right wing has been closing down clinics for fifteen or twenty years now, and it's been hiding from us in plain sight, not on the front page. The name of the project [TGFA] came from the idea of pushing back on right-wing Christians but also—shocking—the liberals too! It would even touch friends of mine in my own circle who thought of themselves as sexually liberated or enjoying a kind of sexual freedom that I could never have.

There's so many places of disconnect in our thinking about Reproductive Justice. Abortion is sexual freedom. I can never have sexual freedom until so many things change. In this way, I see a real divide between me and my closest friends who have more sexual freedom: I'm speaking of gay and queer cis men in particular. If you think about it, it's like some really intense structural hypnotism—it's like a generational teaching or something, for a person, say a friend who loves me, to completely not see me

> as a person with access to the same sexual freedoms that he has, to really want, need, and enjoy the things for himself, but deny me.
>
> There's cruelty there.
>
> And it's very effective how the right, the Christian right or whoever, could isolate abortion as something divorced from sex or humans and just make it about a baby. They really were effective over a long time of dehumanizing the pregnant person. It was so effective that even in my own house, even in my own block with the gayest, with the queerest, most outlaw-y feeling people, I could still not be a whole person to them without them even realizing it.

The link between Reproductive Justice and sex work, the sex trade, and street economy has always been woven into how I move and think in the world. When I was a part of NYPAEC in New York in the 1990s, I saw Reproductive Justice in our bathrooms, which were stocked with syringes, extra hormone doses that people left for others to use, wound care kits, and plenty of space to do makeup before going out—alongside condoms, new clean underpants, and socks. A decade later, when we were collectively writing our Reproductive Justice statement at YWEP, we were able to make a clear link to the activities we did in our bathrooms, bedrooms, and street corners to police targeting and body autonomy. From YWEP's 2008 Reproductive Justice statement:

> Our vision of Reproductive Justice is the complete physical, mental, spiritual, political, economic, and social well-being of girls, transgender, and queer peoples. We want the power & resources to make decisions about our bodies and sexuality for ourselves, our families & our communities.
>
> Reproductive Justice means harm reduction. It looks like non-condemning, just, and accessible treatment. It looks like an end to the police state, an end to sexual violence, harassment, gender profiling, and brutality. It looks like an end to the prison industrial complex and the militarization and gentrification in our communities.

> Our Reproductive Justice movement work denounces violence against our constituents. We demand an end to the criminalization of young mothers who use drugs or have forced abortions/sterilization and experience poverty. We stand in solidarity with those killed due to misogyny, sex or gender, age or race/ethnicity and victims of femicide and transphobic violence.
>
> Although society blames us, we call out the systems that are responsible. We are here to fight against misogyny and hold our oppressors accountable. We support acts of rebellion and resistance; all girls building and keeping sisterhood and fighting for Reproductive Justice that acknowledges the realities and complexities of our lives. To people in the sex trade everywhere, we say: it's easier for our oppressors to try and take us down one by one—but if we stand together as a group, nothing can stop us.

Moments before this book went to press, *Roe v Wade* was overturned. My phone rang off the hook with sex workers and movement activists who had been planning for months or even years for what we knew would eventually happen. While many in the public didn't believe this decision would happen, we prepared for *Roe*'s overturn because we knew that *Roe* didn't protect our bodily autonomy. Liberatory Harm Reduction practice has always included supporting people who do not want to carry children and supporting those who do, with efforts from abortion doulas to birth doulas, from providing clinic defense to demanding that clinics provide trans and gender nonconforming young people and adults with access to whatever health care is needed, regardless of age. In a long text thread about the loss of *Roe* and harm reduction practice in action, Viva Ruiz of Thank God for Abortion said to me:

> It's devastating and it's also just one more day. We will keep prioritizing care for those who need abortions and for those

who provide abortions. We are rooted in Liberatory Harm Reduction, so we are not bowed by *Roe* being overturned. Of course, we have tears and we have feelings about this lovelessness, this brutality. But NOTHING can dissuade us from finding our way back to each other. Our resolve is bigger in the face of this violence. Abortion was out of reach for so many before *Roe* was overturned. *Roe* was an illusion—it was shaky, and it fell.

Now is a moment to rebuild trust among each other and have a real coalition that fights for everyone, not just some—led by Black women, BIPOC, trans and GNC people, disabled people, sex workers. We need our strategy and our tactics to lead this work because our leadership is happening, has always been happening.

Liberatory Harm Reduction says it's not a one-size capitalist, linear, meritocratic path to victory. LHR points instead to what Angela Davis is speaking about—we are living on a continuum of change: "I think that even those struggles that did not conclude successfully, that were not victorious, help us to develop agendas for the future." LHR and Davis remind us that even within loss, there are wins to be made. We ask ourselves, *How are we helping one person access abortion today*? and then take that action every day. We will normalize breaking unjust laws because it's on us to care for us—no matter what. If we touch one person, it's a victory. Every day, we will save our lives and fight for our collective liberation.

revolutionary love notes

These Revolutionary Love Notes are from sex workers and people working to end the criminalization of those targeted as sex workers, who have helped establish and grow the harm reduction movement. They are also legends within the Reproductive Justice movement and because—as Deon notes below, erasure is real—they are also widely unknown with the public health sector of the harm reduction world. Their work, from starting one of the first syringe exchanges in the country (Women with a Vision, in 1986) to being stalked and harassed by a Christian-based housing program and suing the state of Arizona (Monica Jones), is crucial to understanding harm reduction.

But I Cannot Be Silenced:

Conversation with Monica Jones

I first learned about harm reduction when I was a street-based sex worker—from a trans woman who did a training on digital sex work, and from undocumented trans women who were telling me how to survive out here. These are the rules you need to know, for example, let the trade know that you're trans before you hop in a car, make sure you know where you're going, always have condoms on you. If the police stop you, just keep walking until they tell you to stop. Don't give out any information and just say you're just walking through on your way to your friend's house, on your way to the pawn shop. So, those were like my first introduction to harm reduction.

Sylvia Rivera and Marsha P. Johnson started STAR, which was a harm reduction project, housing girls who were getting out of prison, helping them get safe access to the outside through writing letters. But we also realized, *Who's going to heal the healers and the people who are doing the harm reduction work?* We're giving so much of ourselves. And when we have a mental health crisis, who can we call on? Say a trans sister is like working, working, working—let's get her a trip somewhere else where she can detox and replenish herself so she can continue this work and help avoid burnout. Because we put so much into each other people, just turn away from harm reduction because being burned out is real in this work.

We have to talk about violence that is happening to trans women, and offer tools, but we are also at risk ourselves, plus we also have to talk about prison abolition work. It's all a part of harm reduction, and it all affects Black trans women—especially in sex work—double or triple because of all the layers of harm, plus the demands of leadership.

Trans women need to be centered in harm reduction and we also need to be taken care of in a way that is more holistic, especially for the ones out here doing the peer-to-peer work. They are the ones going out at two o'clock at night because Susie got arrested or Susie is in a domestic violence situation and needs to get into a hotel. And then that person then has to go to work at 10 a.m. but been up for five hours with Susie. Is it okay for that person to take that day off, and we have someone else step in? We need to make sure that we build a sustainable environment for trans women to do their work.

Shira: How do we create sustainable harm reduction organizations for sex worker-led projects?

Monica: Take an organization doing serious harm reduction work. Let's say they have enough staff and have enough income to support a sustainable staffing, enough trained staff so that the executive director, who is Black and trans or Black and queer, can step to catch their breath and come back five days later replenished. The funder has to understand that our executive director just had burned out and understand that the staff is stepping in with confidence. We have to make sure that we heal the healers and also create retreat space for harm reductionists. I want to see someone buying property, like a nice cabin like in Northern Arizona or upstate New York, where someone, for instance a group of trans folks, can just go, relax, and get themselves together.

What led me to that work as a Black trans woman who engaged in sex work was this really interesting moment when I was going to Arizona State University to become a social worker. I heard about this social work professor working with the police to arrest people in order to get them services. To me, that's totally fucked up, and that's not what social work is about. Social work is meeting people where they're at and going from there. I said, arresting people doesn't sound right. I had a conversation with this social worker to tell them that they were causing more harm in the world, and that decriminalizing sex work will also combat sex trafficking. I pointed out Australia, New Zealand, the Netherlands, and all these other places where trafficking is looked at differently. He flat out disagreed with me.

But I cannot be silenced. I need to let people know. So, I got involved with fighting to decriminalize sex work and to end trafficking through doing my own organizing work. I became this poster child for this whole movement. I thought we were fighting the power, but then I realized I was going hungry because I was advised not to do sex work while I was doing leadership work because of the media attention, which made me a target for the cops. Not working affected my mental health and not working made me dependent on handouts.

My story was really empowering, but it also was taken from me and used as a narrative against me, too. The positive side of this movement and work is building connections to other organizers, to other trans women, to other Black trans activists, to other sex workers' rights activists. Also, I got connected to scholarships, went to the International AIDS Conference, and talked about the intersectionality. I connected those dots while I'm still in school to become a social worker. I connected the dots of intersectionality and how that plays a part in the criminalization of sex work and how all these little key pieces fit in. Those are really some good upsides.

From the work we built, we can see the studies of how many Black and Brown people are being arrested, and we were able to connect it to immigration too. For so many immigrants, a prostitution charge means no visa, no chance of becoming a citizen—so we have to connect our fights. Building that community and the collaboration work is a really great upside to this movement.

Right now, I am doing a tiny-housing project in Tucson. What trans people need is access to housing that meets them at the outer threshold. We are in the beginning stages of doing tiny-housing projects. We're going to start our demo project of what our vision of a tiny home will look like for trans people and sex workers. Also, there are many people who might not need housing at this point but might need access to treatment or therapy that we may not provide; we can work with other organizations that can provide that. We plan to have a big center in the middle of the tiny-home community for people to come, get some rest, take a shower, eat a hot meal, and go back to whatever they were doing. When they're ready for sustainable housing, then we can provide them access to the tiny homes.

We are also doing policy work, which was our original formation: a policy organization. We are doing the Universal Periodic Review (UPR) and the Commission on the Status of Women (CSW).

What do people need to know about BIPOC harm reduction focused on BIPOC sex workers?

The myth that Black people are more transphobic must end. We are also looking at individuals from a holistic approach and really trying to get our staff together so that we don't create more trauma for people when they're trying to get help. Hopefully, we can pay for Black trans people to go to college to become therapists, to get them the resources, to sort of come back to our organization, to work for our organization and lead.

I also want people to know that whatever they know about me from my court case and national fight to decriminalize sex work, there is a whole individual underneath of that. There is me, Monica Jones: the aunt, the cousin, the daughter, the social worker, the person who loved and who lost, who knows pain, who also knows really good empathy, and is a really great friend. And it's those things that really makes me a really great harm reductionist—all those things about my experience with houselessness and work in the system, my experience with being a person with disability, learning disability, and fighting through all these systems to get where I'm at now. My experiences of sexual and domestic violence make me understand and see other situations and everything else—it's all of this that makes a good harm reductionist and advocate.

Erasure Is Real:
Conversation with Deon Haywood of Women with a Vision

This interview is with Deon Haywood, a Black lesbian from New Orleans who has been one of the most important leaders in my harm reduction universe for the last thirty years. Women with a Vision (WWAV) was started in the late 1980s. It was the brainchild of Danita Muse, who then approached seven other women about the idea of supporting their community because of the AIDS epidemic. At the time, nobody was really talking to the African American community here, nobody was talking to women, yet women were the backbone of the community. The founders of WWAV knew women were the head of household, responsible for caring for everything from children to parents to siblings to other community members, the people that needed to be reached around HIV and drug use.

Shira: Tell me about how Danita started WWAV.

Deon: Danita was a substance abuse counselor for the state of Louisiana and worked in the state-run substance abuse program. She thought they should talk with drug users and take a harm reduction approach even if they didn't call it that. A couple of years later, we became connected to people who were in the harm reduction world, like Dave Purchase, Imani Woods, and others. Imani Woods came here and did a training for us around sex work and drug use and crack use. She came to New Orleans, and she stayed with us for like two weeks, spent like two weeks with us, just hanging out and really talking to community, talking to people who weren't really on the side of harm reduction, who kind of didn't get it. We were going to some of the early harm reduction conferences, like in Cleveland and Miami. I took every single thing home from the conference because we didn't have any resources here. We brought syringes home. We brought vein care kits.

Our syringe exchange started pretty early on. We tried our best to work with the state and the city of New Orleans. New Orleans was a little bit more agreeable to helping us get rid of dirty syringes, so we had kind of an agreement with them. That agreement fell through because they wanted to do it for the research only and not really care about community. They didn't give us these things because they believed in it, they were trying to just test it out on us. Danita sent the two hundred or three hundred thousand dollars back.

I'm very grateful that they modeled that way of leading for me back then. I was the only one working full-time, and so there were times where they didn't take pay so that I could have pay. That struggle exists for organizations of color, especially those led by women. We definitely had a hard time after giving the money back, and we were fine not having it and figuring out how to make it work, which is a form of harm reduction in itself: just navigating how you're going to do this work.

WWAV has been around for thirty years. I think it's our ability to organize, to be present, to be relevant, and to still have an idea of how we serve and work with our community. We were already doing the work before we were incorporated. As far south as we are, nobody we knew was talking about harm reduction, or we didn't meet any harm reductionists here—they were from either the West Coast or East Coast.

Somebody interviewed Danita about two years ago, and she was like, "I didn't have the word *queer*." She was lesbian-identified. I know now that the number of people who've given their time, their energy, and their life to harm reduction were People of Color and Black folk. It didn't pop out of your [white people's] ass. No. You've had a framework to work with even when you didn't know you had a framework to work with.

Tell me about the No Justice campaign.

The No Justice campaign was about fighting the state's solicitation, crime against nature statute, which was the selling or offering of oral or anal sex. The unique thing about this law and this particular statute is that the law had been around for two hundred and something years, and people have tried to fight it multiple times. It was always around gay men, and those men were always white gay men because I don't think any Black men had the resources to try to fight the law.

Then the law was revised to target street-based sex workers, which helped New Orleans get money. They got city money and state money for every person who was in jail. It was very easy, like low-hanging fruit. We saw a lot of people could be targeted even while not doing anything.

We challenged that law because we saw the big picture and were out publicly about what we wanted for sex workers in our community, and who sex workers were in our community. After the No Justice campaign and after people were removed from the sex offender registry, that was the time when trafficking became the big thing for people for all the reasons we know.

We just kept saying, "No, this is what sex workers are." Many of them are not trafficked, and most women we work with and people we knew, including trans people, weren't people who were trafficked; they were people who were surviving or just needed to make a living. We continued on with that, just doing regular outreach about sex work, talking to different people, and even had a voter engagement program. We included all of these things that made people feel like they had the power to do something.

This is how capitalism works. This is how our society works. We put the value on the things that we can get money from. Sex work? It's not always like that. Sometimes people are in charge of themselves, and I know the world has a hard time dealing with that. Since so many people that have been targeted and hurt and all the things you can name in the name of trafficking, they know that shit is not working.

Let's talk about anti-criminalization as an answer to the anti-trafficking movement.

We don't want to legalize it [sex work] because we've seen that before. People of Color, poor people—anybody that the system can target, it will target, even when something is legalized. We saw that with the No Justice campaign. We saw that through the War on Drugs. We've seen all of those things over the years. People are still targeted when things are legalized. We want to decriminalize, to end criminalization of it, because we want to remove it from the books altogether. For example, the crime against nature statute is still listed because lawmakers refused to move it, so the police can randomly charge people, which forces them to go through the system just to be told, *Oh, we can't charge you, and you're free to go*. We want to have all of that removed from the books and completely decriminalized.

I think the anti-trafficking movement is playing into people's fears and also causing a lot of harm. It gives organizations, state- and city-run agencies, and large nonprofits trafficking money. It keeps people in this cycle, and it's not helping them at all. I just feel like they've done more damage. Especially for a government that doesn't want to raise minimum wage or fix the wage gap between men and women, or between Black women and white women in this country. Nobody takes that on, so we're not doing anything but causing more harm to people who've been harmed already. Trafficking legislation conflates consensual sex work and people who make the decision to be involved in sex work with trafficking. I'm not saying that trafficking didn't happen or hasn't happened, but the system that they have in place is not working. It hasn't changed anything except added more incarceration, which seems to be what is always the end result.

Sex workers have their finger on the pulse of most things in our community. They know what's going on. If anything, decriminalizing sex work will actually be an asset to people who are trafficked. I strongly believe that, given what I know about the way community works and the connections that take place in the community.

We also know that sex workers are healers; they are parents; they are caregivers, too—not only trying to care for themselves but everybody in our communities. And I think more than not, nowadays, people have a different idea of what sex work is. I think people are starting to get it and starting to understand people don't want you to save them. They just want you to get out of their way so they can make a living for themselves in a way that feels comfortable to them.

What do people need to know about BIPOC harm reduction?

I just want people to know that it is a part of our culture, Black culture, to care for one another, it is our very survival in this country, and, given the history of Black, POC, and Indigenous people here, our survival has been about us using harm reduction methods. I want to see this story told so people know that harm reduction didn't just pop up five years ago, or because your teacher brought it up in your classroom, or because you got a job and y'all think this is popular to talk about. Some of us have been doing this for a long time. WWAV is thirty years old and still present and relevant, and we're still here doing harm reduction.

When I think about the connection, it's how older people in our community was like, *Oh, we made this medicine, and this will help people in our community do this, or this will help you not get this.* These are all the things that we've been using to care for ourselves when no one else did.

I Believe(d?) in Violence

Many of you reading this may be aware of my long relationship with Mariame Kaba. Mariame and I first began to overlap when I was in my mid to late teens and living in New York City. We were both a part of a youth leadership development program called The Door on the Lower East Side. Interestingly, even though the organization was not explicitly a harm reduction program, it functioned like one: its goals were to meet the needs of young people, whether they were street-based and/or houseless or doing complex community organizing work.

Mariame and I were having vastly different experiences in the world and in our personal lives when we were a part of The Door. I was fighting for my life at night in the park, which wasn't too far from the apartment Mariame lived in with her family. Even though we never met in person, I was one of the "outdoor kids" the program helped, and she was one of the "indoor kids" doing leadership work and organizing other young people. Being a part of that program shaped each of us and helped us form key ideas about harm reduction and created long-term beliefs in youth leading the work. We have always believed the idea that "young people are the future" is bullshit, because we know that young people are our leaders right now. We were both accessing The Door for different needs. I was getting meals and help figuring out how to sleep rough as well as advice for getting through high school.

For me, just knowing that other young people like Mariame were in the same building working on changing the system gave me a sense of power, like I could do that too.

Even though I barely attended high school back in the small town outside of Philadelphia where my mom lived, when I was there, I was vocal. I ran a poetry zine, and I also started a recycling program (the school district did not recycle at this time). Instead of giving the money away that we collected from recycling, I will be honest and tell you that I also kept (stole?) some of the money from the collection cans and used it to orchestrate punk shows in random buildings on the weekends. The five-dollar cover charge to see five mostly terrible bands battle (for what victory I still don't know) gave me enough cash to get back to New York City and buy drugs or food. Somehow, I also had two jobs at retail stores and was managing to sleep with whoever would pay me. I was busy as fuck. It helped that I had a lot of time during the day, because I was barely present in school, but the assumption by teachers and guidance counselors that young people who aren't making it in traditional public school models are lazy or up to no good is really based in adult fears and projections. Outreach workers from Streetwork Project realized that if I knew how to negotiate a price for sex or drugs that I also knew how to talk my way through a college interview. Those outreach workers realized that if I could hold five jobs and keep everyone guessing about where I was sleeping, I could balance a semester's worth of classes and work to pay my tuition.

A friend and lifelong harm reductionist who works with young people explained to me how harm reduction helped them think about healing from childhood sexual abuse:

> Harm reduction responses to childhood sexual abuse ask us to dream what we would have wanted to happen as children and create new ways to support each other and build structures in our communities to prevent, address, heal, and shift cul-

tural norms. Harm reduction helps us attend to the impacts, wounding, health, and healing with love, care, persistence, gentleness, humor, consistency, and take things at our own speed and on our own terms. Harm reduction loves us all.

I have worked so hard to reclaim my body from the experience of childhood sexual violence. I believe that my involvement in the sex trade, street economy, and sex work helped me explore my boundaries and reclaim my "no." Harm reduction helped me process the experiences I had when I was younger because rather than kicking me out of places when I was high, it encouraged me to be there. That experience of being welcome, wanted, and safe no matter what state I was in was irreplaceable in my life. Harm reduction spaces and community showed me I was worth investing in and gave me space to practice boundaries through peer-to-peer communication with other survivors, other drug users, other people in the sex trade. Seeing my peers show up at a program meant, somehow, that I was also alive.

Years later, one night at the park, my feelings about violence crystallized into a belief system—one that did not change until twenty years later, when I began working at YWEP and needed to find nonviolent solutions because now I was part of an organization that was already heavily targeted by police, and it was an organization that I loved. Mariame, a longtime believer that we can't use violence to end violence, and I became thought partners and started to write down where we were being successful in our violence transformation approaches. This became the basis for the workbook titled *Fumbling Towards Repair: A Workbook for Community Accountability Facilitators.*

When I left home, I went looking for safety, for people like me. My people were in that park. We were queer and trans, and we were all using drugs. Most of us were trading sex for money. On this particular night, a friend's boyfriend came looking for her, full of rage. He had just discovered that my friend was getting paid for sex. He thought this amounted to cheating on him, and he wanted a cut of the cash. Unfortunately for him, he walked into the wrong crowd; we were already angry at him and plotting against him because he had sexually assaulted my friend a few nights before.

We knew we couldn't call the cops. We were underage, using drugs, sleeping outside, and had too much cash we couldn't explain. We thought we couldn't tell any adult what was going on without being forced to interact with the system in some way. When "angry boyfriend" showed up looking for cash, we jumped him. And it worked. He never bothered any of us again.

That experience made me think that violence could solve problems. I spent years writing "Kill your rapist" on every surface I could find and possibly convinced myself that I coined that phrase (I did not). I wrote a piece for a popular feminist zine sometime in the early 1990s that had detailed instructions on how to fight back during a sexual assault, including castrating the attacker. But I really doubled down on my belief when I accidently formed a group that would beat up rapists. I say "accidently formed" because the first incident happened spontaneously at an event where a rapist showed up to party, acting as though he hadn't been drugging and raping people for the last few months. He was wealthy and white, and no survivors I knew would even consider calling the police, let alone press charges. Doing so was too dangerous. So we jumped him that night in a parking lot near the house he lived in. A few days later, I learned that multiple people had been a part of those rapes. So we jumped every one of them.

At the same time, I was working in nonprofits. They were beautiful spaces that were liberatory and precious. I knew that we could not use violence to solve our problems because it would risk those organizations being shut down. I would never compromise critical spaces for young People of Color to get their needs met and gather, so I challenged myself to begin to figure out how to solve problems without violence, without police. I began thinking about harm reduction in a new way, as it applied to violence both systemically and interpersonally. Some of this problem-solving looked like giving out metal nail files to be used as weapons in emergencies. They could be passed off as insignificant during body searches by police and could be easily stored in bras or underpants for easy access if needed.

Because our survival is criminalized, I now believe that violence as a solution is unsustainable. In the long term, it makes us less safe than we already are because it opens the door to the state; violence as a singular strategy backfires because it creates more violence. It may stop an instance of attack, but it may set the attacker up to be more rageful and possibly more harmful. I think that when we are violent, we also harm ourselves. Violence can haunt us.

Yet I do not believe that we can tell anyone, especially sex workers of color, and especially those of who survive childhood sexual violence, that they should not engage in violence unless we have an alternative solution to guarantee their safety and to ensure that their attacker will stop. In the most intimate moments, when it's really going down, I believe violent self-defense is a sacred harm reduction strategy. I was often told that feminist self-defense is different because it doesn't presume that girls and trans people know that we have a self to defend. I have always pushed back on that (as I did with *You can't love anyone until you love yourself,* which seeks to deny survivors the right to love). Instead, harm reduction values tell us we are worth loving and protecting exactly as we are, and, moreover, we learn to love ourselves through how we show love and protection to other people. I believe we know we have selves, and sometimes in a fight for our lives and the lives of our loved ones we have more clarity than ever.

revolutionary
love
notes

This section of love notes from Dominique Morgan and Mariame Kaba weave together Transformative Justice, prison abolition, and Liberatory Harm Reduction. As survivors of sexual violence, prisons and courts are built in our names and the state uses us over and over again to explain its carceral logic. Liberatory Harm Reduction is the daily practice that those of us working to end prisons use to reduce violence every day.

Harm Reduction Is Our Shared Root: *Interview with Mariame Kaba*

Mariame Kaba is an organizer, educator, and curator. Her work focuses on ending violence, dismantling the prison-industrial complex, Transformative Justice, and supporting youth leadership development. She is the founder and director of Project NIA, a grassroots organization with a vision to end youth incarceration. Mariame has cofounded multiple organizations and projects over the years including the Chicago Freedom School, the Chicago Taskforce on Violence against Girls & Young Women, the Chicago Alliance to Free Marissa Alexander, and the Rogers Park Young Women's Action Team (YWAT) and is the current cofounder and codirector of Interrupting Criminalization alongside Andrea J. Ritchie.

Shira: Do you remember where you first heard about harm reduction?

Mariame: I think I didn't hear the term *harm reduction* until I was well into youth work; I would say, probably in the early '90s, maybe, is when I started hearing the term. And this was when I was still in New York, doing work with young people on a volunteer basis. It wasn't through my job or through my work because I was teaching, and I was working in a domestic violence organization. I think that when I went to Sanctuary for Families in New York City in '94 is when I got more of a social service harm reduction primer.

Before that, I was just doing harm reduction work, I think, but I didn't have a term for it. I was working with some young people who were substance using at the time. I didn't really have language for trading sex for money and survival, so, it was young people who were "prostitutes"—that was the terminology we used; they called themselves "hoes." I didn't have a framework of sex work at that point yet.

I was really young. I was in my early twenties. So, that's when I started to practice it. The more formalized approaches were introduced to me, frankly, more like social service interventions. That's how I got [formally introduced] to harm reduction. I went to a training when I was at Sanctuary for people who were getting certificates in addiction counseling. And it was there that people were talking about using syringes, clean ones, and how it was a good idea to offer people choices, and that kind of language. That's how I became formally introduced to harm reduction.

So, many people may not know that we were actually in the same youth program when we were both teenagers. That program was called The Door, and in many ways, it was a harm reduction–oriented project—even though they didn't necessarily claim it.

I have to say that my interaction with The Door was really very much an experience of youth-led and youth-driven work that involved them mainly just providing us with a space.

I didn't actually partake of any of The Door's actual services for young people. I was doing leadership development stuff—though that wasn't the language we had. But they worked with all teenagers who needed a space to be able to organize around police violence, around racism, around things like that. I think there are lots of other people who came up alongside me who have a very different experience.

There were those of us who kind of were on one track. And then there were young people who were at The Door for actual services, who were living much more precarious lives than I was. I had my family. I had a safe and stable place to sleep. I had a great school to go to. I was there because we didn't really have any places to hang out when we needed to have meetings in the city, and they let us hang out in their space.

That in and of itself is harm reduction—meeting young people where they are at and working with them whether they had housing and want to organize or they were houseless and wanted a bus pass. I'm bringing up The Door because you and I have talked about this before, that we have this a shared origin story that created a deep alignment in our work and lives.

That's right. I do think that the fact that I was interacting with young people who were precariously housed or "at-risk," as though it was just a casual thing—it wasn't like we were interacting through a shared program. It's like, everybody was there. And some folks who were living very precariously became friends of mine. I actually was able to become friends with people who I probably wouldn't have become friends with in other settings, just because we were in the same place. And some of those young people did join us and participate in things we were organizing.

They all had various challenges that they had to overcome, but they would come and hang out and have food. They would add in, provide a different perspective, different from what we would have thought about ourselves. So, I think that was also an important thing that may not be articulated as harm reduction but is in fact just a natural place to make connections with people, nonjudgmentally.

Do you think that informed your organizing philosophy as a whole?

It hugely did. Because first and foremost, what it did for me very early on, and I could see that it happened to me again many years later when we were trying to build the Chicago Freedom School in Chicago, where people kept saying to me *certain* young people will be coming here and *certain* young people will not, just as a given—this is just the way things are going to be. And I don't agree in the sense that you can make spaces where young people access the things they need at the level they need it. And that some of those young people won't disclose to you that they're precarious. And they'll show up and eat the food and contribute, and you won't know that they are actually houseless the whole time.

That happened to me as a kid. I met young people at The Door whom I later found out were houseless and sleeping in the park. They came over to my house. I used money from my parents to give them money for food and rooms. So, it just made it clear to me that, yes, you want to create projects and programs that meet the needs of particular young people, but that you don't assume automatically that certain young people—like those who are houseless—are just not going to want to do certain kinds of things. The issue is, what do you have on offer? Open it up and let people take advantage of the safe space you make for everyone.

Harm reduction from The Door did inform my organizing, I just didn't know that at the time. It wasn't like, *This is now my philosophy of action*. It became part of the DNA of the way that I moved in the world.

What also stuck with me through the years is a resistance to the idea that "difference is determinative." Just because I come from a different place than somebody else does not mean that we cannot figure out ways to work together, or that we cannot contribute in the ways that allow us to bring our unique selves to the process. Everybody doesn't have to do everything in the same way. Your contribution in this really unique way actually is beautiful. And we should be excited that you came to the meeting that one time. And if you didn't show up again, we still got something out of your presence through that one time.

We did this with Circles & Ciphers* when we were working initially. Talking with the founders, we would talk about not needing to force young people to come every meeting. Some of them are just not able to come regularly. And we should be looking at it as *Did they show up to three meetings in a year?* despite dealing with so much shit. That's a freaking huge deal for young people who are disconnected or gang affiliated or in conflict with the law. The fact they showed up that one time is what we ought to be celebrating. Right?

I wonder at what point did you start connecting harm reduction to larger liberation ideas?

I did that first addiction counselor/harm reduction training thing in '94. I did my first official Restorative Justice training in 1996. That first training was social service based and predates the Restorative Justice language that I got later. My origin story of my work focused on Transformative Justice is always rooted in my RJ training that I took in '96. Restorative Justice gave me framing and language around repair, around being clear about how people shouldn't be thrown away, and how to make sure that we're always trying to be in the right relationship to each other.

* Located in Chicago, Circles & Ciphers' mission: "Circles & Ciphers is a hip-hop infused restorative justice organization led by and for young people impacted by violence. Through art-based peace circles, education and direct action we collectively heal and work to bring about the abolition of the prison industrial complex."

Those lessons that I got from those early RJ trainings led me to wanting to know more about RJ. I read more and got myself trained as a circle keeper.* I guess I had already begun to think differently at that point. I must have because the concept of non-disposability, and that language that I used in the late '90s probably is informed as much by that harm reduction language, but again, rooted in addiction, which was very much like, *Everybody is valuable.*

There was a lot of medicalization language at that time about addiction that I remember clearly. It was like, *People are sick and if somebody had cancer, would you throw them away?* So, that's the language that I got. But that was useful for me at that time because I didn't have a language around addiction, though I had tons of friends who used and abused drugs in my teenage years, and many who didn't make it because they passed away from overdoses, AIDS, and other things that decimated my generation of young people in New York City.

And then in the early 2000s, when I came to learn more about harm reduction through YWEP, I could put more of an emphasis on the thinking around *You have to give people a choice.* You have to not be about directing people into decisions you want them to make. You have to step back and really be nonjudgmental, and what does that really mean when you are really afraid for people sometimes. How do you deal with those emotions?

Being nonjudgmental could lead to very serious consequences for young people, so how do you manage your feelings of wanting to really be protective of people who are young? In this case, many of them were under the age of eighteen. How do I reconcile that with my real desire to want to protect people? That's just my nature—it's not easy for me to see someone struggling and just stay in the space of letting them choose for themselves, but

* In Restorative Justice work, the circle keeper is entrusted with maintaining the circle as a safe space for dialogue and for guiding that dialogue.

I trained myself in that way. I would say that helped me, the experience of working with YWEP, young people really honed it, brought it to bear for me very clearly.

A lot of the young people I worked with were very heavy users of drugs. Some of them were in incredibly abusive relationships with partners who were much older than they were—under every kind of law, it would be seen as statutory rape. I think about that to this day. Yet, my work was to be present with them, to be nonjudgmental, to offer lots of resources and lots of support. *If you feel like you need a place to crash, you can crash at my house. Do you have what you need for transportation? Here's some money.* Just trying to be available with resources.

I started using the term *Transformative Justice* officially in my work in and around 2001. So, the time between '94 or '96, ' 96 to 2001, that was a good five to seven years when I was very much thinking of my work as Restorative Justice work.

And then I think I got the TJ language in 2001, I'm pretty sure, because that's when I remember somebody telling me to read Ruth Morris's work. Somebody in RJ was like, *You need to be reading Ruth Morris's work, because this is work that is broader than RJ and links to the conditions that lead to the things that you're concerned about. And I think you're more in that camp.* And this was, I think, even before the community accountability statement that came out of INCITE! So, I started reading about Transformative Justice before I learned about community accountability.

Harm reduction did predate that stuff for me. And harm reduction was always there but not articulated. That's what I would say. It wasn't really until I met you and Lara [Brooks] and that crew in Chicago that harm reduction as a thing became solidified for me. I did not have that as a conscious frame from which I was operating. But once I got that, I was also privy to you all doing that series of workshops in Chicago that were harm reduction workshops. I attended one of them—it was an introduction to harm reduction one.

And that was my, *Oh, things are much clearer now* moment. The language was much clearer. There was a lot of conversation about sex work. It wasn't just needle exchanges. I was like, *Oh, this is a whole thing with the whole philosophy and a whole set of values.* . . . So that's kind of when that became more incorporated in my youth work.

All the things that I see in common, at least in terms of my practice of Transformative Justice and in harm reduction, I see the connections as the ability to be nonjudgmental, the focus on behavior, and actions over morality. Throwing away the idea of *You are a "bad person"* and you need to do all this repenting for stuff. That is not helpful. I remember very clearly during that training around the stuff about sex work that was like, *You have to let people make their own definitions of things.* That was really helpful for my thinking around harm, because I didn't determine in advance what the harm was. I had to work with the person who's the survivor of the harm and let them tell me what they think the harm is. Also, the person who harmed has to come up with their definition of the terms, and then you have to figure out a way to bridge the gap between those realities. But they're both real for the people who are involved.

There was still a lot of "social work" in harm reduction that limited thinking about root causes of harm, even though I knew people like you and Laura Mintz and Lara Brooks and others who were organizers, who also had a harm reductionist frame. I got the emphasis on root causes more through reading about Transformative Justice and practicing it.

I think you're pointing out that public health distilled harm reduction into risk reduction, and that distillation removes the root-cause analysis component and the politicized realities that Liberatory Harm Reduction actually sprang from.

Yup. Because, remember that I wasn't rooted in worlds of harm reduction in the way that you were. So I had to pick it up by literally learning about it through other people and through other frames. I came to it that way.

I want to talk a little bit about the importance of prison abolition to harm reduction and vice versa.

Yeah, I think for me, there were two things. I think the first is that for a long time I've been saying pretty loudly to people that sometimes our work means doing nothing, actually—that the answer isn't the "treatment-industrial complex" and it isn't "treatment not jails." It isn't, *Oh this person is drinking, let's all now put them in a program*, which is just another form of carceral control and capture when it's not voluntary and people are mandated into it.

I think there was a clear kind of harm reduction–inspired understanding of that for me. Those social service things that I went to around addiction served me well to have a language when people were able to then say, *Well, yeah, what about all these people who are doing drugs? We can't just leave them to their own devices.* And it was like, actually, we can, because there are a lot of people who are using who aren't addicts, and people who are addicts don't need carcerality in order to actually be able to live a life that's productive, that's not under capture and control by state institutions.

That was one angle where it was clear that harm reduction really helped me come up with a theory of the case, kind of. So, I was never deluded. From the very beginning, I never got into the mode where I had to be pulled back from the treatment-industrial complex thing. I always was like, *This is a danger, we shouldn't go down this road.* And I think harm reduction helps quite a bit in making it clear to me, and it gave me the lens really early on to not fall for that crap.

I think the other thing is actually a counterfactual, which was that over the years, I've come to hate the concept of people saying *harm reduction*.

The liberalism?

The liberalism of it. I sometimes feel it can be a cop-out, or an unhelpful label—*We're doing this for a harm reduction*. When actually, you can really just do nothing, and that's actually harm reduction. People think we need incrementalism and that that's what harm reduction is. But these motherfuckers don't know anything about harm reduction. It has become appropriated, and in a kind of perverse way I contributed to that when I used to, many years ago, call voting "harm reduction"—but voting isn't harm reduction. It's just a tool that can sometimes be used.

I think, for the most part, people are actually well intentioned when they're trying to pull out harm reduction ideas. They're trying to acknowledge that people need shit, and we need resources and services. We need ways to provide people with things that the system denies them. And how are you going to do that?

In this way, harm reduction becomes this way of talking about not hurting people more. And so, it really makes sense. And I understand it. Yet it does make me get more and more frustrated, that it's being divorced from its roots and being used now as this "cover-all" to implement incrementalism with no analysis of how they are expanding the capacity and reach of the state.

One thing I've heard recently has been people talking about house arrest as harm reduction and how there's so much opportunity now for house arrest because of COVID, and that we should celebrate that as harm reduction. Can we unpack that as why that's so bad? It's so terrifying.

Yes. I mean I was having a conversation with Vikki Law on a podcast a few years ago. I was pointing out the problem with electronic shackling and home confinement as substitutes for the prison, and as part of what people are offering as a different thing than the current. . . . Really, just prisons are death-making institutions.

They are, in fact, totalizing torture chambers. And people say, *Well, incarcerated people prefer electronic monitoring or home confinement to being in a prison.* And my answer to that is, *Yes.* You know what I mean? Yes, because prisons are hellholes. So, yes. But here's where we're in trouble. Because what home confinement does is it doesn't just make captivity more acceptable and more seemingly benign. What it also does is it takes it out of public view, even more than prisons are out of our public view. So, now we're in a position where, like people in Maya and Vikki's book,* your home is your prison. But in our culture, our home is private. So, we're asking people to "not intervene in a private sphere."

So, now, the prison is just a new version of "private" prisons. But currently private prisons are still a space where the public has a say. Your home is not a place where the public has a say. Can you imagine how much more difficult it's going to be to organize with incarcerated people if everybody's incarcerated in their home?

Imagine how much less we'll be able to marshal for people, much less in terms of resources and visibility. It's horrible inside, in prisons, but you get food, which is terrible, but you get it. You are in a position where a few of you get work, even though it's horribly boring and exploitative work and you get paid very little. Some people who are incarcerated appreciate that. You may have some programs you go to. There may be some things for you that the public is responsible for providing, like terrible medical care, for example.

When you put that into the private sphere of the home, the state does none of that. The state doesn't pay for your food, you've got to cover it yourself. The state doesn't actually provide any sort of programs for you. You're responsible for finding a job with an ankle monitor, and the jobs aren't hiring people with electronic shackles. So, you're constantly in a position where it's a differ-

---

* Maya Schenwar and Victoria Law, *Prison By Any Other Name: The Harmful Consequences of Popular Reforms* (New York: The New Press, 2020).

ent form of privatization that is actually putting all the costs on the individual and their family, the costs that would have been covered by the public sphere to some extent, and in this new/old world no one will be providing any of these things.

There are levels to this. You can't organize people from their home, and they can't organize and they don't have people who will be able to fight for them in the same way that we currently fight for incarcerated people and with incarcerated people. The state takes away every possibility of actually providing any resources to you now. You're in a position where the costs are on your shoulders, as somebody who's being criminalized and held captive by the state.

There're just going to be new challenges and new horrors that are going to emerge from this. And if we don't speak to that, then whatever the harm that's reduced is going to be dwarfed in many ways by the new harms that will be created.

That's what is missed when we talk about harm reduction in a flat way. Because some types of harm will definitely be reduced. Yet, then you have to weigh that in some weird way we don't know how to weigh anything against all of the new harms that are going to be engendered. Harms that people don't really know about yet because a critical mass of people aren't experiencing it yet. So, we can't see how it's going to be potentially even more harmful in certain kinds of ways. This is a horrible example of when people might misunderstand harm reduction and shit goes wrong.

Yeah. I think because people often ask me, *What's an example of public policy that's harm reduction?* And I'm like, *Well, it's about the removal of criminalizing laws.* It's about decriminalization. And it's about legalization. But it's not about reform because reform is such a blunt instrument, and its purpose is always to create harm in certain people's lives and to create criminalized survivors because it has to uphold this other part of the illusion of safety.

Legalization is law. And decriminalization is law, too. But people would assume that those are reforms. Legalizing drugs as a reform.

It would be nonreformist reform because it is steps towards abolition. And I think that's where a lot of people are getting a little bit muddled and confused right now in PIC abolition because it's not in and of itself inherently that reform is a bad thing if abolition is within the context of what your larger goals are and the steps you're taking along the way.

If abolition is your North Star, you're going to try to make it so that the reforms you're adopting aren't going to actually, like you said, expand the scope of the thing you're trying to get rid of. So, in your idea of harm reduction, Liberatory Harm Reduction, nonreformist reforms are steps towards abolition. That's the clearest way to put it: *Is this reform getting us closer to our goal of ending prisons and the carceral control of the state?*

And I would also say that the thing that is a potential problem for how people view harm reduction is the need to be clear and to ask, *What harms are being reduced, for whom, and as opposed to what?*

There is also the frustrating confusion of people not understanding that question. For example, mainstream domestic violence policy advocates do this all the time. They say the reason we can't get rid of cops is because survivors call cops. And I'll say, but 60 percent or 70 percent of survivors don't ever engage them. So, what do you got for them?

For me this is so important. It is critical. Because people often misidentify the harm and create the wrong emergency. So, for example, when we're talking about self-injury, that the emergency that people respond to and the crisis they create is around the moment that that young person or that individual is self-harming, as opposed to the emergency of the violence that they're trying to mitigate or address or heal when they're practicing self-injury.

But self-injury is just the coping strategy—and sometimes it's the most adaptive strategy ever. The emergency is not at the time of the making of the wound—that's the wrong emergency. The right emergency is looking at whatever is going on in that person's life that makes self-injury the best strategy for dealing with pain, trauma, violence, and so on. People don't want to get complicated or messy. But it is.

Because I do think that, to me, this is where people get a lot of things messed up and we get stuck. Because people will say, *Well, you got to do something. We got to do something.* That something is what they're calling the harm reduction.

The other thing is, yeah, but sometimes, harm reduction is actually doing nothing. And that also has to be clearly an option. Like nothing could be the best intervention for self-injury in that moment. But that doesn't leave people satisfied. And so, harm reduction becomes a stand in for doing something. It's how people misuse harm reduction.

When harm reduction is viewed as a liberatory philosophy, *no change* is included as a really important part of the work. So, *no change* has to be a critical part of what we do, because change isn't always the best thing.

And that's where the PIC abolition connection to harm reduction to me is most salient. Because it goes to the point where everybody wants an intervention for some reason. In fact, there are times when it's actually the right call to have no intervention, that having no response to somebody doing an act, can be a productive action.

There was a great article in the *New York Times* recently about a man who owns a little army supply store down in the Lower East Side. The story talks about how the pandemic has totally shifted his work and his life and how the community has rallied around him during this time, and people just stop by to buy a key chain or buy things they don't need to keep him in business. One time a young man came into his store. It seems like he was inebriated or something. He swung around something and broke a case that had all this stuff in it. And what did the man who owned the store do? He just told the young man that maybe he should take kung fu lessons and ended up just fixing his own case. And then I think he got the young man some kung fu lessons.

Another time a young man who he knew in the community was stealing from him on a regular basis. Instead of turning him into the cops, he just continues to treat him with respect to the point where the young man was like, *This guy knows I'm stealing from him, I'm going to stop stealing from him.* In the one case, it was an intervention to offer the kung fu lessons. And the other time, it was like just leave it alone and be a human being. Right? It's just stuff.

That is the case sometimes when we're talking about criminalization. Sometimes you don't actually have to do anything big. Respect is the intervention. Kung fu lessons is the intervention. I just wanted to make that connection of PIC abolition and harm reduction, and [bringing] lessons from harm reduction into the PIC abolition world.

His store is a harm reduction setting because it centers relationship building, and it centers community and transformation and a complex understanding of harm in a way that is actually the essence of both PIC abolition and harm reduction at the same time.

Absolutely. Absolutely. Yes. Yes, yes, yes, that's absolutely the case.

I am so grateful for our—I don't even know how many years it is long. I think it's twenty years at this point. I know we had so many differences in how we grew up and what we were experiencing. Just that we've talked about The Door and how that

shaped me, that we were able to think and communicate with each other about these ideas. I get more and more appreciation for that all the time.

Me too, friend.

Harm Reduction Is Grace in Action

When I interviewed Dominique Morgan, she was executive director of Black & Pink, an organization working on prison abolition and to support queer and transgender people who are incarcerated. She is currently the executive director of the Okra Project, a social justice organization with a focus on LGBTQ/GNC people and individuals living with HIV/AIDS, where she works to dismantle the systems that perpetuate violence against Black trans people. Partnering her lived experience of being impacted by mass incarceration with a decade of change-making artistry, advocacy, and background in public health, she continues to work in spaces of sex education, radical self-care, and transformative youth development with intentions of dismantling the prison-industrial complex and its impact on our communities.

My vision of abolition has been something I have been working toward before I had the language for it. Since I became a paid activist in 2014 it's been a consistent experience of, *Oh, that's what that's called!* So, this idea of harm reduction, I feel like I've always done it, going all the way back to being a five-year-old kid who experienced sexual harm.

The questions I asked myself and my community, even as a kid, were, *How can we be more informed in the decisions we're making? How can we mitigate the harm?* As you're healing, you look back and come up with safety solutions and use them for next time.

I'm a huge comic book fan and so I've watched *WandaVision*. There's this character, Monica Rambeau (also known as Spectrum), whose powers are that she can synthesize and look at energy no matter what it is. I kind of feel like folks who have been impacted by trauma gain that same superpower. And I use the word *superpower* when I talk because I am trying to divest from using any language or words that feel like they come from a space that isn't based in strength. Also, interrogating whether strength is always good or bad.

Like from a Disability Justice perspective? Like we don't always have to be strong—we can be interdependent and ask for help?

Yes. And from a Transformative Justice perspective, too. Like with Superman, for example. There are worlds where Superman is very different. All the same powers, but in one world, he's the savior of the world, and in one world, he's the oppressor. So, power in itself isn't bad; it's about our actions, deeds, and position in the world. My being young and being impacted by trauma, I was given that power of synthesizing and looking at energy. It also impeded my experience in some ways. For instance, I'm that person when I get out of the shower, I lay out ten towels, because in my mind, there's a whole bunch of ways for me to slip, fall, and die in here. Thinking, *How bad can things go?* and planning to prevent that. I could die—but what would make a slip-and-fall not be death?

I remember being young and navigating this superpower with my mother, who experienced sexual harm, but she would never verbalize it. My mother was very much against us going anywhere overnight. Before GPS and cell phones, harm reduction practices were, *Mama, this is where I'm at. Mama, I'll call you this many times to let you know where I'm at.* I'm going to do what I need to make her feel safe, while also doing something that I want to do.

I look back at being young in prison and being friends with roommates or girls from the yard. We needed to make sure that they didn't have an episode that puts them in segregation. Because the institution won't give them the medication that they really need, sometimes, we had to get drugs that could stabilize them. Then we would watch them and stay with them, because if the system got her, it would be worse.

Everything I just said is harm reduction. We ask, *How can we make sure that humans that are involved in the situation are okay, as much as they can be okay?* I've watched people, including my mother, fight things that I know in the depths of their soul they wish that they could take out of their lives, but they can't.

I think harm reduction is a tool to help me stay in the lives of the people I cared about and not feel like I had to leave them because it was too hard to be around them at times. Harm reduction was I would have to talk to my mother before 10:00 a.m. every day because I knew she would be drunk after that. Sometimes I had to get up at 6:00 a.m. to go see her and take her to the store to have those moments, because otherwise I would have to choose; I would have to divest from my mother.

Harm reduction is essential because sometimes that's the only way we can stay in community with people we really love and be able to offer grace and not judge them. And like you've been saying with Liberatory Harm Reduction, it wasn't a module from a public health lens. That came later. It was, *I love these people. I don't want these people to go away.*

I've been doing harm reduction my whole life, especially as a kid who just never wanted to be alone. I think that's why solitary confinement hurt me as much as it did. It wasn't that I was locked in the cellar; it was that I was locked away from people. As a kid who did not want to be alone, harm reduction has always been a tool to keep me closer to the people I really loved.

How do you see harm reduction tying into Transformative Justice and abolition?

I think the benefit of my work in Black & Pink was that it forced me to look at abolition and create my own definition. I had to figure out what abolition means for me personally. Harm reduction is the strategic plan. It's a Google Earth moment—it's the GPS because it is the streets, the hills, the valleys, and the rivers that build us this map to get to abolition.

Shira, it's like harm reduction is grace in action, right? At Black & Pink, we're purchasing this land in Omaha that will be a youth campus for queer and trans youth who are system-impacted to come and live. I was thinking about how dreams and faith are like the same fucking thing, right? I grew up with my grandmother saying, *Faith without works is dead.* And I've been thinking all week that dreams without works is dead.

And in this moment, it's like abolition without works is dead and the works are harm reduction. I think a beautiful thing about harm reduction is it's the actionable way we give grace, that we give opportunity, that we center all people. Harm reduction allows every one of these things because it is relational.

Public health is just fucking saviorism. But real Liberatory Harm Reduction is like everyone leaving a situation proud of the outcome they self-determined. For example, since my teens and throughout my life, I engaged in a lot of survival sex work. It's interesting for me to think about my time in sex work because I didn't have access to comprehensive sex education in school, so condoms were not a part of my harm reduction process until the outreach workers taught me how to use them. What does harm reduction look like for sex work without consistent access to condoms? Liberatory Harm Reduction is inherently about ingenuity and innovation. It takes a lot to be present to create something new in real time to make sure that folks are feeling safe, and you might have a grace quotient to figure out how that other person stays safe, too, because the police won't make the other person safe.

I remember myself and other girls and other young queer folks out there, just figuring out how we could all stay alive. I feel like sometimes the amount of harm reduction we can do is, *Are we all going to be here in the morning?* Right? Bail support, bailing people out of jail is harm reduction, right?

If things in my life stay status quo, I will never do sex work again. And I will always be positioned and framed as a good representation of Black trans women, a good representation of formerly incarcerated people. But we have to divest and be okay with us not being the "good" or "innocent." We're just going to be us. We have to really challenge this and ask what does it mean for your solidarity work if you think in terms of "good people" versus "bad."

What are a few concrete steps you want to see people take toward abolition?

I need us to answer *What do communities and people receive as real solidarity*? and do more interrogation of that and a better job of challenging ourselves to be comfortable with divesting from the things that don't actually serve us and the things that make us feel special about receiving services too. Like with calling the police—it's a service, right? I need you to think about how many people have to be harmed for you to be safe.

The message that I want to get out is that the beauty of humanity and the scariest part of humanity and the most frustrating part of humanity are never going to be addressed by just one solution—like abstinence or prison. And we have to accept that this is going to be a hard-fought battle, but we have to be really excited about what's on the other side of it. And if the solution is too easy, then it's probably not the right thing. Abolition isn't going to happen in the five-year strategic plan; a ten-thousand-dollar grant isn't going to solve it.

People, please don't think that you have to solve it all. Fix your shit in your circle of life—and that could just mean listen to the people in your house. But also have a goal to be concerned about your whole block. I'm creating spaces where other leaders are positioned to step up when I'm ready to go and divesting from this idea that I have to have the answer to everything. I don't. I can't.

Center people. At all costs, center people when it's hard, when it's difficult, when it's scary. But I promise you that you will get more out of centering people even when it's scary than centering systems when it's scary. You're never going to get what systems tell you they will give you or what we've been indoctrinated to believe they will do.

Ask, *What does it mean to feel uncomfortable versus what does it mean to be unsafe?* And come up with plans to address either feeling before you engage with anyone else. If you feel uncomfortable, what do you need to do to make sure that you can take care of your needs? If you feel unsafe, create the plan for your safety. But create that plan with a spirit and a desire of transformation and restoration. Realize that doing the work long term means you need to ask yourself continuously, *What is my role in this work?*

Last but not least, train your heart and train your body to listen. We do a lot of turning off. Something will be said that we need to hear, but we just want to navigate the world in a certain way. We need to open up those avenues in our spirit because this is also spirit work, and the more we listen, the more we will be skilled at navigating safety and community. There's a beautiful moment when you figure out how to deeply listen that allows you to really support other people.

Closing

When I reflect on the work of the people who have contributed to this book, I am awed into silence. I am often stunned by the beauty of the people I have met in my journey to find healing and wholeness, and I am humbled in the face of such a collection of bravery that this constellation of interviews and images presents. Mariame Kaba teaches us that hope is a discipline, and I would add that Liberatory Harm Reduction is the discipline of hope.

We must continue to divorce the overfocus by public health on our bodies as sites of disease by embracing the entirety of who we are, each and all of us. This means our organizing strategies must include people who are high in meetings, who are high in therapy, who are in the sex trade and sex working, who are making decisions about their mental health and wellness that may not fit into the medical model. We must continue to demand trauma-centered practice that is more than "trauma-informed care," which profits from our pain and uses liability as an excuse for institutional violence.

As I write this, knowing that my own shame spirals are sometimes too much to bear, I remember that the conclusion of a book about a liberatory practice should also come with next steps that we can take from our beds, from the bath, and from the streets. This book is about developing a practice and reshaping our politic. It is asking us to stay in love with each other's survival and to push back on the systems that shred our values in exchange for flimsy reproductions of our community's precious rituals.

In all my workshops and talks, I close the session by asking people to take a pledge that honors the roots of Liberatory Harm Reduction. As I end this book, I find myself wanting to close out by imagining all our voices combined into a single chant. I ask you to join me in a pledge to the legendary and radical roots of those who came before us—those who survived and those who became ancestors sending messages from the spirit world.

I ask you to promise with me that every time you talk about harm reduction, every time you have a conversation about this critical lifesaving philosophy, about this love letter from our radical comrades, that you remember and that you share with other people: harm reduction was started by BIPOC organizers, by people in the sex trade, by trans people, by the sex workers, by drug users, by young people, by people who were street based, by disabled and chronically ill people, by antiracist activists, who want to see our resilience reflected intergenerationally. They want us to remember that we have everything we need to survive inside our relationships with each other, inside our creative and brilliant community connections, inside our coping strategies, inside our joy and grief. They want us to release the shame that comes with our struggle and live into our complexity. They want us to carry ourselves and each other through the reality of this beautiful mess with rage and glamour. With love and fury. With creativity and despondence. With generosity and curiosity. They don't want us to be anything—anything but *here.*

Afterword

ROSARIO DAWSON

While I was growing up, activism, community building, and leading with empathy were modeled by my grandmother and mother: two perfectly flawed people who survived injustices and systemic abuses alongside their community. These frustrated matriarchs recognized some of their own lack and limitations but didn't let it stop them from reaching out and lifting up others. One of the greatest gifts they instilled in me is that life is not always easy, sweet, or romantic. They were fully activated; they had no blueprint. They saw a need and met it with a solution. They were instinctively practicing Liberatory Harm Reduction and Transformative Justice; it was alive in them before we had the words for it.

There's a 1970s photograph of my mom, Isabel Celeste (age six), and my grandmother, Isabel, that was taken after they had marched in solidarity with Cesar Chavez and the International Ladies' Garment Workers Union (ILGWU), which my great-grandmother Celestina was also a member of. My mom took me to my first march when I was ten, the Pride March in San Francisco, where we were living. She also took my brother and me to work with her at Women Organized to Make Abuse Nonexistent (W.O.M.A.N., Inc.), a community-based domestic violence service organization. I remember feeling how powerful it was that women who had been cut off from every support they knew—family, friends, home, bank accounts—could encounter someone like my mom, often in dire need herself, who welcomed them with love, no judgement, and immediate care.

When we moved back to New York City and my mom became a residence manager for Housing Works (HW) Guerrilla Housing Program, I would volunteer on clean-up days. We would go to an empty apartment that had been secured for a houseless person with AIDS and do flea bombs and clean roach eggs out of the refrigerator. My mom recalls:

> You were there with me. I would meet and interview the new tenant and would find out what their favorite colors were, what they wanted in their new home. Prior to HW thrift stores, we would find people who would donate furniture and household items so our clients could live with their family instead of being in hospice or remaining homeless. HW created a dignified place where disenfranchised people could live at home with family. It was an incredibly triggering and traumatizing time in my life, as we would have to relocate the family when the client died because the Department of AIDS Services (DAS) was only funding the person who was HIV-positive. And then I would meet another family and I would redo the apartment all over again. It was rough, but hands down it was the best job I ever had because it allowed me to really give back.

My mom was also active in local politics and grassroots organizations like ACT UP and, alongside my dad, built the first recycling program in NYC. She embraced transgender family before T was added to LGB, and she's the first known person to distribute clean needles to injection drug users in NYC.

One of the earliest memories of my mom was of her not shaming people who were down and out: unhoused, heroin-using people, living in Tompkins Square Park and discarding their drugs and paraphernalia from the previous night. Mom would come equipped with a broom, sweeper, and garbage bags. She would make us sit on the bench while she picked up the empty heroin bags and used syringes because she wanted us to have a safe place to play. Ultimately, the nocturnal residents of the park started to help her clean up because she was kind to them; she greeted and treated them with dignity and respect. Then one day, my mom saw one of our family members shooting up heroin in the park. She was mortified, because no one knew he was using. Wanting to ensure his safety and the safety of his wife and family, she was motivated to distribute clean needles to him, and ultimately to others, to help prevent further harm to our community. This occurred in 1986, years before syringe exchange advocacy began.

All this activist engagement was never theoretical. *We were saving our own lives.* The people we cared for and advocated for every day were our friends, neighbors, and family members; some identifying as LGBTQ+, some HIV-positive, some intravenous drug users, some unhoused, and all abandoned by society at large. Like my parents' decision to squat an abandoned building on the Lower East Side of Manhattan because the buildings that we could afford to live in were owned by slumlords: their tenacity proved what can be built and created with sweat equity when status quo systems fail us.

Another deeply seated legacy my elders teach me is that focusing solely on successes without embracing our failures isn't going to move us forward. Witnessing my mom work through her anxieties and generational trauma has been both transformative and distressing. At times, my mom's focus on building a loving community for the most stigmatized among us has been triggering, exhausting, and health depleting for her and those closest to her. She has shown me, though, that without creating dignity for the most in need among us, none of us can heal. Today, the community, the chosen family we built around us, is the source of our mental, emotional, and physical health. Did my mom's tireless community building sacrifice my and her own well-being for the greater good? Yes. But my gut tells me this is not a contradiction.

Let me close by saying to you readers what I said to my mom on a recent Mother's Day. Our generational traumas have been compounded by structures fortified to keep us stressed, depleted, wanting, and needing. We do not have to bear alone the burden of healing that hurt and pain inside us and around us. When you have down moments, feel overwhelmed, broken and apologetic, ashamed, guilty, angry, or resentful, return to the stories and learnings compiled in this book. And resting is enough, because you are enough, and it's gorgeous that you are here.

Gratitude

This is the first time I have written anything outside of a collective, and to do it I asked for help from many lifelong thought partners and comrades. Many people who cried and wrestled with me as I writhed with imposter syndrome, writer's block, and health crises have been in my life for nearly three decades.

This book could not have been written without the hand-holding and hard work of Deana Lewis, Mariame Kaba, Kelly McGowan, Laura Janine Mintz, Rachel Caïdor, and ill Weaver.

Thank you to Leah Lakshmi Piepzna-Samarasinha and Jill Petty for your early and critical support of this project.

I am so grateful for my thought partners, with whom I have been building and creating a complex web of care and pushback: Naima Lowe, Jesse Ehrensaft-Hawley, Erica Woodland, Cara Page, Kelli Dorsey, Emi Koyama, adrienne maree brown, Allen Frimpong, Marcus Rogers, Micah Hobbes Frazier, Ryan Li Dahlstrom, Mayadet Patitucci Cruz, Monique Tula, Pidgeon Pagonis, Kumasi J. Gwynee, Lisa Tonna, Alissa Hull, Taylor Casey, Benji Hart, Lara Brooks, Ray Sukin Klauber, Dominique McKinney, Stacy Erenberg, Ejeris Dixon, Abbie Illenberger, Nomy Lamm, Erin Daly, Mary Ann Russell, Beth Richie, Catlin Fullwood, Mimi Kim, Andrea Ritchie. I am grateful to lauren Perlman, who named early in this book's process that what I was really writing about was the beauty of queer chosen family.

Every cell in my body was nurtured and honed by the opportunity to have been in humble learning with New York Peer AIDS

Education Coalition and the Young Women's Empowerment Project, two collectives led by young people involved in the sex trade and street economy that were BIPOC and queer and trans.

J. Maya Iwata spoke this book into existence by telling me to write it when I was twenty-one years old, and I never dreamed it was possible until Mariame basically demanded that it happen, twenty-five years later. Every single activist and youth worker and harm reduction practitioner who saved my life, just by doing the work, even if not with me, made this book possible. I interviewed as many of them as I could.

My chosen family has taught me the balance of devotion and boundaries of keeping each other safe and alive while still allowing me to be introverted and dressed to the nines. I would be nowhere without my harm reduction and Lower East Side lineage that came through a chance meeting of Chloe Dzubilo in 1996.

Proceeds from this book will go to a giving circle in honor of Miss Major Griffin-Gracy and to the grassroots organizing project, Street Youth Rise UP!, led by Dominique McKinney.

Index

About the Author

Shira Hassan is the founder of Just Practice, a capacity-building project for organizations and community members, activists, and leaders working at the intersection of Transformative Justice, harm reduction and collective liberation. She is the former executive director of the Young Women's Empowerment Project, an organizing and grassroots-movement-building project led by and for young People of Color that have current or former experience in the sex trade and street economies. A lifelong harm reductionist and prison abolitionist, Shira is the coauthor, with Mariame Kaba, of *Fumbling Towards Repair: A Workbook for Community Accountability Facilitators*. Shira's work has been discussed on outlets including National Public Radio, the *New York Times*, the *Nation*, *In These Times*, *Bill Moyers*, *Everyday Feminism*, *Bitch Media*, *TruthOut*, and *Colorlines*.